FROM BASIC ECONOMICS TO SUPPLY SIDE ECONOMICS

M. L. Greenhut
Alumni Distinguished Professor
Texas A & M University

Charles T. Stewart, Jr.
Chairman, Department of Economics
Georgetown University

UNIVERSITY
PRESS OF
AMERICA

LANHAM • NEW YORK • LONDON

Political Economy Research Institute
1410 Promenade Bank
Richardson, Texas

Copyright © 1983 by

Political Economy Research Institute

University Press of America,™ Inc.

4720 Boston Way
Lanham, MD 20706

3 Henrietta Street
London WC2E 8LU England

Co-published by arrangement with the
Political Economy Research Institute

Library of Congress Cataloging in Publication Data

Greenhut, Melvin L.
From basic economics to supply side economics.

Includes bibliographical references and index.
1. Economics. 2. Supply-side economics. 3. United
States–Economic policy–1981–   . I. Stewart,
Charles T., 1922–   . II. Title.
HB171.G7495   1983   338.973   83–16734
ISBN 0–8191–3426–0 (alk. paper)
ISBN 0–8191–3427–9 (pbk. : alk. paper)

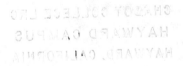

FOREWORD

This book is important because it is about ideas. As Lord Keynes observed almost a half century ago, ideas are more important than is generally recognized. Even in something so practical and political as Congress, ultimately ideas dominate debate and actions. Ideas determine vested interest and ultimately how we are governed and the conditions under which we live.

The adoption of the Reagan Economic Program is a perfect case in point of the ultimate dominance of ideas over vested interest. Fifteen years ago, had you done a survey in the country and sought public opinion as to what caused inflation, government deficit spending and a rapid growth in money supply would not have ranked in the top ten. But because of an intellectual revolution, which brought the ideas of economists and the weight of hard facts to the attention of the public, by 1980 government deficit spending and the process of debt monetization it triggered had been clearly identified by the public as the number one cause of inflation. This idea not only brought Ronald Reagan to Washington, but it made possible the adoption of a set of budgets which elevated the public interest in controlling runaway government spending above the special interest of those who benefitted from that spending and produced spending cuts which would have been unthinkable a decade before.

A similar point can be made with regard to the Reagan tax policy of 1981. Fifteen years ago, the primary focus of tax debate was on redistributing wealth. But two decades of economic stagnation and an intensified debate over the incentives of people to work, save, and invest spawned the idea of stimulating the economy by reducing marginal tax rates. Even critics of the President's Tax Proposals were captured by the ideas that underlay it, and it was a liberal democrat, and not a conservative Republican, who offered the amendment to eliminate the differential marginal tax rates between earned and so-called unearned income, dropping the maximum rate of taxes from 70% to 50%.

It is because ideas have consequences that I commend this book to the reader. Here two well-known economists with academic, governmental and business experience present a common sense, straight-forward analysis of the economic problem, and in the process show how newer perspectives on the economic problems, such as supply-side economics, fit into the traditional framework.

They provide the reader with a tool kit to be used in analyzing the economic process and the impact of government policy.

To me, as an economist who has tried to continue to teach his economic lessons while on temporary assignment in the United States Congress, you are about to undertake the study of the world's most interesting and important subject. I am very pleased that two distinguished economists have undertaken to provide a basic text which can provide you with insight into how the world works. I commend Mel Greenhut and Charles Stewart for their effort, and I commend the product of that effort to you.

Phil Gramm
U.S. Congressman
Texas

PREFACE

This book provides a bird's-eye view of the basic properties of economics. It includes formal (yet simplified) explanations of supply and demand analysis, Keynesian economics, monetarism, and particularly supply-side economics (including its current Reaganomics variation). It provides detailed explanations of our money and banking system, as well as evaluations of the economic progress and problems of other countries. The economic analysis in this book is as precise as that taught in the nation's ivory towers. However, we go beyond purely formal economics by including, in appropriate places, our own values and interpretations of economic effectiveness (with clear indication to the reader that the statements being made are personal judgments). Why is this book important to you? Consider the following beliefs of the present writers.

The stagnation of the 1970's, with high inflation, low growth, almost no increase in productivity, and a greater frequency plus severity of recessions, is no accident at all. To be sure, there were many factors beyond control, such as the increase in oil prices after 1973. But the country's unsatisfactory economic experiences have been primarily the outcome of government policy even though it is surely the case that policy makers did not intend the consequences listed above. Rather the bad policies were (and typically are) the result of ignorance — ignorance of the relevant facts, including a lack of understanding of the nature and causes of the problems with which the policy makers were concerned. Mistakes were also made about the responses of individuals and institutions, and policy makers were unaware of the full range and extent of the indirect consequences of particular actions. Private policy makers, too, are not without fault, but in the recent decades of big government in the United States, the public policy makers have called the tune. Let us illustrate with a few *concerned* notes.

Price support programs for agriculture, intended to help the low-income farmer, have primarily benefitted the large and affluent farmers. They have tended to generate surpluses, which in turn have led to other programs to reduce output, or to "dump" surplus products abroad. These results have adversely affected the exports of farmers in this and other countries as well as the agricultural development of some less-developed nations.

Government subsidies for higher education, and in particular graduate and medical education, have in some cases helped relieve current shortages; in others, they have added to surpluses and assured overcrowding in many fields for decades. All of this leads to waste of human resources and frustration. Subsidy to higher education is a prime example of taking from the poor and giving to the rich.

The school lunch program, intended to provide a nourishing meal to children who might otherwise not get one, grew to the point of reaching 26 million schoolchildren, two-thirds of the population age 5–15 inclusive. Many of the more wealthy among them dump their subsidized school lunch in the garbage.

Medicare and Medicaid were introduced in the mid–1960's to finance medical care for the elderly and the poor respectively. Whereas the poor can be assumed unable to afford medical care, this is not true of all the elderly, at least some of whom are quite wealthy, yet they have the same entitlements as the elderly poor. An unintended consequence of these programs is a large increase in the cost of medical services for those who are not eligible for either program, and an *extraordinarily* large increase in its share of the nation's income with no *significant* improvement in the health of the people attributed to these programs.

Consider our government's assistance for industries adversely affected by import competition. Few industries receiving such assistance have taken advantage of the breathing spell to adjust. Workers in industries displaced by imports have been eligible for more unemployment compensation than if they had been displaced by domestic competition, a policy that might strike other unemployed workers as inequitable.

What about the War on Poverty? If one assumes poverty is a problem that can be largely eliminated by government policy, then the War has failed. The assumption is wrong! The percentage of the population in poverty did decline from 18% in 1964 to a low of 11.1% in 1973 — but it rose to 13% in 1980. Alas, the percentage declined from 32.7% to 18.0% between 1949 and 1964, *without a War on Poverty*, doing this as a result of sustained economic growth. During the 1970's there was essentially no progress at all, even though the amount spent on direct cash income transfers more than doubled between 1970 and 1980. The proportion on poverty levels did not fall because the economy hardly grew, while at the same time the nature of the problem changed.

Who are the poor? A growing share are elderly, disabled, or otherwise lacking the ability to pull themselves above the poverty level by their own efforts. Programs that give them money, or food stamps, or housing subsidies, raise their levels of living as long as the programs continue, and to the extent of their generosity, no longer and no more. Programs to help them are necessary, need to be permanent, and cannot be expected to eliminate poverty; they are a crutch, a life preserver, nothing else.

But the programs aimed at those among the poor who are believed to have the ability to raise themselves above the poverty level have not worked too well. These are primarily education and training programs intended to make teenagers, displaced workers, the unemployed in general more employable through provision of skills. We need to think about their disappointing performance. Were the programs poorly conceived, badly run? Were there not enough jobs to go around? Were target populations unwilling to take advantage of them? Was training through government programs the wrong remedy? There is an answer within these questions. Even had they been entirely successful, they would not have been self-terminating. New generations are continuously growing up, being displaced, becoming obsolete who need help or could be helped to adjust.

Other government policies undermine the effectiveness of our anti-poverty programs: for example, higher minimum wages raise unemployment rates especially for black teenagers. The failure to limit the inflow of illegal immigrants reduces job prospects for some citizens. The availability of income without working is disincentive to work for some individuals. Unemployment conpensation, food stamps, etc. provide the worker with substantial amounts of time to search for a suitable job without having to take an otherwise acceptable job. This is reasonable, within limits, but at some point it allows certain workers to enjoy extended leisure at taxpayers' expense. Where do we draw the line? A requirement that an unemployed worker must work in order to receive benefits would be difficult to enforce without police state methods. Moreover, it would compel the government to provide jobs as a last resort.

Most policies are the outcome of compromises between various groups with different aims, or different perceptions of outcomes, or who seek to appropriate most of the benefits. But the poor results of this competitive process of policy-making are largely attributable to the various sorts of ignorance mentioned above. Knowledge will not eliminate disputes, or assure good policies; well-informed individuals will continue to vie for personal advantage, and the results may be judged inequitable; or they will disagree about values, with some giving priority to public spending on parks, others to schools or highways, still others to private spending. These are, of course, the disagreements democracy is all about.

The present book is a modest attempt to move us toward the informed and intelligent debate over the economic issues which matter in the arena of democracy. It comes, however, with a warning label. Economists are in broad agreement on certain general principles, such as the Law of Demand and the efficiency of competitive markets. But these "laws" apply not to invariant nature, rather they apply to human beings who learn, forget, age, change their minds, their beliefs and values besides their behavior. The ability to predict and prescribe with precision requires application of general "laws" along with specific information. Unfortunately, by its very nature, information is often dated, quite uncertain, tied to prevailing technology, tastes, and institutions. It is simply the case that the learning process is never really finished for an individual, much less for the citizens of a free enterprise nation.

Many have helped us in the writing of this book. We acknowledge our thanks specifically to Mr. B.V. Thompson and the Texas Educational Association, Dr. Steve Pejovich, the Association of Former Students of Texas A&M University, Mr. Richard M. Larry and the Sarah Scaife Foundation, Mr. Robert Smith, Mr. Tom Taylor, Dr. Glenn Beeson, Mr. Phil Trulock, Dr. Ed Feulner, and Dr. Robert Walker for their diverse forms of help and encouragement. We further thank Mr. A.J. Lerager, President of the Lone Star Publishing Company of Austin, Texas, for permitting us to draw freely upon materials included in the book *Economics for the Voter*. We extend final thanks to Mrs. Arla Campbell, Ms. Cindy Hollan, and Mrs. Gwen Stacell for their cooperative secretarial and administrative assistance, so vital to the writing of this book.

March 24, 1983   M.L. Greenhut
                                              C.T. Stewart

CONTENTS

INTRODUCTION TO BOOK
AND TO PART ONE ON
ECONOMIC SYSTEMS

This book explains basic college economics in as *simplified* a form as possible towards the end of applying its principles to current events. In particular, it evaluates supply-side economics and its Reaganomics variations in the context of accepted systems of economic thought. It enters the arena of current events only after establishing the required tools of analysis of the professional economist, as these are prerequisites to logically affirming or disaffirming the policy under discussion. Thus, for example, it is only after Chapter 15 and 16 that we can "scientifically" examine the pros and cons of the tax policy changes effected during the summers of 1981 and 1982. For reasons established at diverse points in the book, the present writers endorse the supply-side amendment to so-called Keynesian economics; in fact, we favor it over the monetarist version in determining what governments of free enterprise nations can and cannot do. As the reader will discover, we also distinguish sharply between supply-side economics and the Reaganomics version of it that began to appear in 1982.

It is vital — at least in the chronological sense of topic-ordering — to note the fact that the first part of this book introduces the reader to the general subject of economics. It does this in part by placing stress on the different economic systems that are prevalent in the world today.

M.L. GREENHUT   C.T. STEWART

PART ONE: CHAPTER 1:
WHAT IS ECONOMICS?

Assume that the level of intelligence on a planet, which shall be called XYZ, is far greater than on our planet. Let their chemists, their physicists, their physicians, their engineers, their dentists, among others, be much more skilled than ours. In fact, imagine that one finds sharper minds, more advanced technology, and even better relations between people living on planet XYZ than those living on earth. We might—in our beginning dream world—even assume that the people on planet XYZ are typically much more compassionate, and much more deeply concerned with the well being of their fellowman than are the people here on earth.

But even in Alice's Wonderland, problems exist! Let us suppose that for some unknown reason no one on planet XYZ has been able to explain how the economy works. Each attempt by the government to promote economic education has failed. The minds of the intelligentsia of planet XYZ have been unable to cope with the problems of the economy.

The people of XYZ are plagued with economic cycles which run from feast to famine, boom to bust, prosperity to depression, back and forth. Economic states change from the full employment (of all who desire and are able to work) to 25 percent unemployment of the labor force. Prices skyrocket and nosedive so that ice cream sodas sell for $1 or more one month, for 10¢ the next. It was in a sense of deep frustration that the President of XYZ and his cabinet, on the advice of selected Congressional leaders, recently decided they must intrude upon people of other planets. In fact, though the policy on planet XYZ had been to remain isolated from the rest of the universe, it was finally decided that a single interference with people elsewhere in the universe was justified.

And so the decision was made on XYZ, in its year 2942, to invade the earth. But, happily for all of us on earth at that time, their planned invasion was not designed as a military one; rather, it was to be a very quiet, peaceful invasion. Through their superior technology, they investigated the backgrounds of all economists on the planet earth. They agreed in advance to select and take to planet XYZ a professor who possessed two charac-

1

teristics: one, the individual had to be a great economist; two, the professor had to have no substantial earthly ties, no family, no loved ones, and if possible, even no friends. This second qualification was required because the people on planet XYZ, as suggested above, were basically good people. Their private invasion of earth would be limited to the disappearance of one economist on earth.

The decision was reached quickly on planet XYZ to bring Professor J.P. Smith of the United States to their world. This professor qualified in all respects. Professor Smith could be described as a great economist and as a loner, without a family. Best of all, Professor Smith had the good fortune of living in the most exciting country on earth, the United States of America. It had the economy most admired by the people of planet XYZ, for it provided the greatest freedom possible for man to fulfill himself. It was also the strongest economy on earth and the most advanced.

On a certain day, just a short while ago, a spacecraft of planet XYZ landed in the United States. No, our radar screens did not spot it; the technology of planet XYZ was so advanced that the craft was able to avoid detection. Alas, however, a terrible mistake was made by its onboard computer. Instead of removing the economist J.P. Smith, an individual residing near Professor Smith's house was literally plucked from earth. In our world of fantasy, imagine that *you* are that person and suddenly find yourself in a spacecraft.

At first, as you glance through the windows of the spaceship and observe the earth receding from you, you are quite concerned with everything being left behind. But fortunately, the people of planet XYZ are not sadists. Your mental state was altered so that you feel assured all people on earth are happy and well provided for. You simply remember the best on earth and accept the fact that you are in a spaceship headed far away.

While you are meditating about earthly things, a very attractive person walks down the center aisle and begins to pamper you with requests: "Would you like steak, chicken, salad, caviar?" Two hours later, well fed, happy, but somewhat tired, you fall asleep. It seems as if an eternity has passed when a loud bell-like sound vibrates throughout the spacecraft. The Captain, in a soft, pleasant voice, gently advises you that you are now within the gravitational field of planet XYZ and will be landing in 45 minutes.

As the craft approaches land, you gasp at a panorama of pastel surfaces, of graceful structures blending harmoniously into the cool greenery of trees, shrubbery and grass, with gently rising mountains as a backdrop. As the spaceship approaches the landing area, you realize that thousands of people are awaiting your arrival. Indeed, as soon as the craft lands, your ears pick up the strains of what you assume to be the anthem of XYZ being played by a band of at least 1,000 musicians.

A young escort suddenly appears at your side and leads you to a stairway that is lowered from the ship. As you begin to walk down the steps, a roar of applause reverberates through the air. You are gratified by the recognition and admiration accorded you. Alas, your thrill at the reception turns to a frightened shiver when one of the dignitaries, apparently the leader or head of the planet, rushes up to welcome the great economist, formerly Professor J.P. Smith of the planet Earth and now Professor J.P. Smith of planet XYZ.

Four hours later, after being wined and dined in ways that make Hollywood extravagances appear to be of pinch-penny order, you are escorted by a pair of very attractive people of the opposite sex to your suite of rooms on top of the Hotel J.P. Smith—just completed and named for you. Your knees have been shaking for an hour or more, ever since President Whatsthename expressed hope that you could complete your book on economics in a few months and begin your teaching before the winter season arrives. Could you dare confess that a mistake has been made? You might look like Professor J.P. Smith, but you are really just an ordinary American voter who does not even know what economics means, much less contains. If you admit the error, maybe these people would be hostile? For all you know, they might be sadists, cannibals, . . .?

It was obvious by their admission testimonials and demonstrations after dinner that they know absolutely nothing about economics, even less than you. It is crazy! They are brilliant and wise about most aspects of life, but they do not even know the name of the paper they use to pay the waiter for his services. They have an economy, they have money, they have jobs, but they are at a complete loss to explain anything related to their economy. Could you bluff your way through?

As you return to your room, then drop into a soft reclining chair and meditate about your fate, you become very drowsy.

WHAT IS ECONOMICS?

Tomorrow morning you will think and decide what to do. Tomorrow morning you will tell them about the error that has been made, or maybe, should you try, in fact, to be *the economist* of planet XYZ?

"THE BUSINESS WORLD ON EARTH"

You awake early in the morning, possibly because you smell the bacon and eggs that have been brought quietly into one of the rooms of your suite and placed beneath a light that apparently keeps the food hot and tasty as long as necessary. Your breakfast is delicious. But, you have to stop this loafing. You have to get with economics quickly, to see if you can pull off "the great impersonation" *or else*. It would seem funny to you if it were not so deadly dangerous. So you drop into that chair again for thoughts — and fall asleep once more.

It suddenly hits you as you awake. Economics deals with the business world. You leap to your feet, run to a desk, sit down, title your manuscript *Economics*, and write your opening sentence: "Economics is the study of people in the business world." You do not know how correct this is; you do not know if it is significant and truly meaningful. Without doubt, the real Professor J.P. Smith could come up with a much more advanced, penetrating definition. But this is good enough for a starting point. You rather like its simplicity, yet its inclusiveness. "Economics is the study of people in the business world." But what is that world about, who comprises it, how does one go about creating a science of economics and establishing scientific laws and relationships? Is economics a science? What is science? The thought staggers you; but, you realize how you must proceed. Why not initially recall the things on earth you do know something about. More exactly, what do people do on earth? What are other sciences about?

It takes but a few moments for you to realize that you had wants on earth, and here too on planet XYZ — wants for food, drink, clothing, entertainment, information, security. Your wants depend upon your physiological needs, your knowledge about things, and the quality of goods as you know or believe them to be. Your perception, logic, past experiences all combine to help you evaluate alternative things. How would good A satisfy you, good B, and others? You recognize that often you wanted something, but had no money to acquire that something. In fact, your actual

4

behavior often clashed with your intended behavior. The desired good may not have been obtainable at the time of day you wanted it. Indeed, your physical needs often changed, even the facts as you perceived them often appeared to change. Then the thought strikes you: are you proceeding logically, by using *yourself* as the center of the universe? Are you identical to everyone else? Can you construct a science on the basis of *your* wants for scarce things? Must not the science be general? In fact, was this not the mistake made by Isaac Newton when he sat in his garden and the apple struck his head? He thought of himself as being at the center of the universe. Einstein indicated that everything is relative. This suggests for economics that, rather than say, "I have wants," you might say, "People have wants." Alas, how are they ordered? Ah, yes! Why not simply start the second line of your book with the words: "It deals with wants of individuals, and these wants are arrayed in an order." But how do we prove this?

How did Newton establish the three laws of mechanics? (These laws are: (1) that each body has inertia, (2) that for every action there is an opposite and equal reaction, (3) that a force is exerted between bodies which is proportional to the product of their separate masses and inversely proportional to the square of the distance between them.) He did not observe them. He could not see this force, these rules, these laws. Obviously, he had postulated (or assumed, if you prefer) that the earth attracted the apple that hit him. At the same time, however, his laws of mechanics included the idea that the apple attracted the earth. Thus the apple weighed something, and the earth weighed something. How long did it take the apple to fall? Why did it take so long? Then you remembered: Newton pioneered the *fluxions*, today called the *calculus* by mathematicians. That system of thought deals with certain changes, in fact the rate of change of objects. One cannot always see the forces existing between either stationary or moving (changing) objects; yet one knows these forces exist. Physicists and astronomers can postulate the existence of certain things, and derive theorems from their postulates. They can in fact test their theorems, indirectly as it were, with the effect of confirming their postulates. Can we do the same in economics?

Fatigue from stretching your mind quickly sets in. But you have too many ideas to stop now. Can you assume a set of *economic wants* arranged in an order, and then deduce a theorem which you can test? If economic wants exist in some order of preference, such that A is preferred to B to C, etc., would it not also follow, for example, that the more A you obtain, the less preferable A becomes? In fact, with increased acquisitions of A, would not A become less desired than B? Therefore, the greater the quantity of A obtained, the less A will be desired. Hence the price of A must go down if the quantity taken is to be increased. You jump with excitement! This simple idea boils down to *your first theorem.* How will you write it? Why, simply that *price must fall if the quantity purchased is to increase.*

Can you test your first theorem as might the physicist on planet earth? Why not! Why not call President Whatsthename and request a lowered price of gasoline for ten days as well as reports on past prices and sales, then later on the new price(s) and sales? Your blood pressure jumps with excitement. You have committed yourself to impersonate Professor Smith.

Your reports on gas sales come in twelve days later. They are shocking! Everything is upside down. Gas sales have decreased even though its price has been cut in half. How could that be? Then you realize that economics differs somewhat from physics, even though it uses the same logical structure as that of the physical sciences or that of mathematics. Because it deals with a changing *social* universe, you might even need a new mathematics, call it *econometrics*, which in effect holds other things constant even though in fact they have changed. Maybe through special applications of mathematical statistics you can determine whether gas sales would have actually increased as prices were lowered *if other things had not changed.* Maybe through such a framework of thought the economist can isolate certain events and identify underlying economic relationships. But you know you are ahead of yourself. Right now it would suffice to uncover and learn elementary relationships only. Keep the science simple! Stay with the immediately apprehended! First focus your thinking on some of the economic systems you know on earth. Then in your next chapter, you can describe the fundamental functions of economic society! Of course, money is central to all economies; so soon after those discussions are complete, you had better explain where money comes from, what banks are and how the banking system operates, what Keynesian economics, monetarism, and supply-side economics are all about, as well as other subjects of importance to the people. After all, that is what Mr. Whatsthename really wants of you.

"ORGANIZATION OF BOOK"

"Professor Smith" never returned; he found the people of Planet XYZ open-minded and appreciative, and we can expect that he became dedicated to helping them solve their problems. Unfortunately, his lectures and speeches were not recorded, or at least no transcript has yet reached the earth. So the book that follows is not his, but is based on speculation by the present authors as to what he might have told us and you about the American economic system and its recent progress had he returned to Washington for the Cherry Blossom Festival of Spring 1983. We can expect, of course, that Smith realized he knew little about the customs and values of the people of Planet XYZ — about their institutions and traditions. In contrast, Smith knew from recollections of history on earth the values and traditions influencing our behavior, the performance of our economic institutions, even the forms of organization that function best in different societies. So we can expect that Professor Smith would begin the book by sketching descriptively some of the main economic systems that had evolved on earth, leaving the people of Planet XYZ free to choose which might be best for them. Then Professor Smith could concentrate on the systems of greatest interest to most economists, those from which the science of economics evolved, in particular the free enterprise capitalist system of the United States. The professor would next provide the readers with a basic understanding of how the American monetary (and banking) system worked, then why the overall economy malfunctioned, and what tools existed or could be fashioned to keep the economic system in good working order.

"FINAL STATEMENT"

Our own book is correspondingly simplified, without sacrificing essential concepts. Yet the reader will still have to devote real effort to understand the principles it develops before being able to use them effectively. The ultimate reward will be not only better management of individual lives, but informed voters who will contribute their voices to improved laws and policies affecting not just themselves, but all of us.

M.L. GREENHUT   C.T. STEWART

CHAPTER 2:
ECONOMIC SYSTEMS

Economies and economic systems stem from the attempts of people or groups of people to organize their economic lives in answer to certain basic economic problems. In fact, let us identify four *basic economic problems* that exist in all nations: namely, 1) what to produce, 2) how to produce, 3) how much to produce, and 4) for whom to produce. Indeed, we can further *classify economic systems* under another fourfold category: the traditional systems we have had on earth, which constitute the so-called traditional economies, the command economies, the laissez-faire or market economy, and the more recently mixed economies we now observe in many countries on earth. What can we say about each? How does each system resolve the basic economic problems?

"THE TRADITIONAL ECONOMY"

The first type of economic system, by its own wording, is based upon tradition. In such a system, decisions conform to the way earlier generations resolved the economic questions. The vast majority of the population is engaged in agriculture. Most production is consumed on the farm or the locality. The system can be described as a subsistence economy. In a subsistence economy cities are small and few in number, trade is limited and the standard of living is low. Methods of production, types of products, levels of output, and ways of life scarcely change from generation to generation.

The traditional economy was prevalent during the Middle Ages. This period began shortly after the fall of Rome in 476 A.D. and lasted about a thousand years. It is referred to as the feudal era. What was called the manor or farm estate emerged then. It was essentially a mini-society within the feudal lord's estate. With over 90% of the working population engaged in agriculture, the manor was a unique type of economic organization. Cities were little more than walled fortifications. But as more and more people moved to the city and the hope of the better life it promised, as trade expanded and the Age of Discovery began, the manorial estate and feudalism in general were doomed in

9

Europe. Similar systems persist today in some parts of Asia and Africa.

"THE COMMAND ECONOMY"

The second type of system is called the command economy. The basic decisions in command economies are made by some central authority. This central authority may be a king, dictator, or governmental agency. Many people feel that parents run (or should run) the household the same way as a command economy. This system characterizes the Soviet Bloc nations.

Command economies have almost invariably been imposed on societies ruled by traditionalism (with a few exceptions in Eastern Europe, such as East Germany). Coincidentally or not, some have instituted modernized versions of the feudal societies of the Middle Ages. For example, a person's residence in the Soviet Union depends largely on the place of birth. A domestic passport system prevails, with passports being valid for five years. Passports contain life history, age, marital status, employment, residence, a personal job history, reasons for separation, etc. Until recently, inhabitants of rural areas were not entitled to a passport, unless recruited for special work. Those without passports were not permitted to visit an urban area for more than five days at a time. Indeed, a member of a collective farm may not even move from one farm to another without permission. The peasantry, some thirty percent of the Soviet population, was tied to the land just as it was in the days of serfdom. Although passports were being issued to rural residents in the mid–1970's, making movement easier, they still needed a registration permit.*

Whereas peasants are on the bottom rung of Soviet society, at the very top are government and party officials. Although substantial income differences prevail, the sharp differences in levels of living are based largely on a vast array of subsidies and special privileges (seats at the opera and ballet, country villas, limousines). Those on top never stand in line.

Must all command economies stratify their members this way? Many economists say yes, many say no. Is their appearance primarily in traditional societies an historical accident, or the

---

*Alec Nove, *The Soviet Economic System* (London: George Allen & Unwin, Ltd., 1977), p. 200.

natural outcome of authoritarian customs in such societies? How much of the limitations on freedom found in command economies are inherent to them? Again, economists and other social scientists disagree. We shall have much more to say about this economy as one of the two polar systems found in industrialized societies today.

"THE MARKET ECONOMY"

Market systems, the third type, are decentralized economic systems in which people or groups of people make their desires known in what is referred to as the marketplace. In the ideal market economy, those who wish to buy and those who wish to sell come to deal with each other. In the process, what is produced, how much is produced, for whom, and at what price it is produced are determined. When one decides to sell something, in effect "a market" is opened. Those who wish to buy what is placed on sale will come to inspect the good. They will accept the price or make a counter-offer, and the other will decide whether to take that counter-offer or not. If the price is too low for the seller or too high for the buyer, the parties may higgle and haggle until they are satisfied with the price. The important thing to remember is that all of this particular kind of trade takes place independently of any central authority, or even of tradition.

"THE MIXED ECONOMIC SYSTEM"

Most systems in this century have been (are) mixed, comprising elements of all the other three, though one of the elements usually prevails over the others. Tradition tends to dominate much of the decision making in many Third World countries such as Thailand and Sri Lanka, although they have well-developed market sectors specializing in rice and tea exports respectively. Other Third World countries, such as Tanzania and India, have introduced significant command elements in basically traditional societies.

How often have you seen a business establishment carrying the "Family Name *and Sons*" in Great Britain, Canada, Germany, Japan, the United States, and other market economy countries you may have visited? Indeed, when feudalism characterized Great Britain and other countries of Western Europe, it was the custom for the eldest son alone to inherit the family fortune. In

11

more recent centuries, other sons, and then daughters too began to inherit some share of the family fortune, besides becoming active participants in the family's business. The increasing equality today of women with men throughout the world possibly portends a significant present (and future) decrease of traditionalism in the market economy. In some market economies, Sweden and the United Kingdom for instance (see Chapter 3), elements of command have grown and restricted the operation of markets. The counterpart applies to command and traditional economies, where use of marketplace relations can be found in some sectors of the economy.

"ECONOMIC INCENTIVES"

What is the fundamental motivation which induces people to produce and exchange goods or services? Answering this important question is not as elementary as one might expect. The factors which distinguish economic systems from each other are not the economic activities each system undertakes, but how decisions are made, and by whom they are made.

The Market Economy

To answer the question raised above we shall assume for simplicity that only two systems are possible: market economies or command economies. Why people produce and exchange in a market economy is simply the individual's "self-interest." People or groups of people in the market economy produce or consume in order to increase their own satisfaction. Consumers increase their satisfaction when they consume more, and producers (including wage and salary earners) increase their satisfaction when their profits and earnings increase. This pressure to increase satisfaction in the market economy makes producers and consumers very efficient at their tasks as well as strongly motivated.

Distinctive Income in the Market Economy

There are different ways of earning or receiving income in the market economy. The most distinctive income earned in such economy is called profit. Unfortunately, previous knowledge about economics has led many to have rather negative views about profits. Some even feel that the profit motive is evil or unfair. But wait a minute; a basic look at profits is in order at this point!

A Note on Profits (Losses)

Profits, we know, are the difference between the amount taken in when one sells a good and the costs involved in producing the good in question. (A fancy way of saying this is that it is the difference between total revenue (TR) and total cost (TC).)

Profits play the central role in market economies. They serve as that signal which indicates to those willing to take a chance where they can best establish a new business. They also stimulate existing firms to become more efficient. Industries making profits attract new investment, and profits, under competitive conditions, lead the market economy to efficiency and growth.

The Command Economy

How is growth and efficiency achieved in a *command economy*? Does self-interest of each individual play the same role? The answer is a sharp "No!" Command economies attempt to replace self-interest as the main motivation for efficient consumption and efficient production. They substitute the social or collective good.* Thus neither production nor consumption are measured by standards of profit or individual satisfactions, but rather by some standard which is considered to benefit the state. The state determines the social good, and is the sole agent for society.

NO PROFIT INCOME IN THE COMMAND ECONOMY

Hard work for the purpose of achieving a higher social good is a difficult pill for many to swallow. So most command economies have tempered their demands for altruism with economic incentives: differences in pay and privileges. There is however no profit income in the command economy, or for that matter rental income as in the United States, since all capital (and business) is owned by the state. The failure to harness individual self-interest strictly for the good of the state has remained a major stumbling block for command economies.

---

*If the command economy is run by a dictator, then it is chiefly the way he conceives of satisfaction and of his (or his country's) profit.

"ECONOMIC PROGRESS IN RECENT YEARS: THE SOVIET ECONOMY"

How has the aggregate economy of the Soviet Union been faring in recent years? The answer is basically well, as evidenced by Table 2.1 below. In particular, the general reader need only note that the USSR has been growing at an average rate among the nations set forth in the table.

TABLE 2.1

AVERAGE ANNUAL RATE OF GROWTH IN REAL GROSS DOMESTIC PRODUCT[a] FOR SELECTED COUNTRIES, 1960–1980

| | Growth Rate | | | |
| | 1960–1970 (percent) | | 1970–1980 (percent) | |
Country	Total	Per capita	Total	Per capita
United States	4.3	3.0	3.0	2.0
Canada	5.6	3.8	3.9	2.8
West Germany	4.4	3.5	2.6	2.6
Sweden	4.4	3.7	1.7	1.4
United Kingdom	2.9	2.4	1.9	1.8
Australia	5.6	3.6	3.0	1.6
USSR[b]	5.2	3.9	5.1[c]	4.2
Yugoslavia[b]	5.8	4.8	5.8	4.9
Japan	10.9	9.9	5.0	3.9
India	3.4	1.1	3.6	1.5
Brazil	5.4	2.5	8.4	6.2

Source: World Bank, *World Development Report,* 1982; for USSR, ibid, 1981

[a]The gross domestic product counts only the output produced domestically by a nation. The output of citizens abroad is excluded. It differs only slightly from gross national product, which can be considered as the total output of goods and services owned by people residing in the country.

[b]Data are for net material product, excluding such industries as public administration, defense, and professional services.

[c]data for 1970–1979

14

We would suggest that a major reason for Soviet progress has been the high percentage share of its total output (call it the gross national product or GNP) that is being devoted to investment. The Soviet Union allocates (by command) 28 percent of its total output to capital improvements compared to 19 percent in the United States. (Incidentally, recent figures indicate that Russia allocates 10 to 17 percent of its GNP to defense compared to about 5 percent in the United States.) Of course, the economic plan of the Reagan administration centers on tax cuts, lower government spending, and regulatory changes designed to elicit substantially greater investment in the United States in the 1980's. What about other facets of the Soviet system?

Consider the housing conditions that prevail in the Soviet Union. The bulk of housing in its cities is owned by the state. The nation's leaders have generally assigned low priority to housing. So the average Russian family lives under very crowded conditions, with little privacy and limited amenities. Families are assigned living quarters by the state, and ordinarily have no say as to the other families with whom they share living space. Housing is typically administered by employing establishments, so that workers are subject to eviction if they change employment. Conversely, the lure of better housing can be and is used by employers to attract workers.

"ECONOMIC PROGRESS IN RECENT YEARS: JAPAN, A FREE ENTERPRISE ECONOMY"

Over 40 percent of Japan's labor force was employed in agriculture in 1950 compared to 12 percent in the United States; by 1980 Japan's agricultural workers had declined to 10 percent of the labor force. Meanwhile the per capita GNP of Japan, which had been one-eighth that of the United States, had risen to almost three-fourths that of the United States. Part of this story is revealed by the almost 10 percent annual average growth of real GNP over the years 1950–1973, reflecting a doubling of family real income every eight years. How do economists account for Japan's remarkable progress?

One vital answer lies in the harmony that exists between Japan's workers and their employers. Since Japan — until recently — lacked a social security system, retirement commonly at age 55 is still based chiefly on private pension plans. In related context, after one year of work in a large firm in Japan, the male employee acquires lifetime tenure in his job. Thus his future is secure provided his company succeeds. Japanese labor unions are enterprise unions concerned with representing blue and lower level white collar workers. They stress improving productivity, maintaining seniority and desirable transfers for workers, assisting management in expansion plans, and the like. Union-management relations typically involve cooperation rather than conflict.

Possibly the most favorable force for "economic growth" in Japan has been its tax structure. Taxes on productive work (income, profit, and payroll taxes) comprise a smaller share of GNP in Japan than in other free enterprise countries, amounting to 21 percent of GNP compared to 28 percent in the United States. Marginal tax rates in Japan have been cut many times since 1950 while the public sector size remained virtually unchanged until the OPEC oil price increases. Quite significantly, the Japanese tax structure is not designed to redistribute income. Moreover, capital gains on sales of securities in Japan are not taxed while other capital gains are taxed at much lower rates than is typical of free enterprise countries. Interest and dividend income carry a maximum 25 percent rate compared to the 70 percent rate in the United States until recently, and the 50 percent top rate now in effect. Small wonder the Reagan administration policy has been designed to effect a real change in the American tax structure, moving our tax structure towards that of Japan.

A basic result of all of the above is a high savings and investment rate in Japan. In fact, a major share of corporate profits is reinvested annually in the company. Thus in place of the 19 percent investment/GNP rate of the United States, we find that post World War II Japan claims a 33 percent ratio. How far up the economic ladder Japan will go is, of course, a matter of opinion. The country is very dependent on imported oil and its growth slowed down after the 1973 OPEC price increase, and again in early 1982 as recession gripped other countries. Japan's exports are highly vulnerable because of their concentration in a limited number of products and markets. Many American economists contend that the more individualistic, innovative daring of American entrepreneurs will combine with an improved business climate, a reduced government bureaucracy, lowered taxes, and better savings incentives to generate a return to economic leadership by the United States. In the meanwhile, Japan is serving as a guiding light.

"INDIVIDUAL VERSUS SOCIAL GOOD"

S.M. Rosen,* who strongly critiques the American economy, asserts that societal interests should, in general, override the private individual interest. I. Kristol notes that:

> "Socialists are persuaded that they have a superior understanding of people's true needs, and that the people will be more truly happy in a society where socialists have the authority to define those needs, officially and unequivocally."**

He goes on to say that to collectivize economic life requires coercion of diverse institutions (e.g., the trade unions, the media, the educational system) besides limiting all sorts of individual freedoms (e.g., the freedom to travel, the freedom to drop out of work, and the freedom to choose the kind of education one prefers). Only then, he asserts, can a "planned society" function efficiently.***

In further support of his position, Kristol later argues**** that Russia, China, and India are responsible for the threat of world famine, not because of geography or demography, but partly because of economics and chiefly because of politics. He contends that agriculture in the Soviet Union has been a disaster area.

The special case of India warrants further mention. Post World War II India was and is a democracy. Agriculture is in private hands. The command economy is a small part of the total. Yet millions are severely malnourished; the very lives of many depend on the timely arrival of a monsoon, on the absence of drought and flood. Why? The "population explosion"? No! Mr. Kristol asserts that India has as much arable land in proportion to population as does France.

---

*S.M. Rosen, ed., "Introduction," *Economic Power Failure* (New York: McGraw-Hill, 1975), p. 45.
**I. Kristol, *Two Cheers for Capitalism* (New York: Basic Books, 1978), p. 13.
***Ibid., p. 14.
****Ibid., p. 40ff.

India's misery in large part is the consequence of a prevalent traditionalism resistant to the changes required for modernization; of entrenched corruption that diverts much food and other aid from those for whom it was intended. But the Indian government has contributed to this, Kristol notes, by subordinating the nation's economy to socialist principles. Agricultural prices were fixed to provide "cheap food for the masses," reducing incentives for farmers to produce food and distributors to market it. Investment in agriculture was neglected while state funds went to manufacturing, steel, machine tools, and nuclear research.

But if socialism is that bad, and if free enterprise is as good as Kristol argues, why do Rosen, Lekachman, and others argue against free enterprise? We shall view the many shortcomings and problems of the free enterprise economy *throughout this book*. In many ways, the real solution to its problems, we shall see, is better understanding by the average citizen of its strengths and shortcomings.

"THE CHOICE OF AN ECONOMIC SYSTEM: HOW DECISIONS ARE MADE: A MATTER OF FREEDOM OR EQUITY"

We have suggested that the choice of an economic system affects (but does not necessarily determine) the personal freedoms of those who live under the system. In fact, a market economy is not necessarily accompanied by civil or political liberty. There are nations characterized by rather illiberal political systems that nonetheless allow free action in economic life. But as Berger pointed out:

> ". . . among those countries that can be called socialist, there is not a single country in which there is democracy. There is not a single country in which human rights and human liberties are even remotely protected against whimsical changes by the state."*

An economic system that emphasizes the command type of decision ordinarily fulfills its goals at the expense of the goods

---

*Peter Berger, "Capitalism and Socialism: Ethical Assessment," in Michael Novak, ed., *Capitalism and Socialism* (Washington, D.C.: American Enterprise Institute for Public Policy Research, 1979), p. 101.

which otherwise would have been produced. Thus if the central authority decides that commodity B, not A, is desirable, it follows that all of the people who would have demanded commodity A must do without the good. They would have to buy (or sell) B instead. The central authority, to be sure, must not then allow any resulting discontent to lead to social unrest. But even if it successfully limits discontent, a major *opportunity cost* associated with command economic systems remains; it is the loss by consumers of the position of dominance they tend to have in determining the goods produced in the market economy.

"A MATTER OF FREEDOM AND EQUITY"

The above comments about an economic system center attention on just how free is the individual in a given economy. The systems which emphasize decentralized markets have often in the past provided the most individual freedom. In contrast, present-day systems involving more central authority appear to allow less personal freedom. They also tend to allow fewer differences in the way people are rewarded. The trade-offs between freedom and economic rewards are clearly important.

What does liberty mean to Americans? In some respects, the basic answer is freedom from government. The American system of government recognizes the individual's intrinsic right to privacy, and encourages private ownership of homes, free of controls by either employer or the state. The fundamental economic role of government in a free enterprise system is not to provide housing, or to provide jobs, but to promote ample and equal opportunity for all. The state is not a guardian for all of us, at most only for those who happen to be incompetent or unfortunate.

It is true that many people still live in squalor in the free enterprise nations of the world. They attest to the failure of the market economy to this point in time to overcome scarcity of resources and consequent limited output, or to distribute output so that all may live in comfort. Nonetheless, one essential difference between the USA and USSR with regard to the poor is the requirement American voters have been placing on their government to promote adequate private single-family housing for all. Moreover, Americans, through private efforts as well as through government, have supported better education for all,

19

given to the poor, and contributed through charitable organizations while promoting selected welfare programs by government. In these ways, the right to privacy, including even the right to be a beachcomber, has been protected. As Nutter* observes about the United States:

John Doe is free to choose his own trade and job, and to shift from one to another as he wishes. If he is willing to bear the consequences and imposes no harm on others dependent on him, he may devote his life to loafing in one degree or another.

The contrast with Russia is sharp: The Soviet constitution stipulates that work is the duty of every able-bodied citizen, according to the principle that whoever does not work shall not eat. In fact, no one of working age is entitled to housing unless currently employed. The obligation to work begins at age sixteen. But that is the way the Soviet Union leaders view the command economy. Must it be that way? Thus far in the history of civilizations on earth, the answer appears to be yes.

"FINAL STATEMENT"

Where individuals specialize, they must also exchange what they produce for what they need. In the market economy, these exchanges are largely voluntary. This is not to suggest that voluntary exchanges do not occur in command economies, only that the voluntary exchanges which do take place are not basic to the performance *of the command economy*. Rather they take place after the economy has determined which goods will be available to its people. Which system is the best for individuals must remain a matter of personal preference. The criteria for evaluating effectiveness include, of course, not only economic values but others as well.

What about some of the economies other than Japan and the USSR? Sweden is closer to a free enterprise state than, say Yugoslavia or, of course, the Soviet Union. How has Sweden been faring? What about Great Britain? It is closer than Sweden to a free enterprise, capitalistic country, yet much further along the

---

*G.W. Nutter, *The Strange World of Ivan Ivanov* (New York: The World Publishing Company, 1969), p. 83.

road to socialism than the United States. What has been Great Britain's progress in recent decades? Most importantly, what about the U.S.A.? It is the leading capitalist country, although much influenced by ideas implemented in Sweden and Great Britain. All three are democratic countries offering a wide range of political rights and freedoms, yet varying in the extent and nature of state regulation and control of the economy. Chapter 3 that follows will focus attention on these countries. Thereafter we will have some understanding of the essential elements of economic systems, and can accordingly proceed toward the ultimate end of evaluating the Reagan administration's economic program. We shall eventually do that in terms of both its short *and* long-run prospects for improving the lives of all Americans.

CHAPTER 3:
PROBLEMS IN THREE
ECONOMIES

"SWEDEN"

Sweden was considered by many people to be proof positive that welfare states are here to stay. The intelligentsia of the world, ever searching for a Utopia on earth, heralded Sweden's socialist economy as the epitome of success. Major changes took place in Great Britain, France, and even in the United States during the 60s and 70s that were modeled in part on the success story of the Swedish economy.

It is well known that Sweden has been endowed with many natural resources (such as lumber, iron ore, and water power). It is blessed with energetic, well-educated people. These advantages alone could not account for the striking gains Sweden made from its low in 1932 to its 1968 peak. Sweden had risen from just an "average European per capita income" status to the top-of-the-ladder where, with Switzerland, it claimed the highest per capita income of all Europe in the late 60s. But a lag exists between cause and effect, both in life and in economic systems. Changes for the worse were slowly enveloping socialist Sweden as the 70s approached.

The slowdown in Sweden actually became manifest during the latter years of the 1968 to 1975 reign of Prime Minister Olaf Palme. Mr. Palme was strongly pro-socialism and anti-capitalism. He contended that the remains of capitalism should be put to rest in Sweden. Thus the harmony that had existed previously between the labor unions of Sweden and the business firms—a basic requirement for the viability of a free enterprise economy—was ended during his administration. Under the preceding regime of Prime Minister Erlander, no significant social-economic state planning had taken place. Apart from the nationalizing of the railroads and public utilities, private enterprise had generally reigned supreme among the industries of Sweden. In many ways, the Swedish economic system had previously been similar to that of the United States, though its income tax did take much greater proportions of the income of the wealthy than did the American income tax. Nevertheless, Sweden still was not a socialist state in the purest sense. Private initiative and private enterprise prevailed notwithstanding the fact that its tax rates on higher incomes were close to punitive levels. Various rebates and allowances were granted to encourage investment and risk taking by businessmen. But "the effect of high personal taxation could not be delayed indefinitely."*

A white collar worker with disposable income of 14 Swedish crowns per hour in 1978 cost his employer 64 crowns; the gap between cost and income of labor of 50 crowns went to the government. Therefore business had every incentive to minimize the use of labor. (It also meant a flourishing black market for labor). Despite a reduced demand for labor by the private sector, government guarantees of employment and income for individuals undermined the restraint of workers in demanding higher wages. Government expenditures to maintain inefficient industries weakened management interest in productivity improvement; high business taxes reduced resources as well as incentives for investment. As a result, a growing share of the labor force has shifted from the more productive private sector to less productive public employment. Egalitarian policies and high taxes created a situation in which government expenditures, and revenues, had to absorb an increasing share of the nation's income.

The consequences can be summarized in the Swedish growth rate in the 1970's, which was the second lowest among the industrial nations of the world and a drop of several places in its ranking in per capita income, which may well continue. By contrast with the 1960's, Sweden experienced in the 1970's:

1. a significant decline in the share of GNP saved and invested;
2. a near-standstill in productivity gains;
3. a decline in industrial output and employment;
4. a marked rise in the rate of inflation;
5. a rising unemployment rate;
6. a worsening balance of trade;
7. rapid growth in its foreign debt, now exceeding $9 billion;
8. continuous growth in government expenditures as a share of the GNP, now over 65 percent;
9. rapid growth in the public deficit and public debt.

---

* A. Shonfield, *The Failure of Socialism* (Washington, D.C.: The Heritage Foundation, 1980), p. 6.

The situation worsened in the late 1970's, for the basic conditions leading to the dismal performance above still prevail.* Sweden's "incomes" policy is still so extreme that workers earning $5,000 ultimately receive $12,000 in disposable income, while those earning $20,000, after paying confiscatory taxes, are reduced to the same $12,000. The average working hours in industry are about 75 percent of what they were in the early 1960's; absence from work because of sickness alone reaches 20 percent of the workforce per day. Employers' taxes on payrolls are about 60 percent of workers' pay; as one result, the number of small and medium-size firms has declined by one-quarter over the last ten years. The firms that remain are in many cases one-man operations. Companies still remaining in the private sector are subject to "codetermination" in management, which means worker representatives on the Board of Directors. In many cases this amounts to having blatantly anti-capitalist union officials helping run private enterprise companies.

"GREAT BRITAIN"

What about Great Britain? That nation had been admired by people throughout the world. Certainly the British people had possessed the highest standard of living in all of Europe up to World War I. By the end of World War II, however, the per capita economic well-being of the Swedes and Swiss had forged ahead of the British. This was not surprising in itself considering the ravages of that war. Yet West Germany suffered from the ravages of the war even more than did Great Britain, but its recovery and subsequent economic health are well known.

Today, after decades of sluggishness (not just a few years of it), Great Britain is among the lowest per capita income nations of Europe. What caused its economic decline? Could it have been the nationalizing of its coal industry, its railroads, steel mills, gas, power, and airline companies? Nationalization after World War II had been effected by a people captivated with the dream of creating "a great world for all." Many believed that greater economic progress and more equality could be provided to all if the nation put into effect economic plans that were similar to the war plans of the allied expeditionary forces.

---

*Shonfield, *op. cit.*, pp. 14–28.

Public ownership of industry does sound good to most people. It will sound good here in the United States when liberal Congressmen and union officials begin to press for codetermination, and then nationalization of, say, the Nation's energy companies. Alas, public ownership is an illusion. Control (real ownership) is placed in the hands of administrators (the bureaucrats) and the union officials who run the company. Great Britain stands as mute testimony to the fact of loss, inefficiency, waste, and a "who cares about the public" attitude that exists when public officials control firms rather than managers who must satisfy private owners.

Beyond its many intrusions by way of public ownership, British government "bombed" industry with regulation after regulation, including wage and price controls. Not only do wage and price controls place bureaucrats on top of bureaucrats—as we shall later see—with nothing produced except paper work and confusion, but they whet the forces of inflation itself. There is, indeed, no logic whatsoever to the expectation that wage and price controls can permanently displace the underlying conditions of supply and demand. In fact, except for war periods, their effect is favorable for six months at the most. After that, results are worse than otherwise would have existed. Furthermore, the overall incomes policy followed by the Labor Party in Great Britain was marked by marginal tax rates on *earned* as well as *investment* income that approached those of Sweden. As a result, Britain's production stagnated, its export industries floundered, and its government deficits and inflation mushroomed.

British labor steadily became more and more militant as jurisdictional disputes between unions in the early '60s served as the forerunner of those which began to plague Sweden a few years later. The entrenched unions sought greater power by monopoly of certain workers, wildcat strikes, and disruption of production. Workers' rights became more important than the "Empire" itself. In fact, the rights of the individual worker—as a member of a union—are now so dominant in Great Britain that even the Thatcher government may fail to arrest the falling British economy. Her government must not only overcome the strong, entrenched labor unions, but also the numerous government civil service workers who want to protect their jobs and their power. The counterpart example in the United States has been New York City, where public officials combined with labor in bankrupting the city.* Can the Thatcher government reverse the tide?

"UNITED STATES"

What about the United States? Let's face it, we are still in trouble! Too many people in Congress and elsewhere, through their regulatory zeal, combined with their desire to plan a better world and to remain in or acquire power, have been sowing the seeds for economic disaster. Take the energy crisis, or the inflation which William Simon so aptly describes as "Made in Washington." What did our recent governments do? Much that has proven wrong—as this book will contend. For the moment, consider one point: By requiring an unduly low price on domestically-produced crude oil, consumption was encouraged. Greater imports followed, along with a smaller domestic recovery of crude than higher prices would have generated. Why—one may quickly ask—would the American government fail to provide incentives for the increased production of domestic crude by American companies? Why would it set up a program that would involve an increase in imports, greater reliance on OPEC oil, greater consumption, and reduced production. Are public officials stupid? We might answer these questions with another question: Why would many in Sweden or Great Britain who favor free enterprise do as they did? Misinformation, bias against industry, and little understanding of the "science" of economics and its basic principles are prevalent there, and in Washington, and elsewhere in the world.

Are American officials (and the public in general) really that uninformed about economics and the free enterprise system? Many are. Without doubt, the economics profession (the profession of these writers) has done a sorry job of educating our college students. Moreover, many of us were actually "planning-oriented" after World War II—at least in the sense of believing in and using Keynesian economics.** Economists have steadily begun to recognize, however, that whenever the nation's leaders

---

*William Simon, A Time for Truth (New York: Berkeley Publishing Co., 1978), pp. 167–169.
**For the moment, regard Keynesian economics as the framework of thought which proposed the idea that full employment and economic progress can be assured by maintaining adequate demand for goods and services; and that adequate demand can be provided by appropriate changes in taxes, government spending, and borrowing.

mix social and political goals with bias and ignorance, everything goes wrong. Witness the inflation and unemployment of the late 1970s and early '80s.

The present writers believe that the Western world, including our own nation, was approaching economic disaster in recent years. The Thatcher government was trying to reverse the Labor Party's decades of leadership. But as will be stressed later in this book, and as was mentioned already, the blocs of unions and civil servants in Great Britain have made effective change there almost impossible. The same holds for Sweden, a pattern that was only slightly reversed while Mr. Palme and his social democrats were out of power in the late 1970's. To say the least, the vested interests of members of strong unions, those in government jobs, those receiving pensions, etc. are hard to break. To be sure, reliance on free enterprise by recent governments in West Germany and Japan has pointed the way to healthy economic growth.

Where does America go from here? Our answer first of all is that if we are to avoid the mistakes of Sweden and Great Britain—originally made in the name of the good life for all—we as voters must learn what free enterprise is about. *And we cannot learn that by discussions of the kind entered in this chapter.* Let us be fair. We have claimed many things in this chapter. We have, hopefully, bothered you, and even angered you because we wanted to promote your desire to probe further into how the world's economies are faring today, especially the American economy. But discussions of the kind entered in this chapter are really empty. If you are inclined to accept our biases and our judgments of what exists and will exist, you simply gained some added "statements and thoughts" to include with your other thoughts. If our statements are contrary to what you hope is the case, you will shortly forget what we said.

True knowledge does not derive from assertions about economics and economic problems, such as we have deliberately set forth in this chapter. In order to understand why we contend that socialism must fail, why we contend that the free enterprise economy of the United States is an endangered species, and why further growth of government will destroy our system of freedoms, we must probe *analytically* into economic relations. We must formally (scientifically) establish principles of economics just as would a mathematician who is charged with deriving fundamental theorems of the calculus. Is it not clear that only after having done this can we (or the mathematician) apply an accepted analytical framework as the means for evaluating this or that program (this or that engineering design)? So unfortunately, we *are* saying that in order to learn about free enterprise, one cannot watch T.V., read the *Wall Street Journal,* or *Barrons,* or *The New York Times,* or a chapter such as this one. In order to learn economics, one must either go to a college and study it there or *work through this book* or one like it. Even then, people will differ in policies preferred.

As we previously indicated, we shall try to simplify our development of economic science as much as possible. We will focus attention only on the analytical tools that are vitally necessary to an understanding of the economic principles which most directly affect all Americans. Yet we must present some analytical diagrams, even though most readers prefer words instead of figure representations. In short, throughout this book, you will simply have to "work with us." But if you do, you will not be like the bank president who (during a social discussion) praised the 1978 farmer's march on Washington in quest of higher price supports and then condemned the minimum wage law. Surely if a bank president does not understand that the two regulations are *analytically identical,* we are in trouble. We should either approve of each on the basis of some special principle (or ethic); or, if sufficiently versed in economics, we should recognize that each involves the same contradiction. Economic analysis proposes that the minimum wage law helps the somewhat skilled white adult while in general increasing the unemployment of young persons, oftentimes black youths. Farm price supports, at the same time, tend to help the wealthy farmer while generating agricultural surpluses. Laws of this kind lead to other laws and controls over people. An enlarged bureaucracy results which often leaves society in a worse position than it was in before. Notwithstanding their impact, high minimum wages are supported by labor union officials and by leaders of the black community; and government-created high prices on farm produce are generally praised by farmers.

"FINAL STATEMENT"

Let us sum up the main point of this chapter. Simply asserting economic effects, such as those claimed in this chapter, actually involves presenting the reader with a set of empty statements.

You should demand proof of our statements before modifying your view of economic policy. Though you may want, for example, to contend that "everyone is entitled to a fair wage," as did Plato, Aristotle, St. Thomas Acquinas, and many others, what would you say if it follows from economic analysis that the fair (minimum) wage law tends to lead to unemployment and hence to more crimes, to more state supervision of the innumerable Americans victimized one way or the other by such a law? All of this is *not* to say that we can't do anything about providing better income shares. It is to say that only after Americans learn economic principles can we, as a people, force legislators and Presidents to alter their priorities. Only then can we expect our nation's leaders to provide minimum, well-directed interferences that will maintain our freedom while providing a fair start, good opportunity, and an acceptable retirement for all.

May we repeat in conclusion our belief that we will be able to present certain formal analytical tools of economics in a comparatively painless way for the reader. Yet, *you* will have to do some work in reading this book. But by the time this book has been completely read, we believe you will be well educated in the basic economics that hopefully all voters and all public officials of a free enterprise democracy want to possess.

INTRODUCTION
TO PART TWO
ON THE MONETARY
ECONOMY

Part Two of the book centers attention on the meaning and place of money in the American economy. It examines the operation of our banking system and the Federal Reserve System's controls over the money supply. The reader will find that banks— as dominated by the Board of Governors of the Fed—actually *create* money, sometimes excessively and sometimes insufficiently. In the initial event, the monetary policy is considered to be expansionary; in the latter event of a slow rate of growth (or even a decline) in the stock of money, monetary policy is called restrictive. Most vital for present purposes is the need to learn *how and when* money is created in free enterprise economies. Later in the book, we shall examine deliberate attempts to generate expansionary or contractionary growths as well as their related impacts on the value of the dollar.

PART TWO:
MONEY AND BANKING
CHAPTER 4:
WHAT IS MONEY?

All advanced economies have one feature in common: money. It is a key to understanding how any complex economy functions. Without money, only simple, poor economies can exist, for specialization and trade is severely limited by the clumsy procedure of barter. What are the basic features of money? What is money? Where does it come from? Who creates it? These are, of course, some of the fundamental questions this chapter must answer.

"BASIC FEATURES OF MONEY"

Money is any quickly recognized *unit of some specified value* accepted readily by people in payment for the things they want. It follows that money *serves as a medium of exchange* which is easily recognized and accepted in payment of goods. Now these two characteristics, call them *unit of account* and *medium of exchange,* allow use of a wide variety of items as money, including gold, silver, even wampum, hides, and arrowheads. You, in fact, may recall from your studies of history that each of these items was used by different people as money. The distinguishing characteristic, we must emphasize, is that the unit of the *commodity* selected must have a substantial use other than as money — thus gold can be used in jewelry, hides in the making of clothes, and arrowheads as weapons.

"PAPER MONEY, COMMODITY MONEY"

A unit of paper money is a medium of exchange, but *not a commodity medium of exchange*. The reason for this is that the paper involved has virtually no effective use *except as money*. A gold coin, on the other hand, is *a commodity medium of exchange*. It has significant use in exchange (as money) and as a good (in jewelry).

As society advanced, paper money was used *to represent* a given quantity of gold. The convertibility of paper money to gold was initially important because it provided a link between that paper money and the commodity, gold. But in time even that link was dropped. Strictly speaking *paper money* has no use other than as money; it is therefore not a commodity medium of exchange. It is not currently tied in the United States on a fixed basis to any other commodity, such as gold.

"OTHER CHARACTERISTICS OF MONEY"

We are ready to compare some of the items that have been used to effect exchange, in order to determine other characteristics of money. Gold, for example, was more widely used than arrowheads. The reason for this had roots in the other uses of an arrowhead. Suppose a tribe suddenly needed more arrowheads for defense (or for killing edible game). One would *literally* see the people's "stock of money" disappearing everytime an arrow was shot at the enemy (or at an animal). For a short while, the value of arrowheads would rise. But as more arrowheads were used in defense or for hunting game, the relative advantages in using arrowheads as a medium of exchange would go down.

It should be clear that substantial changes in the supply of a commodity used as money will alter the quantity of other goods for which that money exchanges. So when the supply of the commodity used as money suddenly decreases sharply, its value in effect goes up *and* the prices of the goods for which it exchanges fall. The converse holds if its supply suddenly increases (e.g., the war ends and mass production of arrowheads takes place.) The sudden increase in supply lowers its value, in effect raising the price of other things.

The demand and supply of a commodity used as money should thus be stable. This is so because either an unstable demand or an unstable supply signifies unnecessary and substantial changes in the price level. Witnessing the disturbing effects of inflation in recent years (or recalling the harmful effects of deflation in the depression years) points to the fact that good money requires a monetary unit that tends to have stable purchasing power. The third feature of money is therefore that it serves as a *store of value*. Let's consider this feature below in greater detail.

"STABLE COMMODITY MEDIA OF EXCHANGE"

The commodity media which have been used the longest have been the ones with *limited secondary uses* — such as gold, silver, and precious stones. They were scarce enough to maintain their value, and limited enough in secondary uses to insure being available as a medium of exchange. When a money maintains its value without undue fluctuations, it can adequately perform its function as "a store of value." This means money is not only *a unit of account* and *a medium of exchange*, but good money is one that has approximately the same future exchange value in terms of other goods as it has today. To repeat, besides being a *unit of account* and *medium of exchange*, money serves as a *store of value*. If prices of other things inflate often and rapidly, it fails this third criterion.

Time, Specialization, and Trade

There is a final, but crucial consideration about commodity media of exchange that should be mentioned here. In some respects, it is the most important consideration. Recognize that the use of commodity money reduces the amount of time it takes an individual to exchange goods in the marketplace. This means more time is available for producing goods. To the extent that our forerunners on earth were not ready to accept paper money or other present-day media of exchange, commodity money therefore served as the vehicle which made specialization and trade between different peoples not only possible but advantageous.

"TOWARDS STRICTLY PAPER MONEY"

Gold, silver, wampum, precious jewels, and other commodities were ultimately replaced by paper money. As societies became more complex, and thus as the demands for money grew, gold and silver supplies simply could not keep pace with the demands for more money. In addition, commodity money was not easily transported. (Imagine—for example—carrying $1,000 worth of gold in your pocket. In the year 1929, $1,000 was roughly equal to 50 ounces of gold. Would not ten $100 paper bills be lighter, more portable, and easier to verify than 50 ounces of gold?) Economic systems had to find other, more efficient media of exchange.

The search for a medium of exchange more efficient than arrowheads, wampum, silver, or even gold led to paper money. Paper money, of course, does not have any intrinsic value; it has value *only* as *money*; so, it is different from the commodity monies discussed above. To be sure, when paper money was first used, it was linked to a commodity money, such as gold or silver. Historians refer to this link as the "instant repurchase agreement." That meant the state would convert the paper into a *fixed amount* of gold or silver at the option of the holder of the money. In most countries of the world today, this "instant repurchase" right no longer exists. It was eliminated during the depression years of the 1930s in most countries. All paper money not convertible into a commodity is called "fiat money," provided the government which issues it also makes it legal tender.*

"MONEY DEFINED FORMALLY"

There are as many definitions of money as there are different kinds of money. A good working definition, however, would go beyond the earlier statements that money is simply anything which serves as a unit of account, a medium of exchange, and a store of value. The definition would have to stress the fact that whatever serves as money must be something that is *readily accepted* by people *in exchange for goods or services*. So money can be defined as anything serving as a unit of account, medium of exchange, and store of value that is readily accepted by the people in exchange for goods and services. Under this definition, such diverse "monies" as wampum, paper currency, and demand deposits (checking accounts) would be classifiable as *money*. By the same token, the definition would *exclude* many claims on wealth which almost serve as money and are called "near" money in economics, such as certificates of deposit and stock certificates. They are excluded since they are not readily (easily) accepted in exchange for goods and services. A better understanding of money can be gained by looking further at the basic roles of money in present-day economies.

"THE BASIC ROLES OF MONEY"

Money has three *roles* in an economic system. To repeat, it serves first as a *unit of account*. In this capacity, it is similar to other units of measurement, such as the yardstick, the centimeter, the ounce, or the liter. Specific units of money vary. For example, the

---

*Technically, legal tender means a creditor must accept it in payment of a debt requiring a money payment; otherwise, no further interest will be due on that debt.

United States uses the dollar, Mexico uses the peso, France the franc. These measures make it easy to express the value of different things in terms of the nation's standard unit of account. When something sells for $25.00 compared to $5.00, the unit of account imparts significant information about comparative values to all potential buyers of the good.

The second role of money is to serve as a *medium of exchange*. The importance of money as a medium of exchange is unique. It provides its users with *generalized* purchasing power. Any study of a well developed economy must center on the importance attached to having a money unit that also possesses generalized purchasing power. This attribute enables individuals to avoid the problem associated with a barter system and uncertain commodity prices. Indeed, as business relationships become more and more complex and interdependent, the efficient operation of an economic system depends upon how well money serves as a medium of exchange. A nation's failure to develop an efficient money would retard its economic progress and development.

The third role of money is to serve as a *store of value*. Stability in the value of money helps it serve best in this regard. On the other hand, if its value fluctuates widely (as when extreme changes in its supply take place), then the store of value function would be fulfilled inefficiently. In present-day economies, the national monetary authority helps control the supply of money. Violent swings in the supply that are not offset by corresponding changes in demand will undesirably affect money's "store of value" function.

"THE MONEY SUPPLY IN THE UNITED STATES"

The money supply of the United States is made up of various types of money produced on the one hand by government, and on the other hand by banks.

"GOVERNMENT PRODUCED MONEY"

There are two broad categories of government produced money: coins and paper currency. With the exception of the penny and the nickel, the small coins minted before 1965 by the United States Treasury were chiefly silver coins, though gold pieces in dollar denominations were in prominent use in the nineteenth century. The paper money printed by the Treasury is called "the U.S. Note" and is quite unimportant today. Table 4.1 indicates how comparatively unimportant is the U.S. Treasury note. There were only $577 million dollars worth of U.S. notes in 1982 compared to $142 billion dollars worth of federal reserve notes. [Federal reserve notes are issued by the Federal Reserve Banks (there are twelve of them in the United States). Look in your wallet and you will find that the paper dollars you have are called Federal Reserve Notes. We will see how and when they are issued later on.] For the moment, recognize further that Table 4.1 indicates that the value of coins in the United States is relatively small.

TABLE 4.1

UNITED STATES CURRENCY IN CIRCULATION
(DEC. 31, 1982)
(MILLIONS OF DOLLARS)

Paper Currency	
U.S. Treasury Notes and other notes (about 60% of this total is being retired)	$ 577
Federal Reserve Notes	$141,984
Total Value of Paper Money in 1982	$142,561
Coins	
Total Value of Coins in 1982	$ 13,597
Total Currency Value in 1982	$156,158

Source: *Treasury Bulletin,* 1st Quarter Fiscal 1983, p. 140

"BANK PRODUCED MONEY"

The most important money we have is the money printed by banks, called demand deposits or checkbook money. When an individual deposits paper money in his bank, that money has been removed from circulation; in its place is the checking account the bank has provided. Via checking accounts, individuals purchase goods from sellers. Any purchase is effected by a simple transfer of an individual's demand deposit with a bank to that of the seller in the seller's bank. (We shall see in Chapter 5, that when the buyer's bank differs from that of the seller, the buyer's bank in effect pays the seller's bank the face value of the check.)

Checking accounts are also created by bank loans. In fact, the largest part of demand deposit money stems from bank loans. (The next chapter will explain how loans are made *and* how this kind of checkbook money comes about.)

Demand deposits account for as much as 70 percent of the total money supply in the United States. They totalled some $363 billion at the end of December, 1982. Coins and paper currency amounted to $156 billion (Table 4.1) which, when added to demand deposits, provided a total U.S. money supply of about $519 billion.

"THE SUPPLY AND VALUE OF MONEY"

To the economist, the most basic money supply is made up of (1) all the coins and currency in the hands of individuals and nonbank business establishments plus (2) the demand deposits (or checking accounts) of individuals and nonbank business establishments kept in the commercial banks of the country. Because of their overwhelming importance in influencing price levels *and* thus the value of money, our discussion of money will center on how demand deposits are created.

We shall find later in the book that the value of money is determined by the same demand and supply forces that determine the prices of goods and services in general. Thus, for example, if we could substantially increase the supply of money just by "snapping our fingers," the value of money would fall. It would fall because as more money is available for acquiring goods and services, prices in general rise. In fact, they tend to rise proportionately to the increase in supply of money. So, *more money* signifies *higher prices* while *less money* signifies *lower prices, all other things equal.* The value of money is less the higher are prices.

"FINAL STATEMENT"

Economists contend that inflation stems from an *excessive supply of money relative to the goods and services being offered* in exchange for money. The statement that government produces paper money and banks provide checkbook money does not account, however,

39

for any relative excess that may exist in the supply of money compared to the supply of goods and services. Rather, the particular reason(s) for a relative excess (or, a relative shortage) of something must be determined by independent analysis. In the remainder of Part Two, we examine the forces governing the *quantity* of money in circulation. Then in the next units of the book, we shall determine the forces that generate large or small supplies of goods and services. The chapters immediately following on the supply of money will focus attention on the ability of the Board of Governors of the Federal Reserve System to, in a sense, increase (or decrease) the supply of money by "snapping their fingers." But first, we must examine how individual commercial banks create money. Thus Chapter 5 inquires into the ability of commercial banks to *create money* by lending demand deposits to customers—borrowers of the bank.

CHAPTER 5:
BANKS AND CHECKBOOK MONEY

Banking is certainly one of the most vital, yet possibly the least understood, business operation in the American economy. Most Americans, in fact, do not think of the commercial bank as a *business corporation*. But a commercial bank *is* a profit-making corporation, just as is GM or Eastman-Kodak. The major difference between a bank and a manufacturing company is that the commercial bank can "create" money whereas manufacturing corporations cannot.

"AMERICAN BANKS INCORPORATED AND THEIR DEPOSITS"

As with any other business, banks may (and typically do) incorporate. Once the bank has incorporated, its primary task is to make a profit by attracting depositors and then investing the money they have on hand. All sorts of organizations, government bodies, and people deposit their money in a commercial bank, and for many different reasons. Some individuals put their money on deposit with a bank for safety and convenience. Other depositors may be interested in the money they can make (interest payments) by letting the bank use their deposits. Fortunately, only two main types of bank deposits require emphasis in a study of economics—namely, checking (or demand) deposits and time (or savings) deposits.

"CHECKING OR DEMAND DEPOSITS"

Once the bank has incorporated and opened its doors, the first task is to attract large quantities of deposits. *Demand or checking accounts* are nothing more than money put on *deposit* with the bank. The unique aspect of demand deposits is that *by writing a check*, the depositor can order (demand) the bank to pay to another whatever the depositor desires—up to the limit of the account. This is why such deposits are called *demand* deposits.

About 75 percent of a particular bank's demand and time deposits come from individuals, business partnerships, and corporations. The way in which the depositor demands payment by

41

the banks is through a check. The money placed on deposit is an *asset* to the depositor (something owned that is desirable), but a *liability* to the bank (something owed to another). Therefore, the bank must keep its depositor's money in such a way that when the depositor wishes to write a check, the deposit can be transferred to someone else. We shall say more about this transfer later.

"TIME DEPOSITS"

The second major category of bank deposits is the *time deposit*. Time deposits differ from demand deposits in that checks typically cannot be written against time deposits. The depositor must keep the money in the bank for a specified period of time. In return, banks pay a fixed amount of interest to the (time) depositor. The money paid (interest) increases during the time the money is kept on deposit.

The most commonly known time deposits today are the *savings accounts* and *certificates of deposits* (CD's). Certificates of deposit generally pay a higher rate of interest than regular passbook savings accounts *because CD's require the depositor to keep the money on deposit for a longer period of time.* As with demand deposits, individuals, business partnerships, and corporations constitute the largest source of the nation's time deposits.

Most recently a hybrid type of account, typically referred to as a NOW account, has become prominent. Those accounts pay interest on deposits of a certain significant size, which deposits are also regularly subject to partial withdrawal by checks. In general, a larger minimum size deposit must be kept at the bank behind the NOW account compared to the demand deposit. For our purposes, these NOW accounts can be regarded as comparatively

TABLE 5.1

LIABILITIES OF INSURED COMMERCIAL BANKS (FEBRUARY 28, 1983)

	Amount in Billions	Percent
Demand Deposits	$ 337.9	25
Time & Savings Deposits	$1,030.4	75
Total	$1,368.3	100

Source: Extracted from the March 1983, *Federal Reserve Bulletin*, p. A.18.

inactive *demand deposits*. (See Table 5.1 for amount (size) of deposits in commercial banks.)

"BANK OPERATIONS"

Now that the commercial bank company has been viewed with particular regard to its main types of deposits, let us examine how this business unit makes a profit. The bank (as a corporation) faces a rather complex dilemma. It has a responsibility to its shareholders to make the highest earnings possible. But highest earnings are oftentimes associated with the most risky ventures. The other side of the dilemma for the bank is to provide the maximum amount of security for its depositors. Some compromise between these competing goals is clearly in order. Thus we can say that the bank faces a "minimax" problem (*minimize* risk yet *maximize* earnings).

"ITS PORTFOLIO"

The major assets of commercial banks are *loans* (55%) and *securities* (20%). Part of the "minimax" problem for the commercial bank centers around the best mix between loans and securities. The best mix signifies that different assets must earn the highest profits while, at the same time, providing the greatest security. With this in mind, the main earning asset for the commercial bank is typically its commercial and industrial loans.

Commercial and industrial loans total about 40% of all bank loans. Table 5.2 illustrates the breakdown of all types of loans made by commercial banks. For our purposes, note that besides commercial and industrial loans, real estate loans are substantial, as are loans to individuals, particularly for the purchase of automobiles.

"A LOOK BACK INTO HISTORY: CREATING MONEY"

The best way to begin a study of a bank's ability to "create" money is to take a look back into history. The medieval goldsmith, it turns out, was one of the first bankers. His was typically the only business establishment in a medieval village that could offer a secure (safe) place to store gold. Anyone concerned about the safety of personal holdings of jewelry and gold was tempted to leave them with the goldsmith for safekeeping. In time, the

TABLE 5.2

LOANS AND DISCOUNTS OF DOMESTIC OFFICES WITH ASSETS OVER $100 MILLION (SEPTEMBER 30, 1982)

Loans and Discounts	Amount in Millions	Percent
1. Commercial and Industrial loans	$316,301	40.4
2. Real estate loans	219,185	28.0
3. Loans to domestic and foreign banks	33,771	4.3
4. Loans to other financial institutions	29,712	3.8
5. Loans to farmers	11,876	1.5
6. Loans to brokers and dealers in securities	7,532	1.0
7. Other loans to purchase securities	4,308	0.5
8. Loans to individuals	133,202	17.1
a. passenger cars	38,015	4.9
b. residential repair	7,746	1.0
c. credit cards	32,281	4.1
d. other retail consumer goods	7,451	1.0
e. other installment loans	17,407	2.2
f. mobile homes	6,714	0.9
g. single payment loans to individuals	24,087	3.1
9. All other loans	26,914	3.4
TOTAL LOANS AND DISCOUNTS	$783,304	100.0

Source: Federal Reserve Bulletin, January 1983, page A72

goldsmith began to realize that many of the people who left their gold with him for safekeeping seldom wanted to *use* that gold. He thus considered the advantage of lending a portion of the stored gold to other citizens, at least for a period of time. At the same instant, he would try to assure himself that there would always be enough gold on hand for return to the few depositors who might need their gold. Obviously, a profit would be made on the gold loaned out.

For example, suppose a person (call him A) enters the gold-smith's shop on the first day of the month and leaves $100 in gold for safekeeping. Suppose A advised the goldsmith not to expect his return until the last day of the month to claim the gold. Now, any enterprising young goldsmith would realize that if the gold belonging to A is *loaned* to another person (say B), and if B is very, very likely to repay the gold before the last day of the month, the young goldsmith would earn extra money in addition to the service charge for the safekeeping of the gold. The way to make extra money is simply to charge B interest on the amount of A's money that is loaned to B. Therefore, when B repays, the re-payment includes the total amount of gold that was loaned plus the additional amount for the interest payment. Whatever that interest payment is, it provides a *profit*. This profit, in fact, is a return to the goldsmith for undertaking the risk of having made the loan in the first place. (Note, profit is the *reward* for con-ducting a risky business venture involving services or products for which there is a need.)

"THE MODERN BANK AS A CREATOR OF MONEY"

While the goldsmith story may be stretching history a little, the example does indicate how modern commercial banks "create" money. They lend a fraction of the money left with them—as demand deposits (and also part of the time and savings deposits in the bank)—to other people. To see how that process works, assume the following:
1. One bank is in operation in a given town.
2. The bank is required to keep 20% of any demand deposits on reserve.
3. All loans that will be made are to be effected in the form of creating additional demand deposits, *and not by giving out cash.*

For the sake of keeping relationships as simple as possible, also imagine that the subject bank has just opened. Do not be con-cerned with such matters as how much money was invested by stockholders, how costly is the bank building, and the like. Rather, we shall focus only on the events that enable one to understand how money (in the form of demand deposits) arises. Let the following events take place:

A depositor enters the bank and opens a checking account in

45

the amount of $1,000 dollars. Table 5.3(a) presents part of the bank's balance sheet. The left side lists the assets the bank gains from the deposit, and the right side lists the liability (the debt) it owes as a result of the deposit. The table is balanced with regard to the cash deposit received and the associated debt to repay that cash whenever the depositor wants it back. More specifically, the cash it received is an asset to the bank, while the demand deposit (the checking account) the bank creates for the depositor represents its debt to the depositor. The basic problem confronting the managers of the bank, as with the goldsmith of yesteryear, is to determine how much of the cash deposited at the bank should be left in its vault, and how much of that cash can be loaned to others.

TABLE 5.3(a)

PART OF THE BANK'S BALANCE SHEET
GIVEN A DEPOSIT OF $1,000.00

ASSETS		LIABILITIES	
Cash	$1,000.00	Demand Deposit	$1,000.00

The actual amount a bank chooses to lend depends partially on the market in which it operates. The Federal Reserve Authorities will establish a minimum percentage of reserves required as security against demand deposits. Recall the assumption of 20% required reserves; this percentage controls the maximum amount the bank can lend.

Table 5.3(b) demonstrates the following: 20% of the original $1,000 deposit ($200) is being reserved under the heading "Re-

TABLE 5.3(b)

THE BANK'S BALANCE SHEET
AFTER TAKING OUT 20% REQUIRED RESERVES

ASSETS		LIABILITIES	
Required Cash Reserves	$200.00	Demand Deposit	$1,000.00
Other Cash Reserves (Excess)	800.00		

quired Cash Reserves." But this leaves $800 in free or excess cash, which is not earning an interest return for the bank and which presumably could be put to work towards such an end.

Look at Table 5.3(c). Notice what has been done: the $800 excess cash on hand was used to support a New Demand Deposit. And an asset called "Loans" is received in the form of a promissory note in exchange for the new deposit liability. Think for a moment about everything that has occurred. $1,000 was received in the form of a demand deposit, 20% of that $1,000 was kept on reserve against the original demand deposit. The remaining $800 served as the basis to create a new demand deposit liability—a *derivative demand deposit* as it is often called. Against that new liability is a new asset (loans). [Because after the new demand deposit of $800 was created, 20% (= $160) is required, not all of the $800 is excess cash reserves; so we refer to them in Table 5.3(c) simply as "Other Cash Reserves" rather than as "Other Cash Reserves (Excess)" as we had done in Table 5.3(b).]

TABLE 5.3(c)

BALANCE SHEET OF BANK AFTER MAKING A LOAN

ASSETS		LIABILITIES	
Required Cash Reserves on original deposits	$200.00	Demand Deposit	$1,000.00
Other Cash Reserves (of which 20% required against derivative deposit)	800.00	New Demand Deposit or Derivative Deposit	800.00
Loans	800.00		

Recognize that the new demand (or derivative deposit) is an *additional* demand deposit created by the fractional reserve banking system. That deposit was *derived*, of course, from the original $1,000 in demand deposits, causing the amount of demand deposits in the bank to total $1,800 at this point in time. The $800 additional deposit will shortly be "used up" by the borrower. All the bank officials must do after the $800 has been borrowed *and then withdrawn from the bank by the borrower(s)* is to make sure that the person(s) who was loaned the $800 will pay it back before the original customer of the bank demands the full $1,000 that was deposited. Clever if done right, isn't it?

47

"MULTIPLE BANK EXPANSION"

Let us now relax the assumption that our bank is the only bank in existence. When one views the entire banking system, the $1,000 in deposits plus the $800 loan will generate still additional loans. Consider Table 5.4: Panel I basically repeats Table 5.3(c) with a slight change in wording for simplicity; in particular we drop the word cash in referring to reserves. What happens when the person who borrowed the $800 from Bank A writes a check to buy $800 worth of goods? Suppose the seller of those goods deposits the $800 check (drawn against Bank A) with Bank B. In practice, Bank B gains the $800 of other reserves from Bank A and simultaneously incurs a new demand deposit liability of $800 to the seller of the goods who deposited the $800 check at Bank B.

TABLE 5.4

MULTIPLE BANK EXPANSION

PANEL I: Bank A After Making Loan			
ASSETS			LIABILITIES
Required Reserves on original deposit	$200.00	Demand Deposit	$1,000.00
Other Reserves (20% required vs. derivative deposit)	800.00	Derivative Deposit	800.00
Loans	800.00		
	$1,800.00		$1,800.00

Panel II: Bank A After Borrower Writes Check			
Required Reserves on original deposit	$200.00	Demand Deposit	$1,000.00
Other Reserves	–0–		
Loans	800.00		
	$1,000.00		$1,000.00

Bank B with New Deposit of $800.00			
Reserves vs. New Deposit	$800.00	Demand Deposit	$800.00
	$800.00		$800.00

(See Panel II.) Note that Bank A loses its $800 of other reserves to Bank B while at the same time Bank A's deposits decrease by $800 as Bank B's go up by that amount.

Let us focus further attention on this last transaction. Observe in Panel II that Bank B is in basically the same position now as was Bank A back in Table 5.3(c). It *must apply 20%* of its reserves against its $800 demand deposit. In other words, it has to keep $160 as required reserve against the $800 deposit, leaving the remaining $640 to serve as the basis for a loan (and hence a derivative deposit). Panel I of Table 5.5 below depicts Bank B's position after it has made the loan of $640. But since we are still talking about a system of banks, we have to ask the question— what happens to the $640 loan when it is checked out and deposited in Bank C? Panel II of Table 5.5 provides the answer.

One concern in your mind might thus be, "What causes the process of creating additional deposits to end?" Another might

TABLE 5.5

MULTIPLE BANK EXPANSION

PANEL I: Bank B After Making Loan

Required Reserves on original deposit	$160.00	Demand Deposit (original)	$800.00
Other Reserves (20% required vs. derivative deposit)	640.00	Derivative Deposit	640.00
Loans	640.00		
	$1,440.00		$1,440.00

Panel II: Bank B After Borrower Writes Check

Required Reserves	$160.00	Demand Deposit	$800.00
Other Reserves	-0-		
Loans	640.00		
	$800.00		$800.00

Bank C with New Deposit of $640.00

Reserves on New Deposit	$640.00	Demand Deposit	$640.00

be, "How does the entire system's expansion of deposits relate to the process of money creation by a single bank?" Let us resolve these questions as follows:

"THE BANKING SYSTEM"

What happened in the *single bank* case was that it loaned what are called its "excess reserves." *Excess reserves* are defined as:

$$\text{Excess Reserves} = \text{Actual Reserves} - \text{Required Reserves}$$
$$\$800 = (\$1,000) - (.20 \times \$1,000)$$
$$\$800 = (\$1,000) - (\$200)$$

Looking again at the single bank example, observe that in Table 5.3(b) excess reserves were $800. In the multiple bank example, the individual bank loaned only an amount equal to its excess reserves; but many banks were involved. In fact, new demand deposits (derivative deposits) were created, and could be created up to the limit where all banks have zero excess reserves.

"THE LIMIT TO DERIVATIVE DEPOSITS"

We can readily determine *how many* new deposits the entire banking system is able to create. A simple formula indicates that the amount of deposits which can be created is a multiple of the amount of excess reserves. This multiple is equal to the reciprocal of the required reserve percentage applicable to the demand deposits. If this reserve percentage is 10% (= 1/10), the reciprocal is 10; if the reserve ratio is 5% (= 1/20), the reciprocal is 20.

Let us continue with the basic example: The original $800 of excess reserves can lead to a total of $4,000 worth of new demand deposits. We see this as follows:

$$
\begin{aligned}
\text{Derivative Demand Deposits} \ &= \ \$800 \times \tfrac{1}{20}\% \\
&= \ \$800 \times 1/(\tfrac{1}{5}) \\
&= \ \$800 \times 5 \text{ (the reciprocal of} \\
&\qquad \tfrac{1}{5}) \\
&= \ \$4,000
\end{aligned}
$$

Remember, each bank will, by itself, typically lend only to the limit of its excess reserves; but when all of the excess reserves of each bank are added, a derivative demand deposit multiple of those reserves arises.* These deposits *in our numerical example* add up to $4,000. This is how banks create money.

The process comes down to this: If—in the nation as a whole—$1 is required against $10 of deposits, $1 of excess reserves can support $10 of new loans (or derivative deposits). If required reserves are $2 against $10, or say $1 against $5, $1 of excess reserves will enable *all* banks operating together to expand the amount of money (that is, new demand deposits) by $5. Again, the total new deposits that can be created are a multiple of the underlying excess reserves in the system, which multiple is the reciprocal of the reserve requirement. *The process can work in reverse.* If a withdrawal of deposits reduces reserves below requirements, banks must reduce their loans by a multiple. The banking system as a whole will reduce the credit by the reciprocal of the reserve requirement percentage times the shortage in reserves.

THE ROLE OF SAVINGS AND LOAN ASSOCIATIONS IN TODAY'S MONEY SUPPLY

Within the last few years, savings and loan associations have increasingly taken on the general appearance of commercial banks as they began instituting checking accounts, styled NOW accounts, and, more recently, money market accounts *and* super NOW accounts. One may well wonder how these permissions and the tendency to deregulate the banking industry will affect the money creation process described above. Without going into unnecessary particulars, let us observe the following:

Savings and loans historically do *not* maintain big vaults to store their cash and related assets. Rather, they use commercial banks for their deposits, for clearing checks, and for their extra cash reserves. To see how it works, let us initially imagine an individual who has written a check withdrawing $3,000 of his deposits in a commercial bank; his goal was to move the money to a high interest paying money market account at a local S&L. In that new account, he will be allowed three checks per month without

---

*It warrants special note that because checkbook money from derivative deposits has exactly the same character as the checkbook money which arose from a cash deposit by a customer, the total of the two types is carried on the books of the bank simply as *demand deposits*.

charge. What happens to the money supply? What happens to the money expansion limits?

Answers to the above questions require our recognizing that the S&L will—upon the deposit of $3,000—credit its new customer with the account and redeposit the customer's check at the commercial bank which holds the S&L's deposits. For simplicity, let that commercial bank be one and the same as the bank whose customer withdrew $3,000. To all intents and purposes, the commercial bank has simply changed creditors (depositors) from the individual to the S&L for $3,000. The bank's reserves, credit expansion potential and deposit liability accounts are all unchanged. However, the S&L also has $3,000 of deposits against which *it* must maintain a small fractional reserve. It can, therefore, lend most of the $3,000, presumably to a builder or an individual buying a house. This money will be redeposited in time back with some S&L or commercial bank. If it goes back to another S&L, that S&L can lend a substantial fraction. So the process repeats itself. If the money goes back to a commercial bank, the process ends just as it would if a check between individuals stayed with a commercial bank, having no excess reserves.

A *multiple* expansion of new credit, in effect can stem from the initial $3,000, the same as if—at the beginning of this chapter's explanation of the money creating process—we had proposed that Mr. A. took $3,000 of money out of his drawer and deposited that money in Bank A. The only difference here is that we have had funds moved from one type of bank to a special type of (intermediate) bank. This process, called intermediation, in the sense that another layer of depositories exists, involves a special *extra* expansionary source of money (checking accounts). It is one reason why the money supply mushroomed so substantially in the early part of 1983 and, in turn, a reason why the Fed in March 1983 advised of its intent to slow down the increasing supply of money in the months to come.

The unique feature of introducing the S&L is that if the commercial bank(s) were fully loaned up, the mere act of switching money to the S&L, redeposited in turn with a commercial bank(s), kept the commercial banks in their original position but gave the S&L credit expansion potential. (Incidentally, the Eurodollar market involves exactly the same process, except instead of S&L's, substitute in your mind *banks elsewhere in the world*).

One final matter warrants mention here. In the days before the super accounts at S&Ls, a shift of money from a commercial bank to a given S&L with subsequent lending, etc. simply shifted ownership of the original checking account from an individual to the S&L and then to the borrower from the S&L. It signified the same final dollar deposits at the commercial bank(s). Meanwhile, the new deposit at the S&L, typically in the past in the form of a savings account, was not called money in the technical sense referred to by the Fed as the M1 money supply. In other words, the supply of money was unchanged, although credit had increased as a result of the intermediation of the S&L. Today, not only is credit increased, but if the money deposited at the S&L is a NOW or similar account rather than a savings account, then the M1 supply of money itself is also increased, as explained previously in this section of our chapter.

"FINAL STATEMENT"

This chapter viewed the bank as a business, and discussed how banks can "create" money. The American banking system was said to be a *fractional reserve system*. This means that banks do not have to keep a dollar in currency against every dollar they have in a demand deposit liability. A single commercial bank subject to fractional reserve banking requirements can lend only the amount of its excess reserves. The banking system *as a whole* can lend a great deal more than that. The *system's* multiplier is the reciprocal of its reserve requirement.* During the 1980's many *savings banks* will be issuing demand deposits, the NOW and super NOW accounts, just as will commercial banks. The principles of creating demand deposits recorded above will apply to them in the same general manner as they do to the commercial bank.

---

*Actually, different requirements apply to different levels of deposits in different size banks. For our purposes, we can think of an *average* reserve requirement and multiplier for the system.

CHAPTER 6:
THE FEDERAL RESERVE
SYSTEM

The Federal Reserve Act of 1913 established the first central bank(s) of the United States, called the Federal Reserve Banks. By central bank we fundamentally mean a bank controlled by a government for the purpose of influencing and regulating profit-seeking, privately-owned banks. This chapter centers attention on central banking. Let us sum up this introductory note by observing that the objective of a central bank is to assist other banks and, in particular, to *regulate* the nation's money supply.

"PURPOSE AND ORGANIZATION OF THE FEDERAL RESERVE SYSTEM"

The Federal Reserve Act established the Federal Reserve System as an *independent* agency of the government. (By independent, we mean *not* directly subject to control by the President, the Treasury, or Congress.) The purpose of this independence was (and is) to insure that monetary policy does not become involved in politics. The Federal Reserve System is organized rather simply. There are twelve *Federal Reserve Banks* located in different regions of the United States. (See Figure 6.1) Ten of these banks have branch banks, making a total of twenty-four branches. For example, there is a branch of the Kansas City Federal Reserve Bank located in Denver, Colorado.

Each of the twelve district Federal Reserve Banks is, in reality, a separate corporation chartered by the federal government. The owners or stockholders of the district Federal Reserve Banks are the member commercial banks in that region (or district). Now, do not confuse the corporate nature of the district Reserve Banks with the typical business corporation. While the structure of each is exactly the same, there is one very important difference. The district Reserve Banks are not profit motivated. Any profit made by the Federal Reserve banks (above a small amount paid to the member banks) goes to the United States Treasury Department.

"FUNCTIONS OF FEDERAL RESERVE BANKS"

The Federal Reserve Banks perform many important func-

FIGURE 6.1

DISTRICT AND BRANCH TERRITORIES

tions for their more than 14,000 member commercial banks. The functions of the Federal Reserve Banks include implementing the monetary policy of the United States, examining and supervising the member banks in their district, providing banking services for the U.S. Treasury, issuing Federal Reserve Notes, and clearing checks as explained below, *to name but a few.*

THE BOARD OF GOVERNORS OF THE FEDERAL RESERVE SYSTEM

The Board of Governors of the Federal Reserve System acts as the supervising body for all twelve district Reserve Banks, even though each of the Reserve Banks is independent. The main purpose of the Board of Governors is to formulate a single monetary policy for the United States which all twelve district Reserve Banks must follow. The Board, in addition to this major task, has regulatory responsibilities over the activities of commercial banks and the operations of the district Federal Reserve Banks. The Federal Reserve Banks are independent of the Board of Governors when it comes to administrative matters within their respective regions. However, when it comes to formulating the monetary policy of the United States, the Board of Governors has central authority.

"MONETARY POLICY"

What does *monetary policy* mean, and in what way does the Board of Governors control this policy? By *monetary policy* we simply mean determining how much money is put into the flow of economic activity, or how much money is taken out of the flow of economic activity. We know that if people have more money, they will spend more, and if people have less money they will spend less. Thus the flow of money gets bigger in the first case and smaller in the second case. Very simply put, that is all there is to monetary policy. Of course, regulating the amount of money being added or taken out of the system is not so simple. As will be seen, the Board of Governors has three main options which it can use. (Glance only at the bottom part of Figure 6.2 for the moment.)

FIGURE 6.2

THE FEDERAL RESERVE SYSTEM
RELATION TO INSTRUMENTS OF CREDIT POLICY

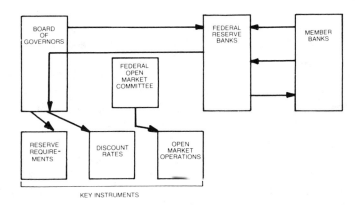

"THE REQUIRED RESERVE RATE"

The Board of Governors has the power to set the required reserve ratios for commercial banks. Recall that these reserve ratios represent the minimum amounts of money that banks must keep as security against their demand deposit liabilities. The Board of Governors has the power to set and vary the minimum reserve requirements on demand deposits. A *high* reserve requirement reduces the amount of excess reserves that the bank has—i.e., it lowers the total amount of demand deposits the bank can create. *Low* reserve rates do just the opposite, creating larger quantities of reserves. These excess reserves can be calculated easily. For simple example, take a cash deposit of $100 under a reserve rate of 10%. We derive:

$$\text{Excess Reserves} = \text{Actual Reserves} - \text{Required Reserves}$$
$$= \$100.00 - \$10.00$$
$$= \$90.00$$
$$\text{Potential New Demand Deposits} = \$90.00 \times 1/[\tfrac{1}{10}] = \$900.00$$

The above excess indicates that through the process of *bank creation of money*, $900.00 of new money could be created. In turn, under a 20% requirement:

$$\text{Excess Reserves} = \text{Actual Reserves} - \text{Required Reserves}$$
$$= \$100.00 - \$20.00$$
$$= \$80.00$$
$$\text{Potential New Demand Deposits} = \$80.00 \times 1/[\tfrac{1}{5}] = \$400.00$$

Using the multiple bank expansion formula, notice that the increase of 10% in required reserves reduced the actual amount of demand deposits that could be created by more than 50%, from $900.00 to $400.00. It should be clear that the greater the amount of new demand deposits that can be created, the greater will be the amount actually created, *ceteris paribus*. By the Monetary Control Act of 1980, the Fed was given the power to set reserve requirements for all depository institutions—all commercial banks, mutual savings banks, savings and loans, and credit unions. The first $25 million of all accounts subject to checking privileges (including telephone transfer and automatic transfer from savings) will be subject to a 3% reserve requirement. On all balances above this amount, the Fed can vary requirements from 8% to 14%, increasing this under extra-ordinary circumstances. Because of the sweeping nature of the change from prior practice and the inclusion of depository institutions previously subject to a particular state's reserve requirements alone, the new requirements are being imposed only gradually. Eight and four-year phase periods are being used, depending on the type of depository institution involved.

Changing the reserve requirements rate may appear to be a very effective method for controlling the amount of money, but it is *not* the control that is most often used. Changing the required reserve rate is an awesome device from the individual banker's viewpoint. Bankers would have a hard time predicting when and how often new reserves are needed. This would disrupt ordinary banking procedures. (Remember the goldsmith example? Can you visualize how difficult things would have been for a goldsmith if he could never estimate how much gold should be kept on hand?)

"THE DISCOUNT RATE"

Among the privileges member banks have is that of borrowing from the Federal Reserve Bank (henceforth Fed). The *discount rate* is the percentage rate charged by the Fed to the banks that wish to borrow from the Fed. The necessity for this borrowing by member banks can result when temporary funds are needed in order to meet unexpected banking conditions. Such funds provide a safety mechanism to provide banks with money available for loans during periods when money is in extremely tight supply. Though bankers will use the so-called discount "window" to procure funds from time to time, other sources of funds (the federal funds market discussed later) are used more often. In any case, when the discount rate is high, banks reduce their borrowing; thus they do not expand demand deposits as much as they otherwise would. As suggested above, though the discount rate is used to influence the banks' ability to expand demand deposits, it is not the most important method of control. In fact, it serves essentially as a signal to banks of intended (or expected) changes in monetary policy and/or the level of interest rates in the weeks to come.

THE FEDERAL RESERVE SYSTEM

"OPEN MARKET OPERATIONS"

Open market operations is the method most often used by the Federal Reserve System to control how much money is put into or taken out of the circular flow of economic activity. This method primarily involves the buying and selling of U.S. Government Securities by the Fed. It works in the following way:

The Fed may buy securities from individuals, dealers, or banks. In each case, its purchases increase the money stock. How does that happen? It happens in the following way: Suppose the Fed buys securities from banks. This transaction means the Fed receives securities from the banks and in return gives the banks a claim against it. In practice, the claim it gives is a demand deposit at the Fed. This same demand deposit (debt of the Fed) takes the form of reserves for the bank (just as the cash the banks keep in their vaults). Increases in bank reserves tend, in turn, to enable new loans by these banks.

Consider Table 6.1. Panel I provides the original picture. Again, we use simple numbers, as we assume the bank only has $20.00 cash reserves in its vault, nothing on deposit with the Federal Reserve Bank of its district (the Other Reserves under Assets in Panel I), and owns $200.00 worth of securities. We also

TABLE 6.1

BANK A BEFORE THE FED BUYS
GOVERNMENT SECURITIES

PANEL I

ASSETS		LIABILITIES	
Cash Reserves	$20.00	Demand Deposits	$100.00
Other Reserves (with the Fed)	-0-	Accounts Payable	120.00
Required Reserves	$20.00		
Loans	-0-		
U.S. Securities	200.00		
	$220.00		$220.00

BANK A AFTER THE FED HAS BOUGHT $100.00 WORTH OF U.S. GOVERNMENT SECURITIES

PANEL II

ASSETS		LIABILITIES	
Cash Reserves	$20.00	Demand Deposits	$100.00
Other Reserves (with the Fed)	100.00	Accounts Payable	120.00
Required Reserves $20.00			
Excess Reserves 100.00			
Loans	-0-		
U.S. Securities	100.00		
	$220.00		$220.00

BANK A AFTER LOANING EXCESS RESERVES OF $100.00

PANEL III

ASSETS		LIABILITIES	
Cash and Other Reserves	$120.00	Demand Deposits	$200.00
Required Reserves $40.00		Accounts Payable	120.00
Temporary Excess Reserves $80.00*			
Loans	100.00		
U.S. Securities	100.00		
	$320.00		$320.00

*In general *these excess* reserves are temporary because as we noted in Chapter 5, when a $100.00 loan is checked out by the borrower, the Bank (A in this case) typically loses the $100.00 of reserves to another bank, $80 of which is excess in the present case. If the borrower happens to write his check in favor of someone who uses the same bank, Bank A, the reserves become permanent to that bank. But the end result remains the same since that bank, *in effect,* replaces the next bank (say, Bank B) in the sequence of the next loan.

make a special assumption that the bank had a small debt (called an account payable) on some office supplies it recently purchased; and we do not list its other assets and liabilities. Next assume the Fed buys $100.00 in U.S. government securities from this bank. This creates excess reserves of $100 in Panel II. These excess reserves allow the bank to expand its demand deposits by $100 (Panel III). *So the banking system's ability to create demand deposits expands when the Fed buys U.S. Bonds from a bank.*

Suppose the reverse had happened. Start with Panel II and assume *now* that the Fed sells $100.00 in securities to Bank A. Then we would move from Panel II back to Panel I, where we see that the bank would have lost its excess reserves and could not expand its deposits. *In practice, the banking system's ability to create demand deposits decreases whenever the Fed sells U.S. Bonds to a bank.*

Let us return for a moment to the *purchase* of securities by the Fed. Purchases by the Fed from *dealers* or *individuals* have effects similar to that of Fed purchases from banks. In such cases, checks by the Fed will be deposited by the dealer or individual with their banks. These banks thus gain new reserves at the Fed. If, instead, the Fed *sells* securities to dealers or individuals in the open market, checks are drawn against the buyer's banks; so the reserves of these banks fall, and money tends to become tight. Open market purchases by the Fed therefore *increase* the reserves of banks; open market sales *decrease* them.

Using the New York Bank to Control Monetary Policy

The actual buying and selling of government securities is handled through the New York Federal Reserve District Bank. The powerful Open Market Operations Committee (see Figure 6.1) determines and directs a basic part of the monetary policy of the United States, serving as an arm of the Board of Governors of the Federal Reserve System. This committee in effect controls the "squeeze on" or "easing of" money. A tight monetary policy results, for example, when the system starts selling its securities; through these sales, it dries up the excess reserves of banks. (Go from Panel II to Panel I in Table 6.1.) A loose monetary policy— as depicted in Table 6.1 by going from Panel I to Panel II— involves purchases of government securities by the Federal Reserve Bank of New York.

M.L. GREENHUT   C.T. STEWART

The Federal Funds Rate

The Federal Funds rate depends fundamentally on the total excess reserves in the system. This rate is actually the rate of interest charged by banks which lend money to other banks in need of reserve funds. By buying government securities, the Fed increases the amount of reserves in the system thus causing the Federal Funds rate to decline. A drop in that rate is generally followed by a fall in the prime rate of interest, the interest rate charged by banks to top quality borrowers. Other rates typically follow in step. The converse holds on Fed sales of government securities. Their sales tighten reserve positions. Thus the Federal Funds rate rises, and the interest rates charged the public also go up in general when the Fed sells securities.

The Federal Reserve Note

The quantity of Federal Reserve Notes in circulation reflects the public's need for cash. To appreciate this condition, recall from Table 6.1 that part of the bank reserves are kept as cash in the vaults of the banks and the rest with their district Federal Reserve bank. Then, for example, let us imagine it is December 5, 1988. People normally need more cash on hand during the Christmas season. If necessary, the Fed will purchase securities in the open market in order to provide the reserves that will support heavy withdrawal of cash from the nation's banks. In turn, bankers will draw upon the extra reserves they then have (or otherwise had) at their Federal Reserve District Banks. The District Banks, expecting this withdrawal, would *in effect* have already cranked up their printing presses. On demand, they ship the required money in the form of newly printed Federal Reserve Notes to the commercial banks. These banks place money in their vaults. We can expect the general public will soon go to their banks to draw this cash out by writing checks against their deposits.

Recognize that since the Federal Reserve Notes originally represented *excess* reserves, the removal of this money to the vault and then to individuals' wallets does not place the typical bank in deficit reserve position. Then after the Christmas season is over, merchants deposit the excess cash they now have on hand with their own banks. These banks then have on hand excess cash over the amount they normally keep in their vaults. They then send

63

the excess cash (the extra Federal Reserve Notes) back to the District Banks, where those in good condition are stored and the others destroyed.

It follows that if the Fed next decides to constrain future bank lending, it can sell securities to decrease the excess reserves noted above; if it wishes future expansion beyond the present money level, it can buy additional securities; if the present level appears appropriate, the Fed will generally balance off its open market purchases and sales in the weeks that follow.

Stable Money Supply

The aim and purpose of monetary policy is to maintain the amount of money and credit needed to keep the economy growing, thereby increasing employment. The role that money plays in all of this is rather straightforward. When there is more money in the circular flow of economic activity, households spend more. More spending by households in the product markets means firms will be demanding more land, labor, and capital thus generating increased demand for goods and services. The economy must expand.

It would be misleading to imply that monetary policy is predictable *and always works*. Monetary policy, and its implementation, actually differs from the textbook type of example given above. No, this is not to suggest that monetary policy is a failure— but only that it is far more complicated and imprecise than the above discussions may have implied. We shall say a great deal more about its shortcomings in Part Four, after Keynesian economics has been set forth in detail.

"CHECK CLEARING"

A final matter under the control of the Federal Reserve System might be briefly noted here for interested readers—namely, the clearing of checks. Others can go directly to the Final Statement.

Figure 6.3 shows the check clearing mechanism in operation. Let us note in its connection that the Federal Reserve Bank of New York handled some 5.2 million checks on a single day in 1974. Notice we said "checks," *not* "dollars worth of checks." The Fed also maintains special amounts to clear the checks of banks that are not members of the Federal Reserve System.

FIGURE 6.3

CHECK CLEARING

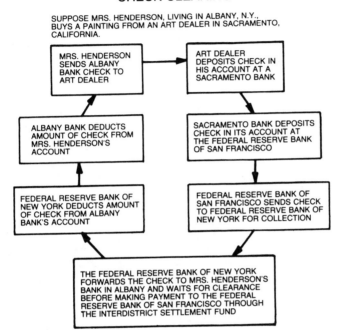

SUPPOSE MRS. HENDERSON, LIVING IN ALBANY, N.Y., BUYS A PAINTING FROM AN ART DEALER IN SACRAMENTO, CALIFORNIA.

MRS. HENDERSON SENDS ALBANY BANK CHECK TO ART DEALER

ART DEALER DEPOSITS CHECK IN HIS ACCOUNT AT A SACRAMENTO BANK

ALBANY BANK DEDUCTS AMOUNT OF CHECK FROM MRS. HENDERSON'S ACCOUNT

SACRAMENTO BANK DEPOSITS CHECK IN ITS ACCOUNT AT THE FEDERAL RESERVE BANK OF SAN FRANCISCO

FEDERAL RESERVE BANK OF NEW YORK DEDUCTS AMOUNT OF CHECK FROM ALBANY BANK'S ACCOUNT

FEDERAL RESERVE BANK OF SAN FRANCISCO SENDS CHECK TO FEDERAL RESERVE BANK OF NEW YORK FOR COLLECTION

THE FEDERAL RESERVE BANK OF NEW YORK FORWARDS THE CHECK TO MRS. HENDERSON'S BANK IN ALBANY AND WAITS FOR CLEARANCE BEFORE MAKING PAYMENT TO THE FEDERAL RESERVE BANK OF SAN FRANCISCO THROUGH THE INTERDISTRICT SETTLEMENT FUND

"FINAL STATEMENT"

This chapter has provided a brief look at the Federal Reserve System *and* how it operates. The Board of Governors of the Federal Resrve System is responsible for determining and implementing the monetary policy of the United States. The purpose of monetary policy is to insure that a sufficient amount of money is available in the circular flow of economic activity (economy). The Fed possesses three "tools" it can use to control the money supply. They are changes in reserve requirements, the discount rate, and open market operations. Open market operations (i.e., the buying and selling of government securities) is the most important tool.

The other side of the coin to money controls—fiscal controls and policy—must next be evaluated. But to do this, an understanding of the basic ideas of J.M. Keynes is necessary. His theoretical framework serves as the basic subject matter of Part Three of this book.

APPENDIX TO CHAPTER 6:*
LIMITS ON THE FED'S
ABILITY TO CONTROL
THE MONEY SUPPLY AND
INTEREST RATES:
1981–1982

In actual practice, money expansion is more complicated than was outlined above. This is so because the cash people wish to hold and the amount placed in time deposits serve as leakages similar in effect to the reserve requirement itself. To fully understand the limits to the Fed's controls, we must go deeper into the money multiplier than we did in Chapter 5. Readers not interested in these finer details may turn directly to Chapter 7.

"THE MONEY MULTIPLIER"

As the quantity of demand deposits in the nation increases, people tend to increase their holdings of currency and time deposits as well. Imagine that over a period of one year, demand deposits have increased by $5 billion. Would you not expect that savings deposits would also increase during that period of time, say by $4 billion, and also that the amount of coins and paper currency in circulation would become greater, say by $1 billion? In other words, is it not likely that as banks, firms, and people increase their overall activities, thus bringing about greater quantities of loans and demand deposits, our savings and holdings of currency are also increased? *But* this means that the simple multiplier formula 1/RR% is incomplete. Currency withdrawn from the bank is like an added reserve requirement, unavailable as a base for new loans. And the reserve requirement against time deposits further diminishes the amount of extra demand deposits that a given dollar's worth of demand deposits can create.

It is further fundamental to a penetrating insight into our monetary economy to recognize that the Fed does not really control excess reserves directly. It is basically responsible for only the size of member bank Federal Reserve accounts and the stock of currency. In fact, there is no assurance that whatever the excess reserves are, they will be used as planned when the Fed increases reserve accounts. How effective is the Fed?

"THE MONEY SUPPLY IN 1980–1981"

The Fed cannot *determine* the money supply *in the strictest sense of the term* for diverse reasons.

First of all, just altering the reserves in the system does not control the private sector's demand for funds. Hence, the Fed does not *determine* the number and size of bank loans over short periods of time.

Secondly, changes in the relative holdings of cash and deposits can offset the Fed's policy for a while. For example, an unexpected-temporary high rate of holding currency depletes reserves while forcing interest rates upward; it thus affects the new loan quantities that would stem from a given action of the Fed.

Third, there exists an additional monetary phenomenon basically outside of the Fed's control, namely the fact that its purchases and sales may, at any moment in time, involve private individuals relatively more than banks *or vice versa*. The result is that different short-run money supply effects derive from a given dollar's worth of open market operations by the Fed.

Fourth, we note that shifts from M2 or M3 money into M1 money *and vice versa* can also make the Fed appear to be unable to control the money supply in the short run.* Money market funds, included in M2, which have grown spectacularly, are subject to neither reserve requirements nor interest rate limitations.

Finally, and equally disturbing is the fact that a two-week lag exists in measuring reserves against deposit liabilities.** This lag signifies that a policy decided at one point in time *cannot* be realized in full, *ceteris parabus*, until two weeks later.

The upshot of all of the above has been erratic bursts and decreases in the money supply, as changes have gone above and

---

*M2 and M3 moneys include pure savings accounts and certificates, as well as large denomination ($100,000) CDs. M1 money, actually M1b, consists of cash and all checking accounts.
**Suppose a bank's deposit liabilities on *March 10* are $100 million and that 12% must be kept on reserve against these liabilities. By present practice, the subject bank must have $12 million dollars in reserve *as of March 24*, i.e., two weeks later.

below targeted levels. The general concomitant is a public outcry against the Fed and claims that the Fed follows inconsistent practices. People have reacted with waves of optimism/pessimism concerning the Fed's real intent. In fact, during the 1980–81 period, many complaints were heard questioning the Fed's *intent* to control (or not to control) the prevailing inflation, and whether or not it was in favor of *increasing unemployment*. Why interest rates after the 1981 tax cuts were higher than supply-siders expected is partly explainable from all of this. Only a few words on this matter are needed here.

"THE HIGH INTEREST RATES OF LATE 1981–1982"

Money funds and, in general, buyers of stocks and bonds tended to add an *uncertainty premium* to their supply of (loanable) funds during late 1981 as well as in 1982 and early 1983. Interest rates rose originally, and then, in effect, remained at higher levels than the moderating inflation of that period would otherwise have indicated. At the same moment, the forecasts of rising public debt with its corollary, large government demands for loanable funds, added to the expectations of many of higher interest rates in the future. The upshot of these forces was a more limited supply of loan funds than that which otherwise would have occurred, especially long-term loan funds. So rates did not fall significantly at the same time that a recessionary decrease in "private industry" demands for money was taking place.

Sooner or later Fed policy does have its effect, and correspondingly so will the Reagan tax cuts and any budget spending cuts. Equally vital, the falling rates of inflation will carry over to the rates of interest. At the time of this writing, in March, 1983, we would challenge the forecasts by some economists of continuing high interest rates throughout 1983. We project instead falling interest rates for 1983 via moderating inflation and the other forces mentioned above. We shall return to this subject later in the book where we shall also forecast a *strong* economy recovery in 1983, and in particular about the time this book will first appear in print.

INTRODUCTION TO PART THREE ON KEYNESIAN ECONOMICS

The recent overall growth of federal agencies is evident in the table below. In particular, note the substantial 71.9% increase in the number of employees of the Health and Human Services Department and the 99% growth of the Department of Labor. Perhaps surprisingly, the number of personnel in the Tennessee Valley Authority (TVA) rose the most—137.6%—along with another old line agency, the Federal Deposit Insurance Agency, which increased 114.8%. Of course, these agencies employ relatively few people, a condition that tends to make their percentage growth appear to be great. When one compares the size of the FDIC with that of the Environmental Protection Agency (which grew from virtual nonexistence in 1965 to its present size), one senses some of the changes witnessed during the seventies. The decline in NASA along with the veritably unchanged size of the Department of Defense further attest to the changed policies of the federal government during the seventies.

The substantial growth of the federal government that is evident in the table (in fact, the role beyond that of providing for the national defense and assisting in the development of our transportation network) first took place in the nineteen thirties. It was essentially the outgrowth of what is referred to today as Keynesian economics, a system of economic thought which *in effect* assigns to the federal government the role of regulator of the economy. The explanation of the causes of recessions and booms, and why the federal government should intervene in a free enterprise economy (as set forth by the famed economist Lord John Maynard Keynes) serve as the subject matter of Part Three of the book.

TABLE 7

THE GROWTH AND DECLINE OF FEDERAL AGENCIES†

This table shows how the number of civilian employes at major federal agencies has grown or decreased since 1965 (or from the date the agency was created).

	June '65	June '70	June '75	June '82	% growth (+) or Decrease (−)
Agriculture	113,017	102,447	120,999	127,293	+12.6%
Commerce	33,668	33,396	36,228	35,248	+4.7%
Defense	1,033,775	1,193,784	1,041,829	1,045,388	+1.1%
Energy	0	0	19,647	18,537	—
HHS*	87,316	108,044	147,125	150,090	+71.9%
HUD	13,777	15,190	17,161	14,568	+5.7%
Justice	33,222	39,257	51,541	55,949	+68.4%
Labor	9,527	10,991	14,834	18,956	+99.0%
State	24,454	24,779	23,785	24,387	−0.3%
Transportation	55,907	65,985	75,035	62,376	+11.6%
Treasury	88,761	92,521	121,546	121,919	+37.4%
CPSC	0	0	303	696	—
Action	1,104	1,317	1,864	605	−45.2%
EEOC	0	850	2,183	3,212	—
EPA	0	0	5,447	12,623	—
FDIC	1,544	2,478	3,103	3,317	+114.8%
FTC	1,157	1,330	1,661	1,622	+40.2%
ICC	2,427	1,755	2,115	1,530	−37.0%
NASA	34,049	32,548	26,447	23,497	−31.0%
NRC	0	0	1,970	3,897	—
OMB	524	633	673	632	+20.6%
OPM**	3,789	5,508	8,157	6,651	+75.5%
SBA	3,751	4,269	4,796	5,117	+36.4%
Smithsonian	2,334	2,641	3,746	4,477	+91.8%
TVA	16,797	22,244	28,423	39,913	+137.6%
USIA	11,628	10,262	8,809	7,926	−31.8%
VA	167,059	168,719	213,143	240,575	+44.0%

NOTE: The percentage increase or decrease is not figured for agencies that did not exist in June, 1965.

*1982 figure combines the Health and Human Services Department with the Education Department, which previously had been together as the Health, Education and Welfare Department

**Previously the Civil Service Commission

First DOT figure is for April, 1967; First EPA figure is for December, 1970; First CPSC figure is for May 1973; First NRC figure is for January, 1975; First DOE figure is for October, 1977

†SOURCE: *The Washington Post*, September 9, 1982, p. A-23.

CHAPTER 7:
THE DEPRESSION OF THE THIRTIES AND UNEMPLOYMENT

To appreciate present-day problems and understand the economic theory used in Washington today, it is helpful to probe into recent American economic history. We shall begin with the depression years of the nineteen-thirties. This background sets the stage for explaining what is referred to as Keynesian economics, named after the English economist, John Maynard Keynes.

"THE DEPRESSION OF THE THIRTIES"

The gross national product (the total output of goods and services produced in the country) fell from $104.4 billion in 1929 to a low of $56 billion in 1933. The effect of the decline in economic activity between 1929 and 1933 is actually underestimated in Table 7.1 because of the recording of business investment expenditures in gross values, for example before depreciation of capital items is subtracted. Actually, the business investment figure would have been *negative* in 1933 if all capital

TABLE 7.1

GNP AND COMPONENTS IN 1929 AND 1933
(BILLIONS OF DOLLARS)

	1929	1933
Gross National Product	$104.4	$56.0
Consumption	79.0	46.4
Business Investments	16.2	1.4
Net Exports	.8	.2
Government Expenditures	8.4	8.0

consumption allowances (such as depreciation, obsolescence, and loss from destruction) had been subtracted from the gross total of the investment expenditures (goods) of that year. Only *government* expenditures—which can be included as part of the nation's investments—remained basically unchanged during the period in question.

Other signs of the severity of the depression can be cited. Dividend and interest income fell by nearly 50% from 1929 levels. Proprietors' and rental income decreased by nearly 66%. Total wage and salary disbursements were down 40%. Total personal income from all sources decreased by nearly 50%. These data indicate that although workers and salaried employees were hard hit, others were—in a relative sense—even more sharply affected. In any case, this economic debacle left few unscathed. The people who lived then can remember such dramatic events as the bread lines, the closing of banks, and the Wall Street suicides.

What was the cause of this national disaster? Certainly by the end of this part of the book, the Keynesian answer will convey to the reader a rather penetrating explanation of the depression. But first, the present chapter will bring us into the subject matter by *describing* how the depression developed. Our next two chapters, which establish the so-called Keynesian framework, will provide the economist's explanation of the imbalances that led to the depression.

"COINCIDENCE OF CYCLES"

Economic historians usually describe the depression of the thirties as involving a coincidence of different kinds of domestic business cycles, each in the stage of downswing. This coincidence, they say, took place at a time of international and political chaos, which further aggravated the situation.

"INTERNATIONAL CAUSES OF THE DEPRESSION"

A trade imbalance developed during the twenties. The British pound sterling had been valued too high by an Act of Parliament after World War I. This mistake caused Great Britain to lose gold because the price of their goods (in dollars, francs, pesos, etc.) was too high. This overvaluation and its impact on the British and other economies can be explained as follows:

After World War I, the British pound sterling was legislated to contain slightly more than 113 grains of gold, while our Congress set the dollar at 23.22 grains of gold. Thus much more gold was contained in the pound than in the dollar; the actual gold content ratio was such that approximately 4.86 dollars equalled 1 pound. This meant that in order to buy a pound, that is £1, an American would have to give his bank $4.86. (Actually, the value of the pound varied by approximately 2 cents around the exchange rate of $4.86 during the days of the international gold standard. This variation depended on the existing trade balances.) It followed that if, for example, a man's shirt cost £1 in Great Britain while the same shirt sold for $2.93 in the United States, there would be a strong demand for the American shirt; oppositely, the shirt produced in Great Britain—in effect costing $4.86—would be very expensive. Since the prices of goods *in general* were high in Great Britain, the effect of making the exchange rate $4.86 for £1, rather than say $2.93 for £1, was to overvalue the pound. The consequence was a persistent excess of imports over exports by Great Britain; over time, that nation suffered substantial losses of gold in payment for its imports.

Political instability, meanwhile, prevailed in Germany and elsewhere. In fact, the late twenties and early thirties were highlighted by politically inspired gold "flights" from many large and small countries. Gold moved chiefly to the U.S.A. and France. In addition, war debt payments moved gold from Germany to France *and* Great Britain; in turn, the overvaluation of the British pound moved gold from Great Britain also to France and again to the U.S.A.

International Gold Flows and Hitler

The international flows of gold described above set the stage for a worldwide financial panic. This was triggered by Hitler's political maneuvers in Germany. That nation, afflicted by war debt and critical internal problems, was moving dangerously close to communism. In order to stop this trend, many British and others were placing their money behind Hitler. However, well before Hitler took power, most foreigners began to cash in their investments in Germany and move them elsewhere. In this chaotic atmosphere, a major bank in Austria, the Credit Anstalt Bank, failed in early 1931. This bankruptcy was chiefly due to bank mismanagement; however it precipitated a further flight of capital as many financiers withdrew their investments from central Europe, moving them to England. The subsequent prospect of frozen accounts in Germany, and the awareness that the British had invested heavily in Germany, soon made Great Britain also appear to be an unsafe place for investment.

A substantial liquidation of investments in Great Britain followed. The sale by foreigners of British corporate securities meant that gold was moved elsewhere *in addition to* the gold losses stemming from the fact that Britain was importing more than it was exporting. With the loss of more and more gold, the British stockpile fell so low that Great Britain was forced to abandon the gold standard in September 1931.

"Gold Standards Abandoned"

Once Great Britain dropped the gold standard, other nations followed suit. Worse yet from the American standpoint, the series of capital flights just described were taking place at a time not too far removed from our own stock market crash of November 1929. The result was that the capital panic in Great Britain in 1931 spread rapidly to the United States. It helped cause the "Bank Holidays" (closings) of 1932 and 1933. But this brings us too far along in our story. We must first recapitulate what is relevant to this point.

The 1920's were fraught with political unrest and economic uncertainty. In Germany, certain export industries were flourishing, but war debt was burdensome and unpopular. In addition, the Weimar Republic was failing to achieve political and economic stability. High prices in Great Britain—combined with competition from Germany, the United States, and France—placed Britain in a precarious financial position; this was aggravated by her overvaluation of the pound. Intensifying the worldwide disturbances was a drain of gold from small agricultural nations as low world prices reduced the export earnings of these countries. France and the United State were prospering, and gaining much too large a portion of the world's gold supply.

Our purpose is to explain the American depression. What we have developed so far is only a picture of large American exports in the twenties. This was unfortunately followed in the early thirties by capital flights of money—which eventually led to heavy withdrawals of funds from American banks. Economic historians argue that restrictive U.S.A tariff policies helped produce the international financial chaos. Actually, the causes of the American depression went much deeper than international conditions alone, as international relations only aggravated a downward movement that had already originated elsewhere.

"DOMESTIC CAUSES OF THE DEPRESSION"

America was experiencing prosperity on almost all fronts in the twenties. Its export trades were flourishing as were its industries producing goods strictly for domestic use. America's political situation was stable. Important innovations were being introduced, and worker productivity was increasing steadily. On the surface, the only "clouds in the sky" were the increasingly troubled international relations, the development of "sticky" price practices by American industries, a rapidly escalating system of installment buying and debt on the part of consumers, and excessive speculation in the stock market by young and old who thought security prices would continue upward with the industrial expansion.

Uncertainty and Business Investment

Only hindsight permits one to know that serious trouble had been brewing. Danger spots were not only the areas mentioned above, but on the domestic agricultural scene as well. Again, only hindsight indicates the proper stress that should have been given to the fact that residential construction had begun to contract in the early thirties as the explosive post World War I construction boom had naturally reached a limit in growth. It will be seen from the following example (of the behavior of businessmen during the depression) that when businessmen are apprehensive, investment in capital goods is reduced and overall income fails.

The Stock Market Crash and Uncertainty

It is recognized today that the developing uncertainty—combined with undue stock market speculation—were setting up a potentially dangerous situation. Suppose—in the context of uncertainty in world affairs (gold)—the idea also spreads that many stock prices are way overpriced. Add the knowledge that many had been purchased *largely on credit* under "bullish" expectations (that is, expectations that the price will keep on rising). Let the bubble be pricked by some *large* investors selling their stock. Suppose stock prices start downward, broker loans are foreclosed, and other securities are quickly sold (thereby further depressing their prices). The result is the conversion of speculative fortunes into unpayable debts. Add a suicide or two. Do all this and *business uncertainty must inevitably increase and spread.*

The stock market crash, in actual fact, had no inextricable relation to the basic economic structure of the country. American companies were stable, their production was high, and worker skills great. Indeed, their output was in large demand. However, the bursting of the financial "bubble" had a significant influence on the businessman's decision-making process. The same factors that will cause an individual to refuse to invest cash in a security would cause the members of *boards of directors* not to invest cash in a new factory building, or in a machine, or in inventory. While the stock market crash had no direct effect on the underlying *productive* capacity of the firms in this country, it had, to say the least, a strong indirect influence through businessmen's expectations.

"THE BOTTOM OF THE DEPRESSION"

Industrial employment and output remained high as the nation moved into the thirties, but the bottom was ready to fall out. Business capital investments were ready to plummet; and indeed the counterparts to stock market losses and foreclosing of loans were already appearing in the consumer fields. As a result of all this, loans for investment and consumption purposes were decreasing in the early 1930's. Foreign trade was becoming more precarious, and the U.S. government, contrary to the advice of J.M. Keynes,* was concerned chiefly with balancing the budget and revising tariffs. No *other* economist was convincingly recommending a substantial increase in government spending.

One gains from these data a picture of a confused mixture of events, but a picture in which all signs pointed downward. Among other things, it should be stressed that a rapid expansion in construction had taken place in the twenties. However, this construction as noted previously had seemingly reached its natural peak during that period. It was therefore also headed downward

*John Maynard Keynes, professor, Cambridge University.

at this time. It is clear in retrospect that the basic economic signs pointed toward a deep depression. And with depression and its substantial unemployment, a new reason for government intervention arose: namely, to extricate a free enterprise economy from the trough of depression and its accompanying mass unemployment. The *how* to do this was suggested by the macroeconomic theory of J.M. Keynes. It proposed in effect that the government should spend and spend, as will be explained throughout this unit of the book. Not only did the *size* of the public sector (government) change as a result of his theory, but so too did the *type* of government expenditures. However, before presenting his theory, a few brief remarks about types of unemployment are in order because Keynes' theories apply to some but not all types of unemployment.

"UNEMPLOYMENT: TYPES AND CAUSES"

There are four major types, and hence causes of unemployment, one of which is attributable to depressionary periods of time. We shall look at each separately.

"SEASONAL UNEMPLOYMENT"

Seasonal unemployment is just what the name implies. Take the Christmas season for example. Stores hire additional employees then in order to meet the increased demand for goods and services in the market. After that season is over, they lose their jobs. Some farm workers are seasonally unemployed at certain times of the year, as substantial demand for their services exists during the harvest season but not at other times. People who become seasonally unemployed are those who are not working because of the nature of their work.

"FRICTIONAL UNEMPLOYMENT"

Frictional unemployment sounds rather involved, but is not. People who are frictionally unemployed are merely switching from one job to another. Therefore, if someone is looking for a better job (having left a former job), that individual is classified as *frictionally unemployed*. He remains in this category until starting work on a new job.

79

THE DEPRESSION OF THE THIRTIES AND UNEMPLOYMENT

"CYCLICAL UNEMPLOYMENT"

The emphasis of Keynesian economics is on the business cycle—the ups of economic activity during boom periods and its downs during depression periods. Cyclical unemployment results from a "down" in economic activity. But what causes the "down"? It may be the consequence of misguided government monetary and fiscal policy. For example, suppose the Fed has provided funds to finance substantial deficits over the years. Suppose in order to limit inflation, the Fed suddenly enacts a very restrictive monetary policy (as was done in 1979 and 1980); this would tend to cause a sharply decreased demand for goods and services in the product market. As demand falls, firms experience a decrease in sales, which causes many of them to cut back on their scheduled production. This means less demand for land, labor, and capital in the factor market.* Less demand for the factors of production signifies unemployment. More specifically, this is called *cyclical unemployment.*

"STRUCTURAL UNEMPLOYMENT"

Structural unemployment results (1) when technology changes so that certain jobs are no longer needed, (2) when resources are depleted (mines), or (3) when there are major long-term changes in demand (e.g., from peace to war). Past examples of structurally unemployed people include street car conductors, silent picture movie actors, Klondike gold miners, and most recently the reduced demand for aerospace engineers in the American space program.

Structural unemployment is in many ways the most serious of the four types of unemployment. Consider aerospace engineers, whose skill requires a substantial amount of education. Such education is very costly, demanding, and time consuming. Unfortunately, the person trained as an aerospace engineer has a comparatively limited background for other types of work. If he was unemployed, this person would need *retraining* for other jobs requiring comparable levels of skill. But try to imagine the psychological-social problems of a person who studied and worked many years to become an aerospace engineer, only to find out that no demand exists for that skill. It would be difficult (to

---

*Labor and other inputs of production (land, management, and capital).

say the least) for the individual to forget the four to five years of college training required to become a highly specialized engineer. It would be difficult not only to contemplate but to *have to* change careers. It is the training-retraining requirement that makes structural unemployment especially serious. It also presents one of the most difficult employment problems confronting the nations of the world.

"FULL EMPLOYMENT"

The preceding remarks centered on the four major types of unemployment; but we have not yet defined what a "state of unemployment" is, or conversely what is meant by "full employment" in the American economy. Many people probably think that full employment entails nothing less complicated than 100% employment. But that would be impossible. Full employment—to the economist—actually means that the number of unemployed is at a level considered to be *acceptable.*

Many in the United States believe that frictional and seasonal unemployment—which cannot be avoided—total as much as 6%–7% today, equivalent to full employment in their view. Many government economists still speak in the 1980s in terms of 5% or even 4½% unemployed as *full employment.* Depending upon the economist, full employment is defined as "that economic state where the unemployed represent a certain accepted minimum amount of the total number of people desiring work at a fair wage, considering their skills."

"MEASURING THE UNEMPLOYMENT RATE"

The government arrives at the rate of unemployment by dividing the number of people classified as "unemployed" by the civilian *labor force.* The labor force, in turn, is arrived at by adding up all of the individuals counted as employed (excluding the armed forces) and all those listed as unemployed. In other words, it equals the number of people working plus the number of people actually seeking positions for which they would qualify if the position were open.

The Present Day Work Force in the United States

In 1981 there were 108,670,000 people in the United States civilian labor force. Of this number, 8,273,000 people were counted as unemployed, establishing an unemployment rate of 7.6%.

Let's return to the full employment concept. *Full employment* means that the unemployment rate is not greater than 4½% or 5% or 6% (again depending on the economist who is speaking about full employment). It also means that practically all of the unemployed are *frictionally unemployed*. (Recall that the much smaller seasonal-structural unemployment are also included, and that there is no cyclical unemployment in a state of full employment.)

FIGURE 7.1

THE HISTORY OF UNEMPLOYMENT

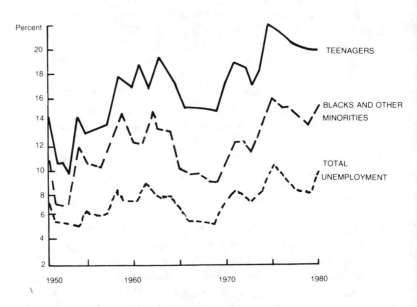

SOURCE: ECONOMIC REPORT OF THE PRESIDENT
JANUARY 1980. PP. 237. 238.

Observe in Figure 7.1 that since the mid-'60s total unemployment has risen rather steadily above the once widely accepted 4% level. Notice further that the unemployment of teenagers and minorities has *always* been well above that level.

M.L. GREENHUT   C.T. STEWART

"FINAL STATEMENT"

Keynesian economics centered originally on the problem of *cyclical unemployment*. But the Keynesian framework of thought actually presents much more than a theory of unemployment. It provides, in fact, a generic overall view of the inner workings of the entire economy. As such, it is believed to be utilizable not only in altering rates of cyclical unemployment, but in changing the tendencies toward structural and other types of unemployment. We must probe initially into the analytical structure of Keynesian economics before the economic problems of the 1980's can be evaluated.

CHAPTER 8:
KEYNESIAN ECONOMICS:
A SIMPLE MODEL

There are certain tools of economic analysis which help explain the interaction between those who *demand* and those who *supply* goods in the marketplace. But let us emphasize that these tools are designed only to provide an easy way of looking at real world events or conditions rather than to depict them perfectly and completely. Economists refer to their approach as abstractions (or simplifications) of real events. The use of abstractions (or models) is very common is science. In fact, people use abstractions every day. For example, the typical street map presents views of a city without indicating hills and other pictures of the city. From it, the motorist learns what he needs to know. In similar form, the weather map in the nation's newspapers is an abstraction in diagrammatic form. From it, predictions are made.

FIGURE 8.1

EXAMPLE OF A MODEL—A WEATHER MAP

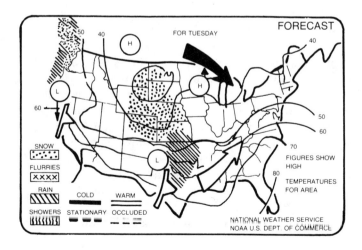

KEYNESIAN ECONOMICS: A SIMPLE MODEL

All abstractions (models) have certain characteristics in common, be they used in a science or for everyday purposes: (1) they are simplifications; (2) as they are simplifications they do not include all characteristcs of the original; (3) many of them are used for the purpose of predicting something. *Economic models,* in particular, often have *prediction* as their primary role.

"MODELS AND LESS THAN MAXIMUM TOTAL OUTPUT"

A basic question must be raised before proceeding. How can economists construct a model, and what insights can it be expected to provide? Since economics focuses on the use of scarce resources, an economic model obviously should provide insight into how firms allocate land, labor, capital and entrepreneurial leadership. Most vitally, the more general economic models are designed to answer the four basic questions, what is produced, how much is produced, how it is produced, and for whom it is produced. These are the essential questions we noted that all economic systems must resolve. What causes a free enterprise economy to run into trouble, and produce smaller amounts than it otherwise could, was the particular problem studied by John M. Keynes. This chapter and the one that follows provides his theoretical framework of thought.

"PROFITS, COMPETITION, AND EFFICIENCY"

Profits play a central role in signaling *what goods and services* producers should offer for sale in the product market. Not only do businessmen produce goods and services which they expect will provide profits, but inefficient (high cost) producers (who make less profit than others) are sooner or later forced out of the market. It is the competition from more efficient (lower cost) firms that pushes the inefficient ones out of the market or forces them into more efficient practices. While this process is harsh for inefficient firms, the consumer benefits. Simply put, competition for sales in the product market compels rival sellers to be as efficient as they possibly can; at the same instance, it causes our economy to expand and sometimes to contract.

M.L. GREENHUT   C.T. STEWART

"THE CIRCULAR FLOW, PROFITS, SALES, AND INVENTORIES"

Firms produce goods and services for sale in the product market. In addition, businessmen regularly consider and reconsider plans to increase sales and profits. To increase sales, they usually must enlarge their scale of operations. This, in turn, necessitates greater investment.

Industrial activities designed to increase sales can take two "investment" forms: First, firms may have to purchase new plants and equipment in order to expand their output. Second, they may also plan on holding more inventories over certain periods of time. It is the competition for sales in the product market that compels managers of firms to plan their inventories and new output carefully. If more is provided for sale in the product market than consumers wish to purchase, *unplanned* investment in inventories must result and profit levels will fall.

As noted, we do not imply *unwillingness* on the part of business managers to carry inventories. Rather, our words simply reflect the idea stressed in Keynesian economics that *unplanned* inventory stock stems from *unanticipated* unsold output. Continued excess of *actual* over *planned* inventory levels is a condition which, *if widespread,* can easily lead to recession.

"CASH FLOW AND INVENTORIES"

Firms acquire the funds necessary to expand production capacity and output from their own profits and from the savings of households. In terms of a simple circular flow of economic activity, money not spent by households for consumption is money saved. These savings frequently take the form of deposits at commercial banks or savings and loan institutions. The American banking system makes these savings available for the use of investors in the form of loanable funds (capital). The important point to remember is that loanable funds represent money that is *taken out* of the circular flow by households. If loanable funds are not returned to the circular flow, an imbalance between saving (money taken out) and investment (money returned) occurs. This imbalance will cause the economy to contract. However, we are getting ahead of ourselves, a review of what has been said thus far would be helpful at this point.

KEYNESIAN ECONOMICS: A SIMPLE MODEL

Business firms regularly adopt sales and production plans. These plans are generally designed to increase output and sales in the product market. To effect this, firms often invest in new plants and equipment. Unfortunately, any output planned for sale but remaining unsold raises actual inventories above planned levels. Annual investment in new output by firms is subdivided into (1) plant and equipment *plus* (2) planned investment in new inventory *plus* (3) any unplanned inventory investment that may result from smaller than expected sales in the product market. It could be that total investment is reduced by an unexpected, sustantial volume of sales in the product market. In short, business investment over a period of time equals new investment in plant and equipment plus or minus the change in inventory stocks.

"MONEY INCOME SAVED AND INVESTED *OR* NOT INVESTED"

Any money saved (removed) from the circular flow is money *not spent* in the product market. What we have to be concerned with is whether the money saved returns quickly to the circular flow or is withheld. Imbalances between what is taken out of the circular flow (savings) and what is returned (business investment) *cause the economy to expand or contract*. This relationship between saving and planned business investment requires close study.

"THE NATION'S SAVERS AND BUSINESS INVESTORS"

Savers and business investors are *not* necessarily the same people. The plans of people who save and of businessmen who invest in plant, equipment, and investories can, and *oftentimes, do, differ*. These differences, as already suggested, have a significant impact on the circular flow. To see the matter more precisely, a large box will be utilized. Let that box contain all of the goods and services under production in the economy—those produced for sale to households and those designed for sale to other economic sectors, such as to domestic governments, foreigners, and other business firms in general. For the time being, let us forget about the government sector and the foreign sector and imagine all output being acquired by households (consumers) or private business firms.

88

Divide the large box into two parts: Let Part A consist of all of the goods *and services* intended for sale to consumers (households)—call Part A *consumer goods.* Then Part B of the box consists of all goods *and services* intended for sale to other business firms—call Part B *investment goods.* Henceforth, the word goods will include services, though we shall occasionally add the word services for purposes of emphasis.) The entire output box is drawn as Figure 8.2.

FIGURE 8.2

BUSINESS OUTPUT

Everyone who helped produce goods contained in Figure 8.2 received an income. The income generated from the production of consumer and investment goods must be equal in value to the consumer and investment goods acquired. In other words, *total income is the same as total output.* Equivalently, the sum of profits, losses, rents, interest, wages, and overtime pay (whether it is inadequate, fair *or* excessive compensation for work) always equals the total value of consumer and investment goods produced. This holds true even if some of the investment goods were not voluntarily acquired, such as unplanned inventory investment. Any output produced for sale, *even if not sold to others,* has provided an income to workers, landlords, etc., as well as profits (or losses) to firms. Figure 8.2 can thus be used to represent the *plans* of firms to produce consumer goods (Part A) as well as the plans to produce *output* not destined for sale to consumers, namely the capital or investment goods output (Part B) produced that year. Remember, goods produced equal income received.

Our simple model focuses attention next on the idea that households can do two basic things with their income: (1) consume it or (2) save it. The box in Figure 8.3—"Consumers' Preference"—reflects these two possibilities. Part A is the amount of income householders choose to *consume*; Part B is the amount of income they choose to *save*. By definition then, economists are saying that people use their income to consume goods, or they save their income by *not* purchasing goods. What they buy out of the total output (income) produced in one calendar year is called *consumption*; what they do not buy out of that same total is called *saving*. *[Any output that is* not *bought by households out of the total produced remains in the hands of business firms. Since that which business firms retain (buildings, machines, "and inventories") is called "investment goods," saving in a given period of time must equal the investment goods created in that period of time. That is, saving must equal all output produced that is not sold to consumers. Saving must therefore equal actual investment goods.]*

FIGURE 8.3

CONSUMERS' PREFERENCE

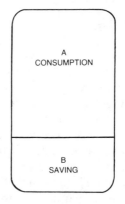

"SAVINGS EQUAL INVESTMENT BY DEFINITION"

Place the boxes of Figures 8.2 and 8.3 side by side, as in Figure 8.4. Let us refer to the left-hand figure, Panel I, as *business output*, and the right-hand figure, Panel II, either as *consumers' preference* or *consumers' decision*. Let us further use the terms *consumer goods* and *investment goods* in Panel I, and the words *consumption* and *saving* in Panel II. *If we further assert that what is consumed in Panel II can only be consumer goods, then the saving under the consumers' preference box must equal the investment (goods) of the business output box.*

FIGURE 8.4

SAVINGS EQUAL INVESTMENT

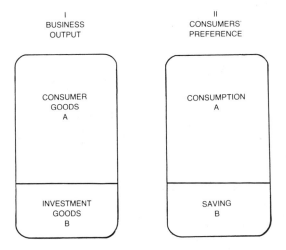

As a matter of definition, saving in the consumers' preference box is the exact mirror image of investment goods in the business output box. In terms of the circular flow, Part B of consumers' preference represents savings of households, typically placed in banks; while Part B of the business output box represents the produced (investment) goods of that period in the hands of firms. You may have already sensed that when the savings and *planned* investment of business firms are equal, the circular flow is in balance. Thus, for the economy to remain stable, savings must equal planned investment. Equivalently, if what is taken out of the flow as savings is exactly put back into the flow as business firms' planned investments, the economy is stable. How, then, can imbalances occur; and what causes GNP levels to rise and to fall?

"INEQUALITY OF SAVING AND INVESTMENT"

Realizing that savers and business investors are different people, assume that consumers decide to buy more consumer goods than were produced for sale in Part A, Panel I of Figure 8.4. What this means is that the consumption decision of consumers (Part A of Panel II) involved intended consumption of more goods than were planned for sale (Part A of Panel I). More specifically, imagine that some of the B section items of Panel I consist of women's apparel which retailers were planning to hold as inventories to attract customers to their stores. But suppose women shoppers buy more than was expected. In order to meet this unexpected demand, some of the B section items of Panel I, Figure 8.4, are sold. Such consumer purchases can occur only if consumers decide to save less. Figure 8.5 will help indicate what we are saying. The section marked A' in Figure 8.5 represents the extra women's apparel that is being purchased. Therefore, the B section in Figure 8.5 is smaller than the B sections of Figure 8.4. How does this help explain business upswings or downswings?

FIGURE 8.5

CONSUMERS PREFERENCE

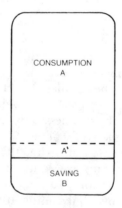

CONSUMPTION
A

A'

SAVING
B

M.L. GREENHUT   C.T. STEWART

"PLANNED INVESTMENT GREATER THAN ACTUAL SAVING"

When women purchase more apparel than retailers expected them to buy, the additional consumption will change the size of the Business Output investment goods section. Such additional consumption can only occur at the expense of some of Part B of the business firm's original output box (Figure 8.4). That is to say, Part B of the Business Output box (including planned inventory) must be reduced by exactly the size of Part A' of the Consumers' box (Figure 8.5). The total produced, let us stress, is unchanged. Consumers, however, have caused the use of the goods to change. Phrased alternatively: *the Consumers' Preference box (Figure 8.5) gives us their plans; and their plans equal final results. Our model, therefore, makes consumers the determining force in what happens. When the women consumers purchased more of A than was expected, businesses were left with less of B (inventory) than was planned. In effect, a decrease (disinvestment) in inventories occurred.*

Unplanned Disinvestment: An Expanding Economy

What is the effect of unplanned *dis*investment? Manufacturers and retailers of women's apparel should be pleased by the unexpected increase in demand for their goods. To replace their depleted inventories, firms will plan to invest more in the future. Thus, we can predict that unplanned *dis*investment will expand the economy. Simply put, an economy expands when *planned* investment (greater than realized investment) is greater than the actual saving by households. Note that *actual* investment (namely, planned investment minus unplanned *dis*investment) equals the realized—or actual—saving by households.

Though we had previously suggested that investment and saving were always identical, we now appear to be saying that they *need not* be identical. Yet this is *not* a contradiction. We are simply saying that *planned investment* may not equal *actual saving*. In our current model, *actual investment* always equals the amount households saved. Two possibilities exist:

(A) More goods may be demanded by consumers than were produced for sale to them. That is, they may save less than expected. Unplanned *dis*investment then occurs. Actual investment equals saving, but planned investment is now greater than saving.

(B) *Output actually produced* for sale to households but not purchased by them *becomes unplanned investment in goods by firms.* These goods remain unsold because households saved more than they were expected to save. Any extra saving must always equal in value the amount of a year's produced output still held by business firms (unplanned inventory investment). Planned investment is less than saving.

Actual investment, therefore, always *equals actual savings,* though *planned investment* may be *greater or less than the savings* of households. The circular flow has thus told us that imbalances between planned investment and actual saving will cause the economy to expand or contract. This result occurs because *planned investments* represent money *placed in* the circular flow for a certain end while *savings* represent the money *taken out* of the circular flow.

We are now in position to discuss the case (B) above where consumers purchase less than they were expected to buy (the opposite of the ladies' apparel case above). Less consumer buying than expected causes actual (realized) investment *and* saving to be greater than planned investment. This state of affairs generates *recession.*

"PLANNED INVESTMENT LESS THAN ACTUAL SAVING"

The original inequality example in this chapter demonstrated that unplanned *dis*investment in apparel took place. What if the reverse had happened? That is, what if consumers purchased *less* ladies' apparel than business managers expected to sell? The result of this state would be an unplanned increase in business firms' inventories of ladies' apparel. (Compare Panels I and II of Figure 8.6. It follows that the *plans* of business managers in Panel I will *not* be realized. Instead, the final picture will be given by Panel II.) In Figure 8.6, less apparel was actually sold to consumers (section A of Panel II) than business managers planned (section A of Panel I). Therefore, the end-of-the-year investment in Panel I would actually include an additional section equal in area to the B′ saving section shown in Panel II. From Panel I we note that the firms' planned investments in inventories and other capital goods equal the saving quantity B of Panel II. This left an unplanned increase in inventory (equal to Part B′, Panel II).

FIGURE 8.6

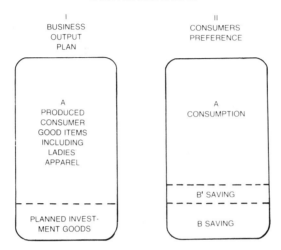

PLANNED INVESTMENT LESS
THAN ACTUAL SAVING

Planned investment B was less than the actual investment *and* savings of B plus B'.

Unplanned Investment: A Contracting Economy

Unplanned inventory stocks induce producers to reduce their future output. A contraction in the circular flow then takes place. This contraction arises in order to protect profit levels in the presence of a decreased demand for goods. The box diagram indicates what causes the economy to contract. *It contracts when unplanned inventory investment occurs.* That is, it contracts when planned investment is less than actual saving.

"FINAL STATEMENT"

It is important to recognize that the box diagram imagined firms selling goods to consumers. Of course sellers offer goods to other firms. Savings flow from households to firms, while "stocks, bonds, promissory notes" go from firms to households. With the nominal dollar savings of people helping to promote a certain level of interest rates, firms may expand or contract their planned investments and in the process lead to economic expansion or contraction. More about this in the chapters that follow. For the moment, let it suffice to say that the people's savings (non-purchased consumer goods out of the income they received) is equal to the firm-to-firm investments.

CHAPTER 9:
KEYNESIAN ECONOMICS:
A MORE COMPLETE
MODEL

Chapter 8 emphasized the firms and households sectors. Clearly, many other sectors can be added such as the banking sector. For our purposes, only two more are needed, the government and foreign sectors.

"GOVERNMENT AND FOREIGN SECTORS"

These sectors can be viewed in the same way as the investment and saving sectors. Specifically, we could treat all government purchases (expenditures) *and* exports as investments, while regarding taxes collected as savings *and* imports as the non-consumption by households of domestic outputs—in other words, also as savings.

We can sum up these thoughts by conceiving of produced goods and services being acquired by consumers, by firms (investment goods), by governments, and by foreigners; in fact, we will include government acquisitions and the foreign sector in the same general category as business firm acquisitions. On the other side, we view consumption goods as being acquired by householders; the remaining output values are then assigned to a section in which we include taxes and imports in the same general category as savings. Let us initially begin by adding the government spending and tax sector to the Keynesian model.

"THE GOVERNMENT SECTOR"

Conceptually the Keynesian system is as simple as its definitions. If the reader would (1) *forget* about individual dollars, individual income receipts (e.g., rents, interest income, etc.), specific tax payments and the like, and simply focus attention on a *total box of produced goods and services*, then (2) classify that output in the categories explained above, the remainder of this chapter will be simplified. Remember, we have a total output of "real" goods and services. We visualize the consumer purchasing a big part of the total, call it "C." We visualize business firms getting part of that

total (in the form of factories, inventories, equipment), call it "I."
Now we visualize the government buying part of the total, call it
"G." We assert that what consumers did not purchase out of the
total is to be considered as not having been used up; and now we
divide that part into two categories, voluntary savings (S) and
involuntary savings—better yet, call the involuntary part taxes
(T). If the total produced is referred to as the "GNP" and sym-
bolized by the letter "Y," we have:

(1) $C + I + G = Y = C + S + T$
(2) $C + I + G = C + S + T$

Subtracting C from both sides of (2) leaves the identity:

(3) $I + G = S + T$

"A DEFINITIONAL IDENTITY"

Recognize that the total expenditures $I + G$ being equal to $S + T$ is a *definitional identity*. This identity provides the final result of a
state of affairs in which the *plans* of different sectors *may differ*.
This definitional identity specifies that all presently produced
goods which were not purchased by consumers will equal the
income received that was not spent voluntarily by consumers.
And the income not spent voluntarily by consumers either was
saved or was taxed.

"GOVERNMENT AND THE SAVINGS–INVESTMENT RELATIONSHIP"

The government sector can be treated in the same way as the
firms' investment goods sector. For example, government purchases of goods and services from firms, and the payments it
makes to civil service workers and to other government employees (policemen, judges, soldiers), can be regarded as *investment
good* purchases. Government removes goods and services from
the product market so that they are not available to the public. To
offset this, tax payments to government can be treated as savings
(part of the income not spent by consumers).

Now, economists can easily show that when government spending is greater or less than revenues, the effect is similar to that
which arises when the *planned* investment of business firms is
greater than (or less than) savings. Although the *plans* of business
managers and savers may differ, as may government spending

and its tax receipts, the sum of I + G must equal S + T. That is, business firms' *realized investment and actual government spending must always equal* the sum of *actual savings and taxes*, in accordance with equation (3) above.

"Government Spending (G) and Tax Receipts (T)"

Let us recap our Chapter 8 findings which dealt with households and firms only. Recall that we might have planned investment (PI) greater than (>), less than (<), or equal to (=) savings (S); of course, realized I always equals S. In adding government spending and taxes to the investment-saving sector, we observed earlier in this chapter that we simply treat government spending (G) as *investment* and government tax receipts (T) as *saving*. We can then say that when G > T, expansion will take place, when G < T, contraction can be forecasted, and when G = T, stability holds, *ceteris paribus*. To simplify and generalize this idea, when:

PI + G = S + T: Stability prevails. No impact on output, employment, or income.

PI + G > S + T: Expansion is the forecast. Output, employment, and incomes go up.

PI + G < S + T: Contraction is the forecast. Output, employment, and incomes go down.

Two caveats (warnings) must be entered: (1) Stable *un*employment conditions (say at 10 percent of the work force) are clearly bad. So, although the word "stability" *implies* something good, it is not necessarily a desired economic state. Correspondingly, expansion may occur at the wrong time and simply signify inflation. A forecast of a contracting economy—though often one which we do not want—may, on the other hand, be a desired forecast.

(2) Government may deliberately have G < T or G > T, besides, of course, having G = T. Final results for government plus firms in relation to households will be identical to those observed with respect to the firms-households box diagrams in Chapter 8 — where we found that goods produced but not consumed represented the investment goods in the hands of businesses; at the same time, that which was not consumed out of the total (income) produced represented the public's savings.

99

KEYNESIAN ECONOMICS: A MORE COMPLETE MODEL

Using the Box Diagrams

Figure 9.1 demonstrates the equality of business plans plus government expenditures with consumer savings intentions plus tax receipts. Observe that Panels I and II are designed to demonstrate that PI = S *and* also G = T. On the other hand, Figure 9.2 demonstrates inequality between business plans and consumer savings intentions as well as between government spending and tax receipts. In particular, Panel I in relation to II is deliberately designed to evidence PI < S *and* G < T. This Figure 9.2 depicts the *plans* of people as they look into the future. Figure 9.3 then depicts the actual result once that future becomes the present. The sum of the intended investment goods spending and actual government spending in Panel I of Figure 9.2 is converted by Figure 9.3 to total the sum of the savings and taxes shown in Panel II of Figures 9.2 and 9.3. This final condition reflects the *fact* that government can clearly spend more or less than it taxes the public—not only by way of plans but by way of final results. In contrast, what businesses invest in is limited to whatever the consumers and government have not purchased. If G > T, I must be less than S, if G < T, I must be greater than S. The result is that *realized* investment plus government spending *must equal the actual* savings and tax payments of households.

FIGURE 9.1

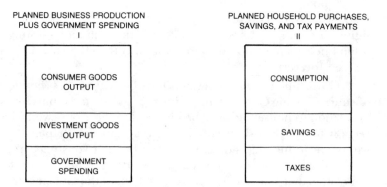

PLANNED BUSINESS PRODUCTION PLUS GOVERNMENT SPENDING — I

CONSUMER GOODS OUTPUT

INVESTMENT GOODS OUTPUT

GOVERNMENT SPENDING

PLANNED HOUSEHOLD PURCHASES, SAVINGS, AND TAX PAYMENTS — II

CONSUMPTION

SAVINGS

TAXES

FIGURE 9.2

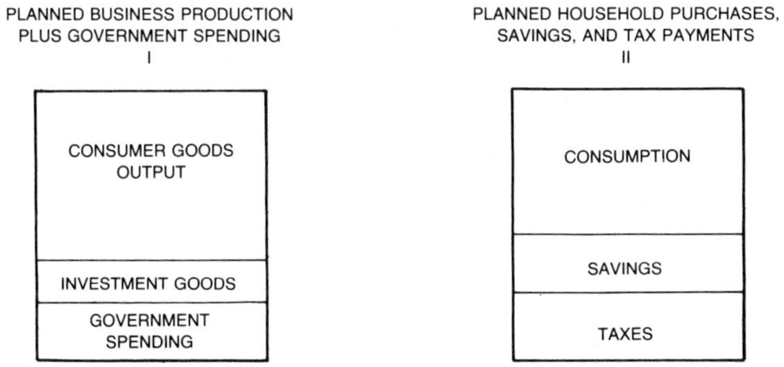

PLANNED BUSINESS PRODUCTION PLUS GOVERNMENT SPENDING I	PLANNED HOUSEHOLD PURCHASES, SAVINGS, AND TAX PAYMENTS II
CONSUMER GOODS OUTPUT	CONSUMPTION
INVESTMENT GOODS	SAVINGS
GOVERNMENT SPENDING	TAXES

FIGURE 9.3

CONSUMER AND BUSINESS INVESTMENT GOOD OUTPUT PLUS GOVERNMENT SPENDING I	HOUSEHOLD PURCHASES, SAVINGS, AND TAX PAYMENTS II
CONSUMER GOODS	CONSUMPTION
INVESTMENT GOODS PLUS GOVERNMENT SPENDING	SAVINGS PLUS TAXES

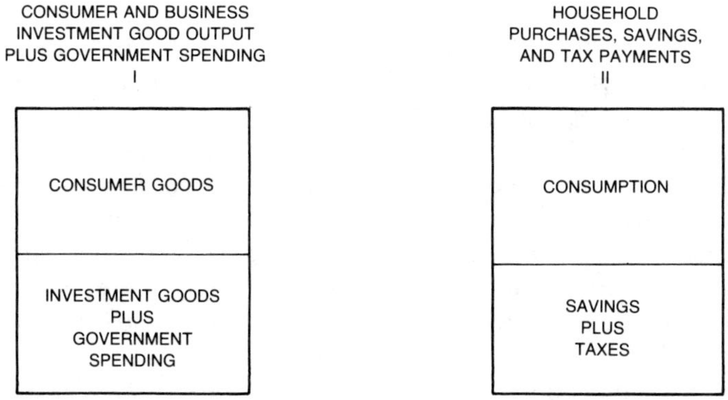

KEYNESIAN ECONOMICS: A MORE COMPLETE MODEL

Contracting Economy

Recognize from the above that if people consume less than the amount of consumer goods being produced (as given by consumption in Panel II of Figure 9.2 compared with consumer good output shown in Panel I), and G is not greater than T by an offsetting amount of investment goods acquired, more inventories will be left on hand at the end of the period than were planned to be maintained by businessmen. So the investment goods *plus* government spending section given in Panel I of Figure 9.3 will be greater than it was in Panel I of Figure 9.2, while being equal to the savings plus taxes total of Panel II of either Figure 9.2 or 9.3. [Remember that in our formulation of the Keynesian model, we allowed people to acquire more or less consumer goods than businesses produced; we did this because firms can use up part of their prior inventory accumulations or be stuck with additional inventories.] Out of the total final income (final output) produced, that part which people did not acquire was not consumed (not used up); this nonconsumed part, by definition, *must equal* the actual savings plus taxes of the people— (i.e., it must equal the S + T segments of the income (output) produced, as given by Panel II of either Figures 9.2 or 9.3).

Expanding Economy

The opposite case of course holds. If people consume more than was expected of them *or* if government deliberately deficit spends (G > T), the stock of goods in which business firms invest will be reduced; the effect is expansionary (anything that makes PI + G > S + T expands the economy). Hence applications by recent American governments of Keynesian economics, which in twenty of the last twenty one years have been characterized by G > T, contributed to the expanding economy of recent years. Unfortunately, the Keynesian idea that aggregate demand is the propelling force and that supply will move along with that demand has not worked. Supply-side shortages (as stressed later in the book) have arisen, with inflation resulting. At the same time, the idea that government can provide public goods to the people at no cost at all (i.e., without a corresponding tax bill) was revealed to be misleading, for the real costs of governmental deficits became manifest to all in the form of inflating prices and declining productivity. For the moment, we stress that if PI + G > S + T, the economy will expand, which is not necessarily good.

"AN EXAMPLE OF THE G + I AND S + T EQUALITY"

To further appreciate the basic relationship, assume a total output (income) of $3 trillion in the year 1983. Let consumption, that is, consumer goods purchased, be $2 trillion. Suppose government spending (in acquiring goods produced by business and in paying judges, policemen, etc.) is $0.6 trillion; then the goods remaining in the hands of firms (that is, investment goods) must equal $0.4 trillion. At the same time because the consumer purchased $2 trillion of goods out of the $3 trillion GNP, he saved the amount x and was taxed the amount y, where x + y must equal $1 trillion, as in Table 9.1. Clearly, the amount taxed depends essentially on government policy. And the amount taxed further determines the amount consumed and saved.

TABLE 9.1

TOTAL OUTPUT (INCOME) IN TRILLIONS OF DOLLARS (FINAL RESULTS)		TOTAL OUTPUT (INCOME) IN TRILLIONS OF DOLLARS (THE CONSUMER VIEW)	
GNP	3	GNP	3
Consumption Goods	2	Consumption	2
Government Spending	0.6	Savings	x
Investment Goods	0.4	Taxes	y
		(Savings and Taxes)	x + y = 1

Suppose your earned income per hour is $10. You customarily consume $8 of it while saving $2 and being taxed 0, as in column II, Panel (A) of Table 9.2. (We are not concerned in column I with the breakdown between government spending and the investment good purchases of business firms.) Change the situation now by having the government tax you $2 on your income of $10. If the ratio of your consumption to your *disposable income* ($8 out

103

of \$10, or ⁴⁄₅) remains substantially the same after the tax is imposed, you would now consume ⁴⁄₅ of the \$8 *disposable (after tax) income* in your hands. Out of the \$10 income minus the \$2 taxes, you now consume \$6.40 of output and save \$1.60 (assuming your tendency, or propensity, to consume is still ⁴⁄₅ of your income and thus your propensity to save is ¹⁄₅ of that income). Column II of Panel (A) of Table 9.2 would reappear for *you* (the individual) as Column II of Panel (B). In comparing Columns I of Panels (A) and (B), we recognize in light of Column II of Panel (B) vis a vis

TABLE 9.2

(A)

I		II	
Output (Income Produced)		Output (Income Received)	
GNP	10.00	GNP	10.00
Consumption Goods	8.00	Consumption	8.00
Government Spending plus		Savings	2.00
Investment Goods	2.00	Taxes	0.00
		Savings and Taxes	2.00

(B)

I		II	
Output (Income Produced)		Output (Income Received)	
GNP	10.00	GNP	10.00
Consumption Goods	6.40	Consumption	6.40
Government Spending plus		Savings	1.60
Investment Goods	3.60	Taxes	2.00
		Savings and Taxes	3.60

Column II of Panel (A), that business firms ended up with more investment goods ($1.60 worth) as a consequence of your reduced consumption (from $8.00 to $6.40 because of taxes).

Government Spending, Inflation, Taxing-Leakage

Government spending has an impact on income similar to that of investment purchases, while taxes operate as an offset (or "leakage") basically similar to savings. The final result of including the government sector with the private sector is not to require investment equal to savings and government spending equal to taxes, but for the total of government spending plus investment to *equal* the total of savings plus taxes. When viewed in the planned perspective of *future effects*, if PI + G > S + T, the economy will expand; on the other hand, if—as would apply to Table 9.2—PI + G < S + T, the economy will contract; if they are equal, the GNP stays the same. *For simplicity*, rather than continue to write PI + G $\lessgtr$ S + T, we shall henceforth use PI $\lessgtr$ S, except when stress on "G" *vis-a-vis* "T" is needed.

"FOREIGN TRADE AND THE CIRCULAR FLOW"

The world's population explosion and the general lowering of trade barriers in recent years have combined to cause a significant increase in exports and imports for virtually all countries. The exports (E) of goods and services from the United States alone rose by $130 billion during the decade from 1967 to 1977, growing from roughly $45 billion to $175 billion. At the same time, the nation's imports (M) rose from $41 billion to $186 billion, from slightly over 5% of gross national product in 1967 to a little more than 7% in 1977. It followed, in turn, that a U.S.A. balance of trade deficit of about $11 billion replaced a balance of trade surplus of $4 billion over this ten-year period.

It should be evident that as E − M changed to a negative value, the American foreign sector was characterized by leakages (imports providing income to foreign producers) greater than injections (exports providing domestic income). The net import balance of trade moderated to some extent the upward spiraling price effects that were taking place in the seventies.

KEYNESIAN ECONOMICS: A MORE COMPLETE MODEL

"THE EFFECT OF E AND M ON THE I + G EQUALITY WITH S + T"

When E and M are introduced into the equation, it is no longer necessary for I + G to equal S + T, except during periods when E equals M. The same reasoning that applied when we added G to I and T to S holds for the foreign sector. For example, if E rises above M, income will rise so that S + T is greater than I + G by the amount of the excess of E over M. In particular, consider the following:

PI + G + E = S + T + M   Stability prevails
PI + G + E > S + T + M   Expansion is the forecast
PI + G + E < S + T + M   Contraction is the forecast

Recognize that the last two inequalities do not tell us whether $G \gtreqless T$, $E \gtreqless M$, or $PI \gtreqless S$. The particular relations do not count because the items on the right side (S + T + M) are all a form of savings (or leakages). Only the total relation between PI + G + E vis a vis S + T + M counts. In fact, the reader can use a short-cut thought system by recognizing that business firms' realized investment is *limited* to the amount that consumers, governments, and foreigners have not purchased. *This is the key to our model.* If the realized I is greater than the planned I, firms have been left with more inventories than they planned to have, so contraction follows *ceteris paribus.* Opposite effects hold when realized I is less than planned I.

To sum up: whatever makes one of the lefthand elements (PI, G, E) > its righthand counterparts (S, T, M) is expansionary, and vice versa. If the lefthand sum is > the righthand one, the total effect is expansionary, as realized I will prove to be less than was planned, although total I + G + E will equal total S + T + M. (We recommend rereading this chapter if necessary for your full understanding of this paragraph).

Economic Policy and the Foreign Sector

What should a policy designed to promote economic stability do about E and M? Our answer is simply this: *any given foreign sector policy depends crucially on all of the conditions prevailing during a given period in history.* For example, consider the mid–1979 period of time. Many economists were asserting that the United States was in the beginning of a recessionary period. At the same time, inflation was running well above the 10% level. One way of combatting *recession* would have been to expand exports (by subsidizing them) and/or decrease imports (by raising tariffs). This would have had the effect of reducing the realized investments of business firms, which is another way of saying that PI + G + E would be greater than S + T + M; the resulting expansion might include employment of previously unemployed persons. Alternatively, *inflation* could have been reduced by increasing the supply of goods in the country, by decreasing exports (via an embargo thereon) and/or increasing imports (by lowering tariffs). This would have had the opposite economy-wide effect to that noted above. But reactions of foreign governments must also be considered. Most economists decided in the fall of 1979 that inflation was a greater problem than unemployment, and to that extent would have favored more imports. They tended only to advocate tight money, encouragement of private investment, *reduced* government spending possibly balanced off by reduced taxes later on, and conservation of fuel, but not trying to change exports or imports because of foreign government reactions.

"GROWTH IN THE PUBLIC SECTOR IN RECENT PERIODS OF TIME: KEYNESIAN ECONOMICS"

Government plays a vital role in free enterprise economies by altering the savings-investment relations. Ever since 1946, the American government has in fact considered itself responsible for maintaining full employment, keeping prices stable, and promoting rapid economic growth.

Keynes' emphasis on government spending was perfectly natural, for governmental tax and spending programs presumably could be changed drastically and quickly by Congress. In contrast, any attempt to induce greater business investments—such as by lowering corporate income tax rates or allowing faster write-offs (depreciation) of capital goods, or by having the Fed move toward lower interest rates—would require follow-up expansionary decisions by business executives in addition to the government fiscal-monetary action. The adage could surely apply that "one can lead a horse to water but cannot force it to drink." This very thought was in fact used during the thirties and subsequent decades to support government spending programs rather than incentives for business investment.

Consumption, of course, also appears changeable in the theory. One way to change consumption is by reducing personal income taxes, and many economists argue strongly in favor of reducing the taxes of the poor. They contend that the tendencies of poorer families to consume exceed those of wealthier families. It would follow, particularly over short periods of time, that any given dollar increase in the "take-home" pay (disposable income) of poorer households by way of reduced taxes should increase that family's consumption more than if the same tax reduction were awarded a wealthy family. Whether correct or not, this device too requires a change in another sector *in addition to government action*. Moreover, it is argued that the spending of poorer families may be fixed by necessity of survival, and that any changes in "take-home" pay would chiefly convert the dissavings of a family (where borrowing is greater than saving) into a zero or slightly positive saving budget.

One conclusion alone was agreed upon by virtually all who favored government intervention in periods of recession or depression and that was simply that one could not look to the foreign sector for help. It was evident that any attempt to increase exports (for example, by subsidizing them) or to decrease imports (such as by raising tariffs*) would be matched by foreign governments. Other nations were also embedded in depression; they too had economists who understood the Keynesian model. Clearly any attempt, in effect, to export one's depression would be matched by other governments.

Government expenditures were only 10% of the nation's 1929 GNP. They increased to 20% by 1941. By the early 1970s, government expenditures had grown to approximately 32% of the nation's GNP. Those employed by the federal, state, and local governments rose from approximately 9% in 1929 to 20% in the 1970s. One out of every five workers in the United States now depends directly on the government.**

---

*Note that if we decrease imports by raising certain tariffs, thereby inducing Americans to purchase domestic-produced goods and in the process reducing the S + M total, the *ceteris paribus* effect is to use up inventories (to make PI > S).

**It is interesting that as of 1972 the two wealthiest counties in the U.S.A. in terms of average income of residents were Montgomery County, Maryland and Fairfax County, Virginia, both essentially populated by government employees in Washington, D.C.

M.L. GREENHUT   C.T. STEWART

"FINAL STATEMENT"

We have completed our view of the impact of the government and foreign sectors in the circular flow. We found that the simple model's idea of expansion resulting when PI > S, contraction when PI < S, and stability resulting when PI = S holds when the government and foreign sectors are included. In the complete model, we simply had to add G + E to PI and T + M to S. In the process, we obtained the same fundamental conclusion. Any action which suddenly makes G or E greater than their counterparts T and M tends to expand the economy. Opposite or alternative relations, of course, would also apply. The key is the sum of PI + G + E vis a vis S + T + M. Viewed retrospectively, the I + G + E total always equals the S + T + M total. The Keynesian model thus centers its main attention on the inequalities formed by different plans (expectations) vis a vis the actual results that take place over a short period of time. When the same differences continue long enough, pronounced expansion, contraction, inflation, or deflation will result. We shall stress inflation and the reasons for it in the unit that follows.

INTRODUCTION TO PART FOUR ON MONETARISM

The inflation of the seventies with high unemployment, high interest rates, and low productivity implied a failure of Keynesian economics. These economic events also helped promote the resurgence among professional economists of a school of thought that is referred to today as Monetarism. This school emphasizes monetary policy over fiscal policy as the central determinant of cyclical swings. Its members propose that the problems of the seventies (and eighties) resulted from an incorrect macropolicy, more specifically an unstable rate of growth in the money supply. Why they believe that fiscal policy is impotent without conformable assistance from the monetary authorities, and why they argue that the stock of money is the key to economic progress *and* that *discretionary* monetary policy is limited, these are the central themes of this part of the book. It sets forth the thought structure of the monetarists in order to learn why they seek marketplace solutions to economic problems, while relegating government essentially to the roles it had exercised before the development and widespread acceptance of Keynesian economics.

PART FOUR:
CHAPTER 10:
THE INFLATION YEARS
AND THEORIES OF
INFLATION

American governments traditionally centered their spending on defense and education. However, increasing emphasis in recent years has been placed on public welfare, health, and the safety of workers. In fact, of all the categories of government expenditure, payments on these programs have in recent years increased the most.

Defense and related expenditures by our federal government amounted to approximately 25 percent of the total $478 billion dollars that was spent by the federal government in 1978, roughly $119 billion. But an even larger amount was designed to maintain the income of farmers, older citizens, dependent children, unemployed persons, and to protect the health of Americans, etc. Defense is now the second major expenditure of our federal government, and cash income maintenance is first.*

The impact of the growth of the public sector has been manifold. It has had good and bad (including inflationary) effects. It was, of course, the severity of the depression years, along with the circular flow theory of J.M. Keynes, that led the nation to use government spending *and* tax receipts to "fine-tune" the economy. The goal was permanent full employment with a stable price level. Unfortunately, the original Keynesian design to have PI + G + E > S + T + M during periods of economic troughs and to apply the reverse inequality during periods of economic boom was transformed into widespread belief that government should stimulate the growth of the economy over *all periods of time*. The post World War II inflation periods reflect an *over*application of Keynesian economics.

---

*The breakdown of a pre Reagan administration federal budget (for fiscal year 1978-79) is presented in Table 10.1.

TABLE 10.1

AMOUNTS IN BILLIONS OF DOLLARS

Function	Current services	Proposed	Increase (percent)
National defense	116.8	117.8	0.8
International affairs	7.4	7.7	3.8
General science, space, and technology	5.1	5.1	0.2
Energy	7.6	9.6	27.1
Natural resources and environment	12.0	12.2	2.0
Agriculture	5.5	5.4	− 1.4
Commerce and housing credit	3.1	3.0	− 4.4
Transportation	17.1	17.4	1.7
Community and regional development	8.5	8.7	2.0
Education, training, employment, and social services	29.4	30.4	3.6
Health	50.3	49.7	− 1.3
Income security	159.2	160.0	0.5
Veterans' benefits and services	18.9	19.3	2.0
Administration of justice	4.1	4.2	3.8
General government	4.2	4.3	2.9
General purpose fiscal assistance	9.5	9.6	1.5
Interest	48.7	49.0	0.6
Allowance for contingencies	1.1	2.8[a]	b
Undistributed offsetting receipts	− 16.0	− 16.0	0.0
Total	492.4	500.2	1.6

SOURCE: Robert W. Hartman, "The Budget and the Economy," in Joseph A. Pechman, ed., *Setting National Priorities: The 1979 Budget* (Brookings Institution, 1978), Table 2-13, p. 53. Copyright © 1978 by the Brookings Institution.
a. Allowance for contingencies includes amounts subsequently reallocated to higher education and urban programs.
b. No meaning.

"MONEY INCOME VIEW OF INFLATION"

Visualize a national income level commensurate with full employment. In fact, assume full employment has prevailed for a while. Then let government expenditures go up and up *as, say, wartime pressures mount.* Given such increased spending, the GNP can move in only one direction, and that too is up. But if employment is already full, output must already be just about as large as possible; and any rise in the nation's income cannot then take the form of more goods. It can only mean higher prices.

The economic period just described is one for which a prior suggestion in this book no longer applies. Recall that Part Three suggested one should think only in terms of the *real* GNP (i.e., the actual physical goods and services produced and the income equivalent of this output). But in order to appreciate problems of inflation and monetarist economic theory, the nation's income should be viewed *in changing money terms;* for clearly an increase in the investment sector (business investment, government expenditures, or even the net export component) will lead, in the Keynesian model, to higher money prices only if full employment already exists, *ceteris paribus.* Of course, all other things need not be equal temporarily—government may restrain prices during a war by selling war bonds, imposing heavy taxes, rationing goods, or invoking wage and price ceilings. Bond sales and heavy taxation reduce income available for consumption, while rationing and wage and price ceilings set a limit on consumer goods spending. These several practices enable the substitution of an increased amount of government spending for some of the previous total of consumption. It is as if the investment *total* goes up just when consumption goes down. In balance, high investment plus consumption could generate GNP at a non-inflated level of income for a while.

When the war ends, however, the "patriotic" buying of bonds (which helped keep consumption at lower values) will cease. Many bondholders will choose to cash in their bonds, and willingness to be taxed will also decrease. Moreover, during wartime, wage and price ceilings and rationing are the "patriotic" thing to accept; however, in peacetime they are considered to be totalitarian controls. Government expenditures will, of course, tend to go down after a war so that some of the restraining controls on consumption can be removed. But if too strong a pent-up demand exists after a war is ended, the reduction in government spending will be more than matched by the increase in consumption, especially if business investment also runs high. This is how it was with the post World War II period in the U.S.A. Instead of the recession that some people had forecasted during the period of industrial conversion from a wartime to a peacetime posture, the American economy was characterized by a continued prosperity that was accompanied by a moderate inflation.

"THE EARLY POST WORLD WAR II YEARS"

Marshall Plan expenditures soon began to replace wartime lend-lease programs . They were, in turn, supplemented by large domestic military budgets, which culminated later on in new outlays for the Korean conflict. Therefore expansionary tendencies continued, as both government and private industrial spending were steadily on the rise—and consumption with them.

The immediate post World War II days witnessed a steady rise in prices and nearly continuous full employment. Downward movements were moderate and short, chiefly reflecting normal contractions in inventory buying. By 1950, the nation's GNP was up to $286.2 billion. By 1954, it stood at $366.3 billion; and in 1959 it was up to $486.5 billion. These and related statistics are shown in Table 10.2.

TABLE 10.2

GNP AND COMPONENTS IN 1950, 1954, AND 1959
(AMOUNTS IN BILLIONS OF DOLLARS)

	1950	1954	1959
Gross National Product	286.2	366.3	486.5
Consumption	192.0	235.8	310.8
Business Investments	53.8	52.7	77.6
Net Exports	1.9	2.0	0.6
Government Expenditures	38.5	75.8	97.6

"INFLATION FROM BOTTLENECKS, SHORTAGES, AND GOVERNMENT SPENDING"

Inflation comes about when the demand for goods increases more than output. This occurs according to Keynes at a time of full employment, though it may also happen in periods of less than full employment when bottlenecks appear on assembly lines and/or in ordering or creating goods. In fact, it may also occur in periods of selected shortages or bad crops, as in the seventies. In any case, bottlenecks have the effect of inducing increases in selected prices, usually of a moderate order. According to Keynesian economics, a pronounced general increase in prices will occur only during periods when *total demand* exceeds the *supply available* at current prices under conditions approaching full employment. Such periods of excess demand are typically periods of excessive government expenditures.*

Price increases at a time of *full employment* may, among other things, be traced to bottlenecks, just as in periods of less than full employment. Similarly, Keynesians would aver that they may be caused by unsound monetary practices, that is, undue expansions of the money supply. During the early post World War II and Korean War periods, inflation in the United States was said to be due to the existence of excess demand at full employment income. To prevent the inflation required an increase in taxes, a greater willingness to save, higher interest rates, or less government spending, or a combination of these approaches. The American government did not want to follow any of these policies and particularly to adopt a smaller budget. It appeared to prefer moderate inflation, being *concerned only with the possibility that disastrous results* (economically or politically) could follow from constraints and curtailments. The price level in the United States was permitted to move upward in 1946–1948 and 1952–1954. The process went something like this:

As income rises, consumption and saving also rise. Further, as prices rise *moderately,* interest rates will rise a little and savings therefore also rise, all other things remaining equal. Thus savings can be seen to be rising on all counts. Investments will also increase further if for no other reason than anticipation of higher prices. Planned saving eventually rises to the level of planned investment. This result comes about through the increases in income. If inflation is moderate, it may go on and on; and all will be well. This is the way many viewed the American economy as the 1950's were drawing to a close.

---

*As we shall see later in the book, supply-side economists contend that inadequate incentives resulting from high income tax rates lead to falling productivity which combine with cash income maintenance programs and government deficits to produce inflation at less than full employment levels of income.

"THE EARLY 1960'S: KENNEDY VS. NIXON, A SMALL CHANGE IN APPROACH"

By the end of the 1950's, the nation's economists had promoted their message through the halls of Congress and convinced the presidential aspirants, John F. Kennedy and Richard M. Nixon, of the relevance of Keynesian economics. The platforms of their parties differed more than did the candidates themselves with respect to proposed (and artful) applications of Keynesian economics. The nation's Democrats and Republicans were concerned then, as now, with the nation's economic well-being. Of course, each party advocated high levels of employment and incomes for all. In addition, each was troubled by the mini-recession of the late '50s.

The youthful senator from Massachusetts—reflecting his party's platform—advocated reduced income tax rates, especially at the lower levels of income.* It was argued that an increase in disposable income would lead to increased consumption, then to increased capital investment, and throughout the sequence to higher levels of well-being in the country. Richard Nixon, in turn, expressed two concerns: one directed towards the Soviet Union, and one centered on the American economy. He too advocated reduced taxes, but primarily reduction in corporate income taxes. Adhering to Republican Party guidelines, Nixon argued that if business is encouraged to invest more in capital equipment, the nation's productivity would rise, incomes would rise, and consumption would also rise. The United States would not only stay ahead of the Soviet Union economically, but militarily as well.

Shortly after taking office in 1961, President Kennedy helped promote an expansionary economic program through the halls of Congress. This program, somewhat surprisingly, contained the essence of what candidate Nixon had proposed. Business investment was to be promoted, not only by accelerated depreciation allowances, but by outright tax credits for investments in new capital equipment. Economists and politicians of all persuasions were accepting the same thought system (e.g., the same

---

*It is significant—as we shall later point out in some detail with respect to the income tax laws—that though the nation's legislators often advocate helping the poor, the big tax breaks established throughout the post World War II years provided tax savings which only the wealthy could use to advantage.

equations C + I + G + E = Y = C + S + T + M) as the basis for understanding the overall economy. To be sure, one group in its applications might advocate more C so as to generate greater Y, while another would propose more I (or more G, etc.) as the preferred vehicle for raising Y.

Why do applications of the same theory differ? They differ because the value judgements of people differ! Chances are the advocate of greater consumption as the prime device to move the economy to higher income levels considers the inadequate consumption by poorer households as the nation's number one problem. This person would believe that by rectifying that problem, increased investment will result and everyone will benefit accordingly. In contrast, the advocate of increasing investment directly does not (necessarily) lack concern about poverty, but rather believes that poverty is best resolved by making sure that greater investment takes place.

Someday the science of economics may be so advanced that a full "cause and effect" sequence will be determinable. Then the total income change in the economy would be predictable as well as the time involved in the process of making such a change. But until that day arrives, disputes will continue to rage as to whether one sector needs more help than another. The present authors would sometimes prefer fiscal changes promoting investment and, at other times, changes centering primarily on consumption or on government expenditures. At still other times, as we shall attempt to spell out near the end of this part of the book, we might simply prefer to work with the quantity of money and the interest rate. The choice would depend on world affairs, on the state of the nation's technology and the arts, the position of the overall economy, and the prevailing state of cultural as well as economic well-being of its people.

"THE L.B. JOHNSON, EARLY NIXON YEARS: A MAJOR CHANGE IN APPROACH"

John M. Keynes had argued that the cost of World War II was borne by those who lived then. He had further argued that the American public debt was unimportant in that if it was ever to be paid off, a simple exchange from taxpayer Paul to bondholder Peter would take place. He also argued that if resources were not

119

being utilized, government spending programs (i.e., projects which would employ idle resources) were clearly costless. For those who feared the public debt as they would private debt, Keynes argued that the Fed could buy up the public debt and thus financial bankruptcy was impossible.

It was in the context of the pleasing thoughts of Keynes that Lyndon B. Johnson's "Great Society" was born. A redistributive zeal prevailed in the country; poorer families had to be helped. Although welfare programs plus expenditures for the Vietnam war added up to large deficits, Keynesian economics had already suggested—a la Roosevelt—that we had nothing to fear but fear itself.

Excessive government expenditures were accompanied by a reluctance on the part of Wilbur Mills and other Congressmen to push for higher taxes. Even President Johnson waited much longer to recommend higher taxes than his economists advised. By the time Congress legislated higher taxes in the late 1960's, prices had begun skyrocketing. By early 1971, President Nixon (shifting the Republican Party's laissez-faire gears completely) *imposed price controls* on the American economy. But artificially low prices and energy controls (for example, the arbitrary low prices set on natural gas sold in interstate commerce) tend to increase demand by shifting the wants of people to the very goods whose prices are artificially low. Price controls can only keep prices where they are during the early months of control. Sooner or later black markets, cheating of weight or quality, and pressure by different groups must generate more and more police and state controls *or* the abandonment of the control program altogether. In fact, price controls work reasonably well only during wartime years when patriotic saving can be substituted in the place of normal demands for goods and services.

The inflation of the '70s was thus marked in part by excessive government expenditures. These large expenditures reflected both President Johnson's "Great Society" program (as continued by President Nixon) and involvement in the Vietnamese War. The expenditures were excessive (the public debt grew) because of the reluctance of Congressmen to raise taxes to pay for the "Great Society" *and* the war. When the controls were lifted (which would have been necessary sooner or later), the forces of inflation shot prices upward.

120

There were many other causes of inflation during this time. "Cradle-to-grave" security—in the form of social security and pension plans—tends to induce individuals to shift their consumption upwards and their savings downward. Credit cards induce increased consumption; *and* excessive government spending raises total spending further. A shift to "governmental production" in the form of more and better highways, an expanding purchase of services by government, and greater paperwork fostered by its bureaucracy will increase the number and size of paychecks. However, no goods are produced for consumers or businessmen. Greater money income without an equivalent increase in saleable goods output results in higher prices.

Relatedly, environmental protection laws entail expenditures *and* income; but goods are not produced and sold to consumers. Raw material shortages in the '70s were due in part to drought. International prices (such as coffee) rose. Monopolistic increases in prices, such as by the OPEC cartel (Organization of Petroleum Exporting Countries), also raised the cost of living substantially—with no increased output. Even though the economy was at less than what many economists claimed was the full employment level, output was not increasing. The effect was more rapid inflation, as if full employment prevailed. [*More about inflation* will be entered in Chapter 13 and 14 where both the circular flow model *and* the theory of the monetarists can be used to evaluate what recently occurred in the United States (and other nations in the world).]

"THE CRITIQUES OF GOVERNMENT ECONOMIC POLICIES BY THE MONETARIST SCHOOL OF THOUGHT"

The Theory of Keynes which centers on the use of government spending to promote full employment has not been universally accepted, nor indeed has the associated view gone unchallenged that increased spending and deficits help create a great society. A small group of economists were concerned in the early 1960's with increased deficits. They began to argue that those who gave up consumer or investment goods during a war that was financed by government deficits did so voluntarily. They *wanted* to obtain Treasury Bonds; hence, economic deprivation was *not* a factor. The real problem from a debt comes later on, when interest is paid on it or when the debt is being paid off. This group of economists, therefore, rejected Keynes' argument that those hurt by incurring war debt were those who gave up consumption goods to finance the war.

Keynes' "Paul-to-Peter argument" for internally held debt where taxpayers pay what the government owes to its other citizen bondholders was also critiqued. *Paul* might be a poor taxpayer and *Peter* a wealthy bondholder. Individual choices are changed significantly when the debt is being paid off. In effect, the future generation *does bear the burden of a war debt,* not those living at the time the debt is created.

Keynes' argument that idle resources were being used when government expansion led to deficits was also criticized by this group of economists. They held that there is always a cost in using resources since public spending reduces the output (C + I + E) available to other sectors. Even when government puts idle resources to work, some are used up (e.g., energy reserves may be depleted). When an unemployed individual goes to work, there *is* a cost. The cost to the individual is the giving up of the leisure that he would otherwise have enjoyed.

Even Keynes' argument that financial bankruptcy would not occur was being disputed by the group of economists in question. They contended that a growing share of the American public debt was in the process of being owned by foreign nationals. More importantly, to the extent that the debt is financed by the Fed, the money supply grows and inflation results. That alone could cause economic breakdowns.

By the time the Nixon years ended, the fears of this group had gained prominence under a much broader framework of thought than that centering on the question: "Who bears the burden of a debt, the present generation or future generations?" Their framework of thought is called Monetarism. Their basic thesis is that the federal government should eliminate its public deficit interferences with the economy. One of the economists along this line of thought, Phil Gramm, ran his campaign for Congress on a Monetarist type of program. He emphasized the need to reduce government bureaucratic controls and spending sharply while curtailing the growth of the money supply. Before probing deeply into what Monetarism is all about, some concepts must first be developed in Chapter 11.

M.L. GREENHUT   C.T. STEWART

"FINAL STATEMENT"

To understand the late 1970s and the 1980s, we must turn our attention to *Monetarism*. Before we do, a last point must be made. What started out as the anti-depression Keynesian system of thought had, by the time of the Johnson, Nixon, and Ford administrations, become the basis for improving the economy every day, every year. *Political* reaction to this application of a theory of economics was delayed, however, to as late a time as California's Proposition 13, if indeed a full change in application has actually yet occurred. Certainly, there were many in the House of Representatives in 1981 who resisted a change in the use of the Keynesian model. It is impossible to say, even as we move into the spring of 1983, whether the Reagan administration (and especially Congress) will return to using the circular flow as an anti-depression guideline alone or continue to use it freely during even rather prosperous times. The Monetarists, we shall see, assert that the Keynesian system of thought should never be used—that it is simply a misleading, or at best a misapplied, economic framework of thought.

CHAPTER 11:
INFLATION — SUPPLY AND
DEMAND

We have used the word "inflation" up to this point in the book without formally defining its meaning. Precise definition and tighter analysis are needed now. The public appears to consider inflation as "a substantial rise in the price of most goods and services." Of course, what is *substantial* involves a value judgment decision. In some contrast, many economists designate an increase in prices greater than 2% as inflationary. They are not saying the prices of *all* goods and services must rise by 2%, nor that prices must rise by that amount or more *each year*. In general, the following elementary definition of inflation will suffice for our needs:

> We define *inflation* as taking place when the prices of a large number of goods and services purchased in the country are rising *and* the annual rate of increase is hovering at or exceeds 2%. Annual rates of price increase—such as the 7% to 13% rates which have taken place in the United States, or the 30 to 70% rates of many South American countries—are clearly inflationary (in fact, very inflationary).

All of the above may strike one as being rather imprecise, and it is! All that needs to be remembered is that inflation signifies a continuing increase in the prices of most goods, and that this increase is sufficiently great to be noticeable.

"HOW DO WE MEASURE INFLATION?"

The next question which typically concerns economists is how to measure, or know, when the prices of most things have been going up. The answer to this is easy. The Bureau of Labor Statistics of the United States Department of Labor measures the general price level. It calculates what is known as the "Consumer Price Index" (CPI). This CPI is nothing more than a measure of the average price of some 400 selected goods and services purchased by households. Which are the 400 goods and services used by the CPI? Actually those selected are supposed to represent the ones you and I might find in our typical market basket.

"COMPARISONS WITH THE BASE YEAR"

The CPI is expressed in relation to some base or index year. An example should help. Suppose we use 1967 as our base year. This means that a given year (often the present one) will be compared to 1967 in measuring how much prices have changed in general. *For the sake of simplicity*, the base year CPI is always assigned the number 100.00, no matter what base year was chosen and no matter how high or low prices were then.

In Figure 11.1, compare the CPI of 100.00 for 1967 with the 1977 CPI of 181.50. Notice that the CPI in 1977 is about 82 points higher than the base year level. This indicates that prices in 1977 were approximately 82 percent above the base year prices of

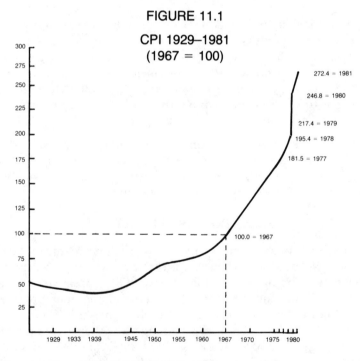

FIGURE 11.1

CPI 1929–1981
(1967 = 100)

272.4 = 1981
246.8 = 1980
217.4 = 1979
195.4 = 1978
181.5 = 1977
100.0 = 1967

Source: *The Economic Report of the President, 1982.*

126

1967. Figure 11.1 traces the historical record of the Consumer Price Index from 1929 through 1981. For example, the CPI was only 88.7 in 1960 compared to 1967.

"INFLATION: THE CAUSES"

Four alternative theories exist, each of which stresses major forces (causes) that account for inflation in such free enterprise economies as the United States. They respectively stress: 1) a large quantity of money, 2) a strong demand-pull, 3) a cost-push, and 4) the so-called "structural cause."

"THE QUANTITY OF MONEY"

The "quantity of money" model of inflation is one of the oldest around. It can be understood readily in terms of the circular flow model. Recall in this context that all of the goods and services produced in the circular flow are either actively acquired *or else become unplanned inventory investment*. The goods and services purchased usually involve the spending of money. The *quantity theory of money* concentrates on the relationship between goods and services produced and the amount of money available for buying goods and services. The relationship goes like this: If the Fed puts more money into the circular flow (this generally signifies more consumer demand), the price level (CPI) will normally go up. The *quantity theory of money* simply states that as more money is put into the circular flow of economic activity (economy), prices (CPI) will tend to rise, all other things unchanged.

To make this point more precise, Table 11.1 below provides selected American data on the quantity of money in circulation and the Consumer Price Index. If the quantity theory of money works, we should find the CPI rising as more money is put into the economy. Table 11.1 does *suggest* that changes in money *are related* to the value of the Consumer Price Index.

"DEMAND-PULL INFLATION"

Demand-pull inflation simply means that consumers demand more (have the willingness and ability to buy more) goods and services than are actually being produced. Since money and demand are so closely related, many economists say demand-pull

127

TABLE 11.1

MONEY AND PRICES

Year	Money Supply ($billions)	CPI
1960	141.9	88.7
1965	169.5	94.5
1970	216.5	116.3
1975	291.0	161.2
1976	310.4	170.1
1977	335.5	181.5
1978	363.2	195.4
1979	389.0	217.4
1980	414.5	246.8
1981	440.9	272.4
1982	478.5	289.1

SOURCE: *The Economic Report of the President*, 1983

inflation results from too much money (demand) chasing too few goods (shortage of supply).

Notice in Figure 11.1 the rather sharp increase from 1965 to 1970 in the CPI. The upward price spiral starting in 1965 was said to stem from demand-pull inflation. In that year the United States was expanding its military effort in Vietnam. The substantial rise in military effort meant more jobs in war-related industries, and the increased employment generated more income to consumers. Naturally, demand went up. But what is bad about this?

The answer relates to the production possibilities of the nation. As more war-related goods (national defense) are produced, less consumer goods are produced. Thus the Vietnam War period (as with all war periods) was characterized as an era of demand-pull inflation. In a nutshell, incomes went up because of war production; but that same war production meant fewer consumer goods could be produced. Prices rise when people with increasing incomes and ability to pay higher prices find consumer items in shorter and shorter supply.

M.L. GREENHUT   C.T. STEWART

"COST-PUSH INFLATION"

Cost-push inflation is rather easy to describe. It simply means that if firms are faced with increases in raw material and other input prices—that is, if the prices of the factors of production (land, labor, capital) go up—they will pass the higher costs on to the consumer in the form of higher prices for the final product. Higher prices must be charged in the product market in order for firms to continue to make the profit they feel is necessary for their survival.

Many argue that one of the main causes of cost-push inflation is organized labor (the labor unions). The reasoning is elementary: When labor unions negotiate higher wage contracts with large corporations (such as the coal pact of 1978), the companies will simply pass the new higher wage settlement on to the consumer in the form of higher prices.

"STRUCTURAL INFLATION"

By *structural inflation*, economists mean that something has changed in the basic nature or makeup of industry, or perhaps the economy as a whole. A change in production or supply conditions typically (but not necessarily) results in higher costs of production; new technology often reduces costs.

Many things can cause structural inflation—such as crop failures attributable to weather and disease, legislated increases in wages, or the exhaustion of high grade ores. Perhaps the most recent important example was that of the Arab oil embargo. The shortage of oil that resulted from the embargo was a major contributing factor to the rising price level of the early 1970's. In fact, the CPI fuel bill measure for July 1973 (before the embargo) was 133.1; while in July 1974 (after the embargo), it had risen to 221.1.

Which Theory is Correct?

Economists are in general agreement that the demand-pull, cost-push, and structural inflation theories are essentially *descriptions* of underlying forces. They argue further that if the Fed would create less money than it does, there would be less inflation. When one studies economics in many American universities, it is likely that the professor will assert that the basic cause of inflation is money being created at a faster rate than goods and services (the quantity theory of money). But this assertion is essentially the basis for Monetarism, as explained in Chapter 12. To understand Monetarism, the principles of what is called demand, supply analysis must be understood. This is the subject to which we now turn.

"PRICES, DEMAND AND SUPPLY"

In free enterprise systems, heavy reliance is placed on the movement of prices to achieve efficiency. This is so because prices provide a link between the conflicting "self-interests" of consumers and producers. The economist explains the "conflict-resolving" operation of prices by use of a competitive market model. In that model, the technical concepts of "demand" and "supply" are designed to reflect consumer and producer valuations of resources. These valuations, in turn, reflect the amounts people are respectively willing and able to buy and sell.

"GENERAL EXPLANATION OF DEMAND, SUPPLY, AND MARKET PRICE"

Economists view economic values through the interaction of demand and supply. They stress the idea that price moves towards a given value called the "equilibrium price." At the equilibrium price, the amount consumers are willing to buy and producers are willing to sell are equal, thereby clearing the market. Because of the importance of the concept of an equilibrium, additional comments on demand, supply, and equilibrium are needed.

Demand

The technical meaning of demand is that it is a schedule of the various quantities of a good or service that consumers are willing (and able) to buy at given prices. An example of such a schedule is provided in the left hand side of Table 11.2. Note that as price falls from $22 to $19 per unit, the quantity demanded increases. Panel (A) of Figure 11.2 depicts the demand schedule shown in that table, so that either the table or figure illustrate what is called the "law of demand" for normal goods. This law states that consumers will be willing to buy more (less) of a good at lower

TABLE 11.2

DEMAND, SUPPLY AND THE EQUILIBRIUM
PRICE AND QUANTITY

	Demand		Supply		
Points on Figure 11-2	Price (P)	Quantity Demanded (Q_D)	Price (P)	Quantity Supplied (Q_S)	Points on Figure 11-2
a	$22	28	$22	34	c
b	$21	29	$21	32	g
e	$20	30	$20	30	e
f	$19	31	$19	28	h

FIGURE 11.2

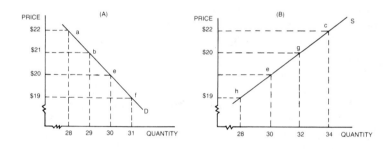

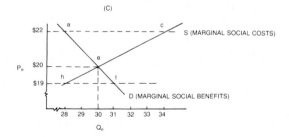

(higher) prices.* So at price $22, consumers would be willing to buy 28 units per time period (per day, week, etc.), while at the lower price of $21, they would be willing to buy one more unit, 29 units in all.

The law of demand states that consumers will be willing to buy more (less) of a good at lower (higher) prices.

The law of demand is illustrated in Panel (A) of Figure 11.2 by the fact that the demand curve representing the demand schedule drops from left to right; that is, it is negatively sloping, a downhill slope. Prices are measured in the figure along the vertical axis upward from zero to higher values; quantities are measured along the horizontal axis, from zero on the left to greater values to the right. Each point on the demand curve thus represents a set of prices and corresponding quantities, with points a, b, e, and f respectively providing the price-quantity sets $22–28 units, $21–29 units, $20–30 units, and $19–31 units. Note that point a is located at the intersection of a dashed line drawn horizontally from the price $22 on the vertical axis *and* a line drawn vertically from the horizontal axis at quantity 28. Viewing point a in another way, the quantity demanded will be seen on the demand curve by moving from the price $22 on the vertical axis to the point a and then dropping straight down to the quantity 28 on the horizontal axis.

It is important to recognize that each point on the demand curve therefore indicates the quantity consumers are willing to buy at a given price. The negative slope of the curve reflects the decreasing valuation by consumers for additional amounts of the good relative to other goods; that is to say, they are willing to buy additional (greater) amounts *only* at lower prices.

Each point on the demand curve depicts the quantity consumers want at a particular price. Example: point b in Panel (A) of Figure 11.2 indicates that consumers will buy 29 units when the price is $21.

Supply

Supply is a schedule of the various amounts of a good or service that producers are willing to sell at various prices. The right side

---

*This statement assumes that other determining factors (such as expectations of different future prices) have already been considered and hence have influenced the quantity the consumer would purchase at a given price.

of Table 11.2 provides an example. Panel (B) of Figure 11.2 depicts the supply schedule given in the table. Both the table and figure reflect the critical idea that producers will be willing to offer more for sale only at a higher price. Thus in the numerical example, producers will offer 28 units at a price of $19, while they will offer 30 units for sale at the higher price of $20.

The idea behind supply is that producers will be willing to offer more for sale only at a higher price.

Panel (B) of Figure 11.2 depicts this supply characteristic by the fact that the supply curve (S) slopes up from left to right: that is, S is positively sloping (going uphill from left to right). As with the demand curve, each point on the supply curve S represents a set of prices and corresponding quantities. Thus points h, e, g, and c represent the price-quantity set $19–28 units, $20–30 units, $21–32 units, and $22–34 units.

The supply curve is positively sloped. A point such as c indicates that the quantity supplied at a price of $22 is found by moving to the S curve directly to the right from a price $22 and then dropping straight down to the quantity of 34 units on the horizontal axis.

Each point on the supply curve represents producers' costs; also it indicates the output to be offered for sale at each corresponding market price. The upward (positive) sloping nature of S reflects the idea that since costs increase with increases in output, it would not be profitable to increase output unless prices are sufficiently higher to meet the higher incremental costs. It follows that the producers' supply curve reflects the increasing costs of additional output.*

The Equilibrium Price

Table 11.2 and Figure 11.2 illustrate how the interaction of demand and supply generate forces that move price and output towards a given value. That value in economics is called the "equilibrium" or "market" price and the "equilibrium" or "market" quantity. That price is set when the amount consumers are

---

*Technically, the supply curve of the individual firm is the firm's so-called marginal costs of production; and the market supply is the horizontal summation of individual marginal cost curves. The term marginal cost and related matters are specialized and not intrinsic to the purposes of this book.

willing to buy equals the amount producers are willing to sell. The equilibrium price occurs at the quantity for which demand equals supply. Table 11.2 indicates that this equilibrium involves a price of $20 and a quantity of 30 units. This equilibrium is illustrated in Panel (C) of Figure 11.2 by the intersection of D and S at point e, where price is P_e and output is Q_e.

The equilibrium price is the price at which the amount consumers are willing to buy equals the amount producers are willing to sell. Price P_e Quantity Q_e in Panel (C) of Figure 11.2 depict this equilibrium.

Benefits Equal to Costs

It is important to recognize that the demand curve reflects the benefits individuals derive from acquiring a good while supply reflects the costs of resources used up in producing the good. This relationship establishes a critical principle, namely that the additional benefits to society of the last unit of quantity purchased by buyers equals the additional costs to society of producing the last unit at the equilibrium point. See again the total Q_e in Figure 11.2(C).* This is the economic meaning of equilibrium price under competitive market conditions. In still other words, exactly the right amount of the good will be produced, not according to the judgment of some government agency, but according to the decisions that individual consumers *and* producers make on the basis of their own value judgments. What constitutes "too much" or "too little" or "the right amount" of a good would *under the above defined market conditions* reflect the judgments of people. The people are those who must sacrifice other goods in order to buy the subject product and those who incur the additional costs of producing that product. Furthermore, *under these market conditions*, the production of "too much" or "too little" of a good is self-correcting whenever prices are free to move in reaction to the judgments of buyers and sellers. Let us illustrate this last vital thought by reference again to Table 11.2 and Figure 11.2C, both of which are repeated below for the convenience of the reader.

---

*This statement assumes that there are no third party ("external") benefits derived from consumption or third party costs from production. Then at the point where demand equals supply, the marginal (added) social benefits from the last unit in the quantity Q_e equals the marginal (added) social costs of producing the last unit making up the equilibrium total.

Self Correcting Market

Suppose price was initially set at $22. Then, according to the table, 28 units would be demanded by consumers while producers would be willing to produce 34 units. This price would result in a surplus output of 6 units; this surplus is reflected in Panel (C) of Figure 11.2 by the fact that demand at this price (point a) is much less than supply (point c). (The surplus of 6 units is provided by the dashed line ac.)

A higher than equilibrium price signifies supply greater than demand. A surplus exists.

REPEAT VIEW OF TABLE 11.2

TABLE 11.2

DEMAND, SUPPLY AND THE EQUILIBRIUM PRICE AND QUANTITY

Points on Figure 11-2	Demand		Supply		Points on Figure 11-2
	Price (P)	Quantity Demanded (Q_D)	Price (P)	Quantity Supplied (Q_S)	
a	$22	28	$22	34	c
b	$21	29	$21	32	g
e	$20	30	$20	30	e
f	$19	31	$19	28	h

AND FIGURE 11.2C

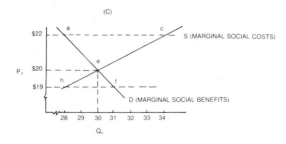

(C)

135

A surplus means that producers cannot sell all they want at the prevailing price. If in our example they produced 34 units, expecting they could profitably sell this amount at price $22, their inventories would increase at the rate of 6 per week, per month, or whatever time unit applies to the demand, supply curves drawn in Figure 11.2. In order to work inventories down to "economic" levels, producers would have to lower their prices. At lower prices they would reduce output *and* consumers would be increasing their purchases. Market price would move towards $20 ($P_e$) and output towards 30 units (Q_e). Thus a surplus (or "too much") would be corrected automatically by a decrease in price, a reduction in quantity supplied, and an increase in quantity demanded.

If on the other hand price were initially lower than the equilibrium price (P_e), demand would exceed supply at that price. A shortage ("too little" produced) would result. For example, if price were initially $19, consumers would be willing to buy 31 units per time period, but producers would be willing to offer only 28 units for sale. This results in a shortage of 3 units per time period.

A lower than equilibrium price signifies demand greater than supply. Queues will form.

A shortage is shown in Panel (C) of Figure 11.2 by the fact that demand at the price $19 (point f) exceeds supply (point h), with the shortage represented by distance hf. *If buyers and sellers are free to react to this situation,* prices will increase towards P_e. Buyers would compete for the short supply, and some would be willing to pay a higher price. Producers would realize that they could increase price. At higher prices, firms could further increase profits by increasing output; therefore, the quantity supplied would increase. At higher prices, some consumers would not be willing to buy as much, so the quantity demanded would decrease. As a consequence of these decisions by buyers and sellers, price would move towards $20 ($P_e$) and output would move towards 30 units (Q_e).

As price rises and profits increase, firms supply more of the good and consumers buy less of it.

Note that under these conditions of price flexibility, price acts to ration short supply over the period during which production cannot be increased. As the price rises, it also acts to correct the under allocation of resources by motivating firms to increase production. In the short run, increased output will be from existing plant and equipment. In the long run, firms will be motivated to use the increased profits towards the end of expanding their scale of operations by constructing new plants and/or using more equipment.

Shifts in Demand and Supply

One final demand, supply curve preliminary is needed before we can turn to Monetarism. Suppose a greater quantity of a good is demanded at a particular price than was previously the case. This condition is referred to by economists as an increase in demand. It is depicted diagrammatically in Figure 11.3(A) below by a shift in the demand curve from curve D to D'. This condition is called an *increase in demand*; it stands in sharp contrast to an increase in *quantity demanded* because of a lower price; note the increase in demand signifies greater quantities demanded *at every price*. The same applies to a decrease in demand. If the demand (taste) for a good decreases, the curve shifts leftward, such as from D' to D, in the process depicting smaller quantities; thus, for example, we have q_1 in place of q_2 at the given price, p*. The smaller quantity noted is not attributable to a higher price. If it

FIGURE 11.3

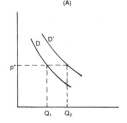

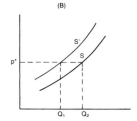

were, we would refer to it as a decrease in *quantity demanded*, where the reason for the decreased quantity is the higher price not the decrease in demand.

The same semantics and applications hold for supply. Suppose curve S is the original supply; but then assume new firms enter and produce the same good. At any given price, such as p*, the quantity q_2 offered for sale is now greater than was the old quantity q_1, as viewed in Panel (B) of Figure 11.3. This represents an increase in supply distinct from an increase in quantity supplied as a result of a higher price.

In sum, greater demand and greater supply require a shifting of the D and S curves to the right, decreases to the left. We shall apply this vital concept later (and the prior ones) to such thought systems as Monetarism. It also fits such problem areas as minimum wages, gasoline prices, and the like, as we shall see. Remember, the words increase or decrease in demand or supply signifies a shift in the demand or supply curve. An increase or decrease in the quantity demanded or supplied signifies a change due to a change in price.

"FINAL STATEMENT"

We have defined inflation in this chapter and recorded some of the explanations advanced about it. Essentially, the so-called theory of Monetarism explains inflation in terms of the quantity theory of money while focusing its attention on relative changes in the demand and supply of money. This chapter therefore had to provide the essentials of demand, supply analysis, a tool of economic thought which we shall utilize often in the remainder of this book. For the present, our central concern is with inflation. In fact, we will see that our concern is really with stagflation, the state of less than full employment combined with inflation. After Monetarism, we shall see what supply-side economics is all about, and then evaluate the solutions advanced for stagflation by the Reagan administration.

M.L. GREENHUT   C.T. STEWART

CHAPTER 12:
MONETARISM

We previously observed that when one studies economics in many American universities, it is likely the professor will assert the basic cause of inflation to be that *more new money is being created than the growth in output* (the quantity theory of money). A typical statement is then appended which holds that if certain costs have already risen drastically (e.g., the price of crude oil), or excessive demand is prevalent (e.g., a war or a new government agency paying out large amounts of income without a related increase in the production of goods or services bought by consumers), the potential for inflation is clearly evident. The professor finally observes that if *the Fed is led by its own evaluation (or via Congressional pressures) to increase the money supply substantially, inflation becomes a fact.* In still other words, *expansion of the money supply* enables the cost-push, demand pull, or structural change forces to generate inflation; this expansion often follows budget deficits.

Whatever the particulars behind a given inflationary period, the "supply of money increasing relative to output" theory is generally accepted by economists as the *basis* for the inflation. Unfortunately, to understand monetarism and the economic policies derived therefrom requires our going well beyond the idea of the relative supplies of money and goods and services. We shall divide this chapter into 2 parts: a section A which provides background data along with the theoretical framework itself; and a section B which relates monetarism to certain policies of the Carter and Reagan administrations.

A. THE MONETARIST
FRAMEWORK OF THOUGHT

"THE RELATION BETWEEN MONEY SUPPLY AND PRICES"

Table 11.1 in the prior chapter indicated that the money supply more than doubled between 1960 and 1975 while the dollar value of output went up threefold. Actually, output itself also increased. So why didn't the increase in output make prices fall? The answer is that the increase in output was much less than the increase in money supply.

139

Table 12.1 converts the money number M and price level CPI of Table 11.1 into percentages with 1960 = 100: This table also adds an output column in percentages based on 1960 so that the three columns can be compared easily.*

TABLE 12.1

A. OUTPUT (O), MONEY (M), AND
PRICES (CPI), (1960 = 100)

Year	O	M	CPI
1960	100	100	100
1965	126	119.2	106.5
1970	147.2	152.5	131.1
1975	167.4	205.1	181.7
1980	200.9	292.1	278.2

B. PERCENTAGE CHANGES

	O	M	CPI
1960–1965	26.0	19.2	6.5%
1965–1970	16.8	28.0	23.1
1970–1975	11.4	34.4	38.6
1975–1980	12.0	42.4	53.1
*Sum 1960–1980 (rounded values)	66	124	121

The last row of Table 12.1 suggests that it was the extra growth in money supply over and above that of output which proved inflationary.**

---

*Probing readers might be advised that the Table further converted the output figures into constant (1972) prices, so that besides being indexed against the common base year 1960, all output figures were purged of changes in prices.

**Of course, adding percentage changes substantially understates the actual percentage change from a base year (1960) to a later year (1980). Since we are concerned only with comparing columns, the error due to our simplifying procedure in the table is unimportant.

This extra growth of about 58% in the money supply was associated with a price increase of around 121%. Of course, there were other forces at work: the huge increase in the price of imported oil resulting from OPEC, the sharp monopoly increases in medical costs that took place over these years, the foreign crop failures which raised the price of some of our farm products by increasing foreign demand for them, and even the disappearance of the anchovy. Also, some cost-push and structural inflation forces were evident which affected outputs of certain key industries. Ultimately all of these forces reappeared in the form of an accomodating government that ran deficits and engaged in an excessive printing of money.

Further examination of Table 12.1 indicates that output increased from its 1960 base by more than the money supply over the subsequent five year period 1960–1965, while prices rose very little—about 1.2% a year. (Why this could occur will be evident to the reader shortly after we have discussed the *velocity of money*.) During each of the following periods in the table, the money supply increased by much more than output: almost twice as rapidly between 1965 and 1970, with average *annual* price increases rising to 4.3%, more than three times the average annual price change from 1960 to 1965. Similar relations apply to the 1970–1980 period with prices rising over 7% a year between 1970 and 1975, and 9% a year between 1975 and 1980.

"THE BASIS FOR THE QUANTITY THEORY OF MONEY AND MONETARISM"

Can one, knowing output and money supply, predict price trends? Or, knowing price trends and output, can economists determine what the money supply ought to be?

In the absence of structural changes, a reasonable estimate of the relations between money, output, and prices can be made if one more thing is known: the speed with which money changes hands, referred to by economists as the *velocity of money*. Velocity of money in circulation determines the relationship between the money supply, total spending and the price level. If each dollar bill is spent once a month instead of once a week, then roughly four times as many dollar bills would be needed to pay for the same amount of monthly purchases at current prices. In fact, most payments are made by check, and it was previously noted that a deposit of $100 typically generates additional money. How much and how fast new money is created depends upon how quickly loans are made and the credits spent. Improvements in banking and financial institutions have increased the velocity of the money supply. That is why prices could rise between 1960 and 1965 even though output had risen more than the money supply.

If the velocity of money is unchanged, changes in the money supply will lead to proportionate changes in prices, provided output is unchanged. This obviously happens only when resources are fully utilized, so that increased demand does not raise output.

It has also been noted previously that changes in demand lead to expansion (or contraction) by causing unintended inventory disinvestment (or investment). But a closer look at demand is needed—in particular, how it relates to the money supply (cash and demand deposits).

"THE MONEY PRICE EQUATION"

Money offered is the money supply (M) multiplied by its velocity of circulation (V), or in composite form MV. If cash and credit were spent only once in the course of a year, the money supply would be equal to the total value of goods and services sold during the year. We would have $M = PQ$ (where P stands for the price index and Q is the quantity of output). But if a dollar bill (or bank credit) is spent once a month, it will buy $12 worth of goods and services in the course of a year ($V = 12$); if spent weekly, it will buy $52 worth ($V = 52$).

The money supply multiplied by its velocity ($MV = 52$ in the last example) equals the total amount Q of goods and services sold multiplied by their average price P. This relation is known as the *equation of exchange*. It is typically written as $MV = PQ$. If MV increases 10% (whether as a result of more bank credit, or greater velocity, or a combination of the two), then PQ also rises 10%. If production does not increase, or rises less than 10%, then average prices will rise. If MV decreases, then either Q (output) or P (prices) must fall proportionately. If output falls, we have a recession; if prices fall, we have a deflation or disinflation. It is the combination of existing cash and checkbook money that people hold for whatever reasons—along with *how long* they hold the money—that accounts for the magnitudes of MV.

"MONETARISM AND THE LAW OF THE DEMAND FOR MONEY"

Monetarist theory essentially involves demand and supply curve analysis. Thus, once the reader becomes familiar with the forces shaping and moving the demand and supply curves *for money,* he will be back on familiar grounds. Let us begin our formal study of monetarism with the *demand for money.*

Economists have specified the price level and three related factors as determining the demand for money. These other determinants are *real income, expected prices,* and the so-called *selected other prices.* Changes in these other determinants move the demand curve for money to the left or right. Meanwhile, the price level, which fixes the value of money, determines what we referred to in Chapter 11 as the *quantity demanded.* Because the price level relates to the price of all goods, it can be considered as a factor influencing the value of a "unit of money."

"THE VALUE OF MONEY (THE PRICE LEVEL) AND THE QUANTITY DEMANDED"

To understand monetarism, first suppose the prices of goods and services rise. People then need more cash and credit to take care of their usual purchases. So, *price levels* determine the quantity of money demanded. Most important, let us recognize that the higher the price level, the less valuable is a unit of money, *ceteris paribus.* When the value of money falls as direct result of higher price levels, people (as with any other good whose value may have fallen) tend to demand more of it, everything else unchanged. Thus the same law of demand relation that we viewed in Chapter 11 for other goods or services applies to money). *The lower the price (i.e. value of a unit of money, the greater is the quantity demanded.* This is the basic relation which must be understood in order to appreciate the theory of monetarism. Remember also that *the value of a unit of money is low when the price level is high.*

143

MONETARISM

"The Determinants (or factors) Affecting The Position Of The Demand Curve For Money"

(A) Real Income

If the real incomes of people rise, they will demand more cash and deposits because they typically spend more at higher than at lower real income levels. Therefore, *real income* is a determinant of the demand for money. A *change* in real income at a given price level, that is a change which is *not* attributable to a change in the price level, shifts the curve in Monetarist theory. A change in real income moves the demand curve to the left or right, as the case may be. *When real income increases, the demand for money rises because people are wealthier and demand more units of money just as they would demand more units of any other normal good. The demand curve for holding money moves to the right as real income rises. The converse holds as people become poorer.**

(B) Expected Prices

Another determinant stressed in elementary Monetarist theory deals with the expectations of people about future prices (hence changes in the future value of money). If people anticipate inflation, they expect the value of money to decline; so they will try to dispose of their money now before part of its value is lost. When householders expect prices to rise in the future, they buy some of the goods and services needed before prices go up. This behavior pattern tends to accelerate projected price increases. It causes the velocity (or turnover) of money to rise. *In effect, the demand to hold money is less when increased inflation is forecast. The upshot is that the demand curve for holding money shifts leftward. Conversely, the demand for money tends to be greater (i.e., the demand curve for holding money shifts to the right) when deflation is forecasted.*

(C) Certain Other Prices (Chiefly the Interest Rate)

Willingness to hold cash and demand deposits depends on the price people are paying for this "liquidity." If 10% can be earned

---

*We stress for probing readers that monetarists think in terms of *real income,* not money income, in order to emphasize that here it is not a change in prices which makes people feel wealthier or poorer, but a change in output (income) itself. So at any given price level (hence value of money), the amount of income produced may have made people feel wealthier or poorer.

on savings accounts, they are likely to hold less cash and less in strict checking accounts than if savings accounts were paying 4%. The available alternatives to holding cash or some type of demand deposit influence the demand for money. The greater the return on a dividend or interest yielding asset (e.g., a stock, bond, a long-term savings account) *vis a vis* what people would otherwise have expected, the less willing they are to hold money (i.e., cash or demand deposits). *At comparatively high rates of return for other assets, the demand curve for money shifts to the left. The converse also holds, of course.*

"MONETARISM AND THE SUPPLY OF MONEY"

Monetarists believe there is a direct link between money and production: an expansionary monetary policy provides people with excess money which results, *ceteris paribus,* in an increase in spending. The increase in spending raises the price level, thereby lowering the price (i.e., value) of money.

"THE DEMAND AND SUPPLY OF MONEY ILLUSTRATED GRAPHICALLY"

Figure 12.1(A) records the *value of money* on the vertical scale. The lower we are on the vertical scale OY, the lower is the value of money; the higher we are on the vertical scale OY, the higher is its value. (Observe the right hand axis O'Y'. It is included for special explanatory purposes. It reads high price level at its lower points, and low price level at its higher points, opposite to the normal procedure. But this OY' axis is a special inclusion designated to remind the reader that the value of money is the inverse of the price level.) We repeat, the lower is the value of each unit of money, the higher is the price level. And more money is wanted (needed) to purchase goods and services as the value of money falls. It follows that greater quantities of money are demanded when the value of money is low (i.e., at higher prices); hence because the D curves in Figure 12.1 are plotted in terms of the value of money, they slope down and to the right.

Demographic factors, such as age, help determine the shape of the demand for money curves given in Figure 12.1. For example, if we assume an older population wants to hold more money than a younger population at higher prices, its D curve would be flatter than that of the younger population at all lower money values.

FIGURE 12.1

MONETARISM ILLUSTRATED

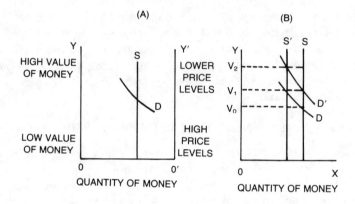

Changes in the Determinants of the Position of the Demand Curve

Assume a change in real income, in expected prices, or in selected other prices. It would follow that the D curve must move to the right or left. Some examples of a shifting demand curve for money follow:

Suppose deflation is *forecast*. Then the original D curve can be expected to shift to the right, such as to D' in Panel (B). It does this because people and firms would then be willing to keep more money on hand, expecting to use it later on at lower price levels when its value is greater. So given the supply S of money, the value of money would rise when people expect deflation; it would rise from V_0 where D intersects S to V_1 where D^1 intersects S. Recognize that prices fall because people slow down their spending as they *in effect* demand more M. In still other words, *the forecast of deflation increases the demand for (or holding of) money, and in the process raises its value as the price level falls. The converse holds since if people forecast more inflation, they would want to spend now; the demand curve for holding money can thus be expected to shift to the left.*

Monetarists view the interest rate as having a similar demand effect, where by interest rate they mean the general rate of return (or yield) on investment in stocks, bonds, and comparable assets. Suppose the return on investment of money in stocks and bonds is comparatively lower than the people consider to be warranted.

They would, accordingly, sell some of their stocks and bonds, in effect seeking to hold more money. Sales of securities lower the prevailing prices in the stock and bond markets. Lower bond and stock prices signify greater return per dollars worth of investment. In still other words, comparatively low rates of return on stocks and bonds generate an increased demand for money; the demand curve for money shifts to the right from D to D^1 in Panel B of Figure 12.1. Most importantly, the increased demand for money slows down total spending, and lowers the price level. *In sum, when stock and bond rates of return on holding non-money assets are comparatively low, the demand for money shifts to the right. This lowers the price level and raises rates on these assets to the equilibrium (proper) level. The converse, of course, applies to the situation where rates are considered to be comparatively high.*

Monetarists often separately stress another determinant that is related to the interest rate. This determinant governs the placement of the demand curve, to the left or right of the D curve drawn in Figure 12.1(A). It includes such factors as credit card availability. Following the March, 1980 restrictions that were placed on the use of credit cards, individual needs for money (i.e., demand for money) increased substantially. As a result (ignoring other demand conditions, such as expected future inflation), the curve D could be viewed in March, 1980 as shifting to the right to D' in Figure 12.1(B). Note further that given the supply (S) of money in the figure, an increase in demand to D' would raise the value of money, which is equivalent to saying the price level will fall. Of course, that was the intended effect of the Fed's constraints on the use of credit and credit cards.

"THE CORE OF THE THEORY"

Elementary demand and supply curve analysis indicates that a *decrease* in the supply of money, e.g., shifting the S curve to S' in Panel (B)—as with an increase in the demand for money—will limit the spending of householders and firms (since less M is available). In the absence of some other real force, such as a decrease in productivity, this will raise the value of money. To appreciate the basic effect, take the low V_o value of money given by the intersection of the D and S curves in Figure 12.1(B). Suppose the supply is decreased to S'. Less money is available; hence less is spent, prices fall, and the value of money rises to V_1.

[Note that we drew our D' and S' curves in such a way as to produce the same V_1 value as a result of either an increase in the demand for holding money from D to D' (with supply fixed at S) *or* from a decrease in the supply of money from S to S' (with demand fixed on curve D).] If next, subsequent to the change from S to S' we further assume that people anticipate deflation because of the Fed's policy of decreasing supply to S', the demand for money will shift to D'. It shifts to D' since people who anticipate deflation tend to want to hold more money: So the price level will then fall again, with the value of money becoming V_2. Monetarism is as simple as that. Just shift the D or S curves for a given reason.

"A SUMMARY TO THIS POINT"

Monetarists regard money as a "good." The lower is the price level, the higher is the price of holding money, and hence the smaller is the quantity of money demanded. In addition, our taste (preference) for other things controls the amount of money demanded at different price levels. If real income increases, the demand curve for money would shift to the right. When we are wealthier, we demand more of that "good" money; the reverse holds if real income falls. Correspondingly, a forecast of deflation or increased charges for using credit cards also shift the demand curve for money to the right, and *vice versa*. The Monetarists' treatment of the demand for money thus corresponds to the classical treatment of the demand for any good. Recognize further that changes in the *supply* of money will shift that particular curve. So as with any other good, changes in the demand for and/or supply of the good affect the ultimate price (value) of that good. To repeat, Monetarists view money as a "good." Let us now view the problem they claim exists today.

B. RECENT APPLICATIONS

"SUPPLY AND DEMAND FOR MONEY, PRICES AND OUTPUT: KEYNESIANS VS. MONETARISTS"

There is some disagreement among Keynesians and Monetarists as to how prices and output are affected by the supply of and the demand for money. The *Keynesians* believe that the money supply acts on the economy through its effect on interest rates. They say that expansion of the money supply lowers interest rates and thereby induces *business firms* to borrow for the purpose of investing in new production capacity and expanded output. *Monetarists*, on the other hand, believe that the effect is more direct. In their view, an increase in the supply of money results in larger money balances than people wish to hold. The result is that *people* will spend their surplus money, and in the process increase their demand for goods and services. This extra spending, as a result of increased money supply, typically causes prices to inflate.

Each of the alternative effects described above does take place in the real world. The difference between any two schools of economic thought typically lies in the *stress* they place on different variables. According to either Keynesian or Monetarist theories, the projected outcome of an increased money supply is an increased output of goods and services *provided the increase in money supply occurs in the presence of under-utilized resources.* If, instead, the increased money supply takes place under conditions of full employment of labor and capital or supply-side limitations, inflation results, *ceteris paribus*, under either theory. What, then, is the real difference between them if the final effects of the theories are the same? Surprisingly, the answer is that a substantial difference arises in their policy proposals.

"POLICY DIFFERENCES"

Keynesians believe that the *level of investment* is the unstable element causing economic fluctuations. They treat the *interest rate* as a major determinant of investment. Accordingly, they center attention on *interest rate policy* for stabilization, while also stressing *fiscal policy* effects—government spending and taxation. *Monetarists* see a more direct employment impact from the money supply, and hence regard the *money supply* rather than the interest rate as the main determinant of economic fluctuations. Therefore, they focus the attention of the Fed on the money supply rather than on the interest rate. The monetarist influence in the country was manifest on October 6, 1979 when the Fed decided to shift its policy target from a low interest rate to a restrained money supply.

Monetarists advocate only a steady small increase in the money supply to match whatever increased output would result in the country from increased productivity. They do *not* want government entering the economic arena actively, just passively. In their view it is the government that destabilizes the economy by interfering with the free market.* Keynesians, on the other hand, believe that private investment is the unstable factor in the economy, and that government must offset its volatility by manipulating the interest rate *and* by fiscal policy (e.g., $G \gtrless T$).

Monetarists thus advocate a government hands-off policy, even during a recession, contending that unemployment would be less *in the long run* if government would get out of the economic arena. Government's role should simply be to provide the right supply of money. Keynesians contend that government can intervene effectively in the economic arena, and in the process would limit the number of unemployed to an effective minimum.

"1979, 1980 AND MONETARISM"

Inflationary expectations were rampant in the United States in the late 1970's. As a consequence, the *demand* for money was shifting leftward regularly, while the *supply* of money was shifting rapidly rightward as the Fed, following Keynesian economics, endeavored to keep interest rates low. The monetaristic induced changes of Fed policy in October, 1979 and March, 1980 were designed to stop these trends. But they were able only to reduce the upward price spiral (i.e., cause a lower rate of price increase) rather than to lower the price level. Here is how it worked!

"GRAPHIC ILLUSTRATION"

The United States of the late 1970's to 1980 is given in Figure 12.2. Note that the decreased dollar value from U_0 to U' reflected a continuing rise in prices due to an increased money supply from S to S'. In turn, an inflation forecast signified a decrease in the demand for holding money to D', further pushing prices upward to the point where the value of money dropped to U''. The resulting increase in prices (say, a 10% rise) was nevertheless

---

*Monetarists further propose that when people correctly anticipate inflation, they adjust accordingly. The result is that money is ultimately neutral in effect as the underlying real economic forces finally prevail. It is the unanticipated government changes in money supply, hence in price levels, that generate the booms and busts.

smaller than the 16% inflation rate that might have resulted if the rate of increase in the supply of money had continued to S″, such as appeared likely before the change in the Fed's policy of October, 1979. The comparatively small relative increase in the money supply to S′ in late 1979 and early 1980, instead of the shift to S″, meant that the rate of inflation, though very high, was less than it might have been. This lower U″ rate of inflation compares favorably to the money value U‴ that expansion to S″ would have caused.

FIGURE 12.2

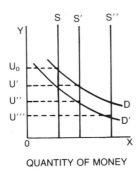

QUANTITY OF MONEY

"AN INTRODUCTORY COMPARATIVE LOOK AT THE CARTER AND REAGAN ADMINISTRATIONS"

Chapters 15 to 19 will center their attention on the Carter and Reagan administrations' economic policies. A few suggestions about their policies can, however, be entered now *chiefly to illustrate Monetarist theory.*

At its inception, the Carter administration was fully tuned to the Keynesian extreme. Its policy was to *spend today* in order to provide "well-being" for all who receive today's bounties. Unfortunately, for reasons to be detailed in forthcoming chapters, the combination of substantial deficits, increased money supply, and falling productivity soon generated what is called stagflation (the state of inflation combined with unemployment). The appointment of Mr. Volcker as chairman of the Federal Reserve System involved a minor swing toward economic conservatism; this change was evidenced on October 6, 1979 when Mr. Volcker

151

announced that henceforth the Fed would control the money supply by controlling bank reserves, and not center its attention on maintaining low rates of interest. By the second quarter of 1980, the results of the new policy were visible in the slowed growth of the money supply; in fact, the rate of growth of the money supply was very low. Unfortunately, the Fed later appeared unable (or unwilling) to sharply limit the growth of the supply of money. In any case, the policy was clearly compatible with the Monetarist view of concentrating on the supply of money. By the end of its term of office, the Carter administration had continued its policy of fiscal liberalism while the Fed was — at the most — evidencing signs of conservatism.

The Carter years may be summarized quite simply by reference to Panel (A) of Figure 12.3. In 1976 the D and S curves for money intersected at a lower price level than in later years. Thus, a comparatively high value of the dollar existed, as represented by P. But at this point in our economic history, the American people had forecast inflation while welfare state practices continued to expand. The result was that the desire to hold money decreased, causing the demand curve for money to shift to D'. So given the supply S, the price level rose — which is another way of saying the value of money fell to P'. However, deficit spending and associated expansion of credit caused the supply of money to increase to S', further raising the price level to the point where the value of money fell to P''.

FIGURE 12.3

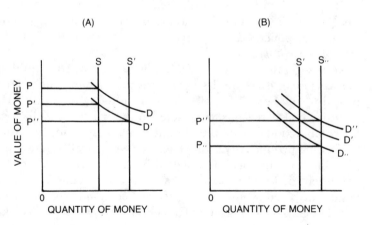

152

The Reagan administration is fundamentally very far removed from the Carter administration in its economic policies. To gain a glimpse of its position, recall that Monetarism is essentially a theory stressing the *demand and supply of money*. As with any other good, whatever increases the demand, raises the price of the good. Specifically: (1) If we expect greater real income (for example, by increased productivity), the demand for money shifts to the right. (2) If we expect moderating inflation through decreased public spending, lowered across-the-board tax rates, and other policies that would encourage saving in place of spending, the demand for money shifts less to the left compared to the past; this is so because future dollars appear to promise greater value than if galloping inflation were forecasted. (3) If rates of interest appear relatively lower than before because of projected lower inflation, the demand for money shifts less to the left than it had in the past. If the total demand effect trends rightward, the value of money rises — which is equivalent to saying "the price level falls". Then if, at the same time, increases in the supply of money are constrained by a tight-fisted Fed, any rightward shift in supply will be constrained, say to $S_{''}$ only, as in Panel (B) of Figure 12.3. Thus Panel (A), which represents LBJ, Nixon, Ford, and particularly the Carter years, converts to Panel (B) according to the Monetarists who speak for the Reagan administration. Ignoring $D_{''}$ for the moment, they propose that if demand shifts from D' to the right to D'' and supply increases only slightly to $S_{''}$, the price level will be projected to remain the same. *Of course,* Panel (B) is only depicting a *possible* state probably well in the future. What about the more immediate future?

We must recognize that during the early years of the Reagan administration people were still forecasting a comparatively high inflation and minor supply-side productivity (income) gains; therefore, the overall demand curve for money was likely to shift further leftward, not rightward. In effect $D_{''}$ applied to the early years of the new administration, as price levels continued to rise.* Significantly, at such time when the slowing down of inflation projected by the Monetarists is perceived to be lasting, we can expect a curve such as D'' to result.

---

*If the Reagan administration tax bill leads to increased productivity rather quickly, *real* income would rise and the actual D curve in a few years could become the D'' curve, i.e., shift to the right (not left) of D'.

153

"FINAL STATEMENT"

Our statements about Keynesian economics and Monetarism do *not* claim that Keynesian theory is invalid nor do they even imply that Monetarism is the correct theory. Each of the economic theories set forth in this book provides insight into the American economy. The really big problem in using economic theory arises from improper applications, and hence unenlightened interferences with the economy. But before considering policy errors, we must apply our theories via specific illustrations of what goes wrong during inflation. This will be the goal of the chapter that follows, which in effect brings us into the field of supply-side economics. After further probing into supply-side economics, the reader will see why on certain occasions the present writers would propose using early Keynesian economics, or supply-side economics, or Monetarism, depending upon domestic and world conditions. The goal of economic policy-making can be a shifting one, we shall propose, albeit if the policy-makers themselves are uninformed, as the Monetarists contend, the best game plan can well be to fix the growth path of money and in general to leave things alone. But first, we must get to the basics of supply-side economics.

INTRODUCTION TO PART FIVE ON SUPPLY-SIDE ECONOMICS

The population listed as living on poverty levels of income fell during the War on Poverty, from 18 percent in 1964 to 12.8 percent in 1968. But it had been falling before then, as the table below indicates:

Time Period	Decrease in Percentage of Total Population in Poverty
1949–1953	32.7% to 26.2%
1954–1958	27.9% to 23.1%
1959–1963	22.4% to 19.5%
1964–1968	18.0% to 12.8%

The total decline in poverty from 1949 to 1963 was 13.2 percentage points, approximately 1 percent a year, the same as took place later during President Johnson's Great Society years.

Charles Murray (*Postwar Social Welfare Policy*, Heritage Foundation) stresses the fact that during the 1970's the percentage of the population whose cash income belonged to the poverty level class *did not decline*.* The lowest level reached in constant, uninflated dollars was 11.1 percent in 1973 after which the ratio rose to 13 percent in 1980, about the same as in 1968, even though we had spent twice as much on direct cash income transfers in 1980 as in 1968, and fourteen times as much as in 1949. Murray further notes that the increased cash income transfer expenditures were concentrated on only about 12 percent of the population in the 1970's vs. more than 25 percent of the population in the 1950's. In three years of the unproductive 1970's (1970, 1974, and 1975) the nation's GNP declined in constant dollars, and the percentage of people in the poverty class increased in each of those years. On the other hand, in the years when the GNP rose, the percentage of people on poverty levels of income did go down. Because the same relations held for the 1950's, Murray concludes that the GNP is the prime determinant of poverty.

---

*Let us note that cash income does not include in-kind assistance.

The conclusions drawn above from the experience of the past three decades may be too harsh. The future never repeats the past exactly. And assistance to the poor can generally be expected to better their lot, not to intensify poverty. Nevertheless, if Reaganomics does increase national well-being (i.e., causes GNP and productivity to rise at faster rates), the War on Poverty will also be won, without increased welfare expenditures. It follows that Reaganomics must be examined strictly as a scientific theory, without preconceived bias that it favors the wealthy or neglects the poor.

This part of the book will inquire initially into inflation and its effects, after which we shall reexamine the Keynesian framework of thought. The school of thought called Keynesian economics is vital to us because the reader will find in Chapters 15 and 16 that supply-side economics (or the Reaganomics of 1981 distinct from its changes in 1982 and 1983) is simply of the same order as President Kennedy's *tax cut* application of Keynesian economics that we described in Chapter 10. What went wrong years after the tax cut was not that the supply-side application of Keynesian economics erred; rather, it was the increasingly profligate spending of the federal government stemming from the apparent success of the Kennedy tax cuts that went completely out of hand. The purpose of the chapters that follow is, therefore, to learn the empirical and then logical meaning of supply-side economics, in particular to determine its relevance for the 1980's. After this part of the book is done, we can focus our attention on the differences between supply-side economics and the changed policies of the federal government beginning with L.B. Johnson's Great Society days, as continued through the Nixon/Ford/Carter years, and as perhaps will again be on stage in 1983.

PART FIVE:
SUPPLY-SIDE ECONOMICS

CHAPTER 13:
INFLATIONARY IMPACTS

Who gains from inflation, who loses? What does inflation do? What does it mean to the economy as a whole? These are some of the fundamental questions most voters have in mind as they ponder the impacts of inflation on their lives and that of the nation in general.

"A BASIC VIEW OF THE CONSUMER AND INFLATION"

Consider initially what inflation does to the consumer. It hurts the average consumer because the general price level typically will go up faster than individual income; thus *real* income per person falls. Let's see how this works!

Assume *you* used to earn $200 dollars a month in a part-time job. Assume further the price of gasoline was then 40¢ a gallon. Your $200 monthly income would allow you to buy (if you bought nothing but gas) a total of 500 gallons of gas. Suppose after working one month, you received a $25 dollar pay increase. This was good news. However, what if the price of gasoline had risen by 10¢ a gallon to 50¢ a gallon? How gratifying or disturbing would recent economic events be *to you?*

Before your pay increase and the hike in gas prices, you were able to buy 500 gallons of gas. After the $25 raise and the 10¢ hike in the price of gas, you could purchase only 450 gallons of gas. The $25 raise and the 10¢ hike in the price of gas actually amounted to a confiscation of 50 gallons of gasoline from you.

How could you have lost when your salary went up? The answer is painfully simple. Your income is the basic resource you use to buy all the things you need. In the gasoline example, your income went up by 12.5% [= ($225 – $200)/$200], but the price of gasoline went up by 25% [= (50¢ – 40¢/40¢]. The paychecks of consumers under conditions of inflation typically yield smaller quantities of goods for them, as in this example. However, before

157

we are able to demonstrate who wins and who loses by inflation, two important definitions are needed. We must define *nominal* versus *real* income.

"NOMINAL AND REAL INCOME"

By *nominal income*, economists mean the actual dollars received. Take the nominal value of the money you have earned on the job. Suppose it is $1,000. If you wished to purchase goods and services in the product market with this $1,000, the general price level (CPI) would determine how much you would actually be able to get. *Real income*, therefore, signifies what your nominal income actually buys in the product market. If the average price of goods and services in the product market is $1.00, a nominal income of $1,000 would therefore buy 1,000 units. This simple relationship can be formalized by an equation:

$$\text{real income} = \frac{\text{nominal income}}{\text{price level (CPI)}}$$

This equation indicates that if prices (the denominator) go up faster than nominal income (the numerator), real income (what the nominal income will buy) goes down.

"WINNERS AND LOSERS AMONG INDIVIDUALS"

The above formula can be used to determine which individuals gain and lose from inflation. The winners during any inflation are those who receive an increase in real income; the losers are those who receive a lower real income. In the gas example, if the consumer had received a 25% increase in nominal income, the same amount of gas could have been acquired as was possible before the change in income *and* prices. If the consumer had received more than a 25% increase in nominal income, a greater quantity of gasoline could have been obtained compared to the past.

The real income equation explains why some of the individuals shown in Table 13.1 tend to win and others to lose during inflation. Consider first the people with fixed incomes: for example, widows who are receiving a set amount of income each year from their deceased husband's estate.* The answer is clear: if

---

*If the widow's assets are chiefly in bonds, her real income falls sharply with inflation.

158

TABLE 13.1

TYPICAL LOSERS AND WINNERS DURING INFLATION

Winners	*Losers*
Debtors	Creditors
People with rapidly growing incomes:	People on fixed incomes:
Young people	Old people
Wealthy people who can speculate in anticipation of inflation	Poor people on welfare
Investors in real estate, precious gems, etc.	Savers (time deposits — CDs)
Tenants with long-term leases	Landlords with long-term lease commitments

prices are going up while nominal income remains essentially the same, real income has fallen.

"IN GENERAL, CONSUMERS AND BUSINESS FIRMS LOSE, THE GOVERNMENT WINS"

As incomes rise, taxes rise. But recognize that federal income (and also state income) taxes are progressive, which means that an increasing share is taken from individuals earning higher incomes. The tax on a single individual earning $4,100 in 1977 was $122, approximately 3% of his (her) income. The same individual with an $8,200 income (twice that of $4,100) would have paid $852, slightly more than 10% of his (her) income. But before proceeding further with exactly how the individual worker loses with inflation, let's first look at business establishments in general.

"AMERICAN BUSINESS FIRMS LOSE"

Inflation signifies a rise in nominal business and individual incomes. But consider the plight of the businessman. By accepted tax accounting practices (where the word "accepted" means government-allowed tax accounting practice), *the firm must lose!* It

159

loses since the amount of depreciation permitted as an expense against income is based on historical cost. For example, suppose a firm buys a building in 1970 costing $100,000. Suppose the building deteriorates so that in ten years it is worthless. On a ten year straight-line depreciation basis, the firm would be allowed a $10,000 per year deduction for depreciation on that building. (Note: after ten years it would in effect have saved $100,000 through depreciation. The sum would enable it to replace the old, "worthless" structure with a new $100,000 building.) But suppose in 1980 the new building costs $200,000 (which would be its price given the 7% average rate of inflation that was taking place during the 1970's). It can then buy only a new half-sized building in 1980. What has happened? The firm's real income went down if its earnings rose only in direct proportion to the inflation.* We shall examine this result in greater detail with the aid of Table 13.2.

Table 13.2 assumes the firm earned a gross income before depreciation of $100,000 in 1970 and $200,000 in 1980. (Gross income is derived essentially by subtracting expenses from sales receipts.) Then in 1970 subtract $10,000 for depreciation and do the same in 1980. Now the net (after depreciation) income of the firm would be $90,000 in 1970 and $190,000 in 1980. Let the corporate income tax rate be constant — suppose we take a rather high 50% tax rate, though whatever rate we would have selected, our results would remain essentially the same. At that rate, the government would take $45,000 in 1970, and $95,000 in 1980. So the *net* (after depreciation *plus* tax) income of the firm would be $45,000 in 1970 and $95,000 in 1980. It looks like the firm has won . . . but consider the following!

Assume the firm in 1970 distributed all of its net (after depreciation *and* tax) income to stockholders as dividends. Suppose the firm in 1980 decides it should give these stockholders the same *real* income as they had in 1970. In place of $45,000, it therefore declares a dividend of $90,000, twice as much nominal income at a time when prices are twice as high. But notice now that the firm had put aside $10,000 in 1970 to be used eventually in replacing its building. It is allowed the same $10,000 depreciation in 1980, and in addition has $5,000 left over after

---

*This in fact took place in the United States.

TABLE 13.2

EFFECTS OF INFLATION
ON REAL INCOME OF BUSINESS

	1970	*1980*
Assumed gross income of a firm (rises at the same rate as the inflation rate)	$100,000	$200,000
Assumed annual depreciation allowed on building that cost $100,000 ($100,000 ÷ 10 years = $10,000 per year)	10,000	10,000
Net income (gross income minus depreciation)	90,000	190,000
Corporation income tax (50% of gross income)	45,000	95,000
Net income (gross income minus depreciation minus tax)	45,000	95,000
Dividends declared (see the section on dividends below)	45,000	90,000
Extra savings (net income minus dividends)	0	5,000
Building replacement needs	10,000	20,000
less depreciation allowance	− 10,000	− 10,000
equals	0	10,000
less extra savings	0	− 5,000
Equals unmet replacement needs	0	− 5,000

dividends are paid. However, the cost of the building has doubled, and $20,000 would have been needed each year in order for the firm to replace its "used up" building in full. The annual amount of "depreciation plus extra saving" has fallen from 10% (10,000/100,000) to 7.5% (15,000/200,000) of the cost of a new building. Either a smaller building must be purchased, or else dividends paid to its common stockholders should have been lowered throughout the inflationary period. Manifestly, the result of lower dividends would have been lowered *real* income for the common stockholders.

Between the years 1970–1976, American industry gained an

increase in gross after-tax income that was directly proportional to the inflation that had taken place over the same period of time. But after adjusting for *under* depreciation and for inventory profit accounting effects (which are of similar order as the depreciation effect), business *real net income* had fallen by 50%.* Business firms had lost out to the inflation. *The government in fact had won!* Note that the income tax received by the government rose *in our example* from $45,000 to $95,000. In other words, government's real income rose $5,000 more than the rate of inflation, and the business firm's ability to replace its building (and equipment) had fallen by the same $5,000.

7% Inflation in the 1970s

The Nixon, Ford, and Carter years witnessed an average of 7 percent inflation. They further witnessed a falling real income for American business firms. The truth is that the Carter administration inherited a problem, just as had the Ford administration and the Nixon administration. The latest problem goes back to the mid 1960's when serious inflation in the United States was first beginning.

"THE BIGGEST LOSER: THE CONSUMER"

Consider now the individual with a $4,100 income in 1970. Let it be $8,200 in 1980. Ignoring the extra tax on social security because of the worker's higher income, and deducting only the income tax that the worker would pay, his(her) after-tax income is $3,987 in 1970 and $7,348 in 1980. Suppose the individual also inherited some common stock (not fixed income bonds) from his (her) father, which provided dividends of $4,100 in 1970 and $8,200 in 1980. Ignoring minor differences in tax treatment, nominal after-tax income in 1970 would have been $7,348 and in 1980 $13,537, as in Table 13.3. Adjusting the 1980 income for the 100% rise in prices reveals that the individual's real income of

---

*See J. Buchanan and R. Wagner, *Democracy in Deficit* (New York: Academic Press, 1977), p. 66. Remember also that our example assumed, for numerical simplicity, a constant (high 50%) corporate income tax rate. If, instead, the rates increased in the example from lower to higher rates, the corporation's loss to the government would have been greater. In fact, there is a higher rate on corporate income in excess of $100,000 than there is on lower income.

TABLE 13.3

THE INDIVIDUAL (CONSUMER) LOSES

	1970	1980
Before-Income-Tax Income	$4,100	$8,200
Dividend Nominal Income	4,100	8,200
Total Income	$8,200	$16,400
Approximate Tax on Total Income	852	2,863
After-Tax Income	$7,348	$13,537
CPI	100	200
Real Income After Tax	$7,348	$6,768.5

$7,348 in 1970 had fallen to $6,768.50 in 1980. What did the government receive? It received $852 from the individual in 1970, and $2,863 in 1980. The government's nominal income more than doubled, and hence its real income also increased. This is one of the things that makes Congress willing to spend excessively, appearing to please all constituents.

Gov't (1970) index of real income

$$RI = \frac{Nom\ I.}{CPI} = \frac{\$852}{100} = 8.52$$

Gov't (1980) index of real income

$$RI = \frac{Nom\ I.}{CPI} = \frac{\$2863}{200} = 14.3$$

It should be clear that a legislator can therefore support government deficit spending without being forced to propose new (unpopular) tax-increasing laws. Those in Congress recognize that firms and individuals *automatically* pay more in taxes. Deficits, we should emphasize, rose in recent years somewhat less than they would if it had not been for the inflation-caused increase in government real tax income. (However, legislation enacted in 1981, and currently under attack, indexes the personal income tax starting in 1985; it will adjust tax brackets in step with changes in the purchasing power of the dollar, ending the windfall tax revenues to government from inflation.)

"THE WINNER: GOVERNMENT"

Government wins against business firms, not so much because tax rates change, but largely as a result of the accounting practices it imposes on business — depreciation on the basis of historical, not replacement costs. It wins against individuals because it applies *higher rates* as their nominal incomes rise — the real value of exemptions falls, and taxpayers move to higher tax brackets even though their *real* incomes have not risen. The effect of the Reagan administration indexing of individual income tax rates as of 1985 will be to stop the government wins, individual loses effect of inflation. By indexing tax brackets — adjusting them and exemptions for inflation — and allowing current cost (replacement cost) accounting, the government would be reduced to the private sector's position, and would thereby be motivated to curtail its spending proclivities in an attempt to control inflation.

"JUSTIFICATION FOR INFLATION"

One might wonder how American voters permitted the federal government to stimulate the fires of inflation over the last decade when only the government wins. The answer, of course, is two-fold. Americans were told (and many believed) that inflation was caused by greedy unions and greedy Big Business (Chapter 14 will explain why this is not so). They were also told (and many believed) that government was seeking less unemployment and could easily achieve this goal in exchange for a little inflation. A trade-off between the two existed, which was referred to by economists as the "Phillips Curve." Their argument went as follows:

"THE INFLATION-UNEMPLOYMENT TRADE-OFF"

It is clear that unemployment can be reduced only if there is a demand for more workers in the factor market. We know that the

FIGURE 13.1

TRADE-OFF THEORY OR PHILLIPS CURVE

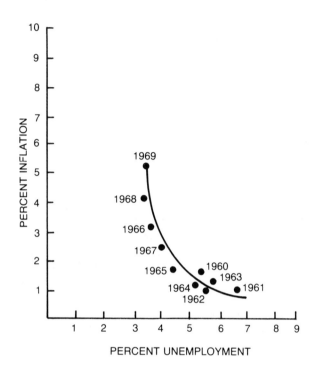

PERCENT UNEMPLOYMENT

demand for workers in the factor market goes up if and only if a greater demand for goods and services has taken place in the product market. Moreover, this demand typically rises when people have more money to spend for goods and services. What can cause all of these upward moving events to happen?

For one thing, by monetary and fiscal policy, the government can put more money into the circular flow of economic activity. If it does, the theories of inflation discussed previously indicate that the general price level (CPI) will go up. On the other hand, if the government tries to reduce inflation, this will cause consumers to spend less in the product market, which will, in turn, reduce the demand for goods and services. The reduction in demand for goods and services must then cause a decrease in the demand for

165

labor in the factor market. The effect of this reduction in demand is increased unemployment. Figure 13.1 indicates that throughout the 1960s unemployment fell when price levels were more inflated. Chapter 14 will demonstrate however why the Phillips trade-off curve of Figure 13.1 broke down in the 1970s.

"FINAL STATEMENT"

We should enter the qualifying statement that *only* the income tax aspects of inflation were examined in this chapter. We did not evaluate the benefits derived by Americans from selected spending programs. At the same time, note that we stressed here the fact that inflation involves a decrease in real incomes. This conclusion warrants emphasis because the problem up to the Reagan administration's tax victory had been becoming more and more serious. A major question is: "How much inflation and how much government is *too* much?" Another is whether inflation necessarily ends in recession and unemployment? Forthcoming chapters will provide answers to these questions. In particular, Chapter 14 will consider the question of whether inflation leads to stagflation, and maybe worse yet, to depression and large-scale unemployment.

CHAPTER 14:
INFLATION,
UNEMPLOYMENT, AND
STAGFLATION

It has already been noted that a trade-off appeared between inflation and unemployment during the 1960s. In effect, take your pick. A little more of this for a little less of that. Indeed, in the ivory towers of many economists, the trade-off (Phillips curve) was used to justify deliberate inflating of the economy as unemployment was considered the greater evil. Of course, the inflation of the 1960s was moderate compared to that of the 1970s.

"THE BREAKDOWN OF THE INFLATION-UNEMPLOYMENT TRADE-OFF"

During the middle part of the 1970s, the trade-off policies designed to reduce unemployment, which included work-training programs, employing more bureaucrats, encouraging more and more consumption and service activities, and willingness to deficit spend even at the risk of some inflation, became suspect in the eyes of many. Prices kept going higher and higher, but so did unemployment. How was this reversal of prior history possible?

"GOVERNMENT REGULATIONS CUT OUTPUT"

Monetarists, in particular, began to stress that as the government in Washington expanded, the related government *output* was in the form of more and more regulations. This *output* does not provide more goods and services for sale in the market. Expenditures on welfare, Uncle Sam's regulations of agriculture, the costs of the nation's environmental protection laws, and the increased supervision of the energy industries all signify income going to government employees without a corresponding output of goods and services to be sold in the product market. This administrative cost of the federal government alone was estimated at $3.2 billions for 1976. But it was a small part—less than five percent—of the total cost of federal regulation for that year, estimated at $66.1 billions. (See Table 14.1.) The remainder is the costs of compliance with regulations, imposed mainly on business (and passed on in part to the consumer via higher prices); part of this cost is also imposed directly on households and governments themselves.

TABLE 14.1

ANNUAL COST OF FEDERAL REGULATION,
BY AREA, 1976
(MILLIONS OF DOLLARS)

Area	Administrative Cost	Compliance Cost	Total
Consumer safety and health	1,516	5,094	6,610
Job safety and working conditions	483	4,015	4,498
Energy and the environment	612	7,700	8,372
Financial regulation	104	1,118	1,222
Industry specific	484	19,919	20,403
Paperwork	—[a]	25,000	25,000
Total	3,199	62,906	66,195

[a]Included in other categories.

SOURCE: The estimates of administrative costs shown in this table were derived from Murray L. Weidenbaum and Robert Defina, *The Rising Cost of Government Regulation* (St. Louis, Mo.: Center for the Study of American Business, January 31, 1977).

Not only do all compliance costs of government regulations fail to generate increased output, but in many cases the reverse is true: costs go up, output goes down, productivity falls. Environmental Protection Agency rules and required business expenditures raise costs while decreasing final goods output.*

---

*Weidenbaum and DeFina, *Ibid.*, estimated the annual cost of EPA regulations at about $8 billion, of which 99% was cost of compliance.

These and other regulations (many of which are, of course, well based) are nonetheless inflationary, for compliance costs are mainly paid out as income to labor, which increases the demand for saleable goods and services. They should be imposed on the business world only when *clearly conceived and obviously desirable and necessary.* Laws providing income to many who do not produce saleable final goods output are inflationary unless government restricts the money supply, and such restrictions could cause unemployment if carried out at the wrong time.

A special note on government regulations

A caveat for the above is in order. Not all regulation cuts output or raises costs (and some that do may still be justified). We previously stressed that profits and relative prices serve as guidelines for economic decision makers, leading to efficiency and growth. But they do this only if they are competitive profits and competitive prices. Vigorous and healthy competition can only prevail under a system of laws, subject to appropriate regulation. Businessmen might otherwise successfully conspire to monopolize production and trade. Cutthroat competition, subject to no law, is not in the best long-run interests of consumers. Laws and rules with enforcement provisions are necessary to prevent restraint of trade, unfair competitive practices, monopolization. Where business self-regulation through competition is impossible, as in local monopolies of water supply or telephone service, regulatory bodies are needed to force monopolists to price and produce as if they were competitors. Regulation may be sought to compel decision makers to take into consideration the external costs they impose on others: pollution, noise, occupational hazards. In markets where the costs of learning by experience may be too high, or the time required too long, or the price of ignorance too high, e.g., food and drugs or certain occupations such as medicine, some regulation—not necessarily by government since it could be by the appropriate industry—*is* needed. Regulation that creates and preserves competition can harness even the baser motives of avarice and greed into the service of society.

The problem stressed by most monetarists and supply-siders is not the existence of regulation, but regulation that works against rather than with market forces, for instance price ceilings on domestic oil and gas which discouraged domestic output, encouraged consumption, and increased imports; or the counter-productive pathological risk aversion which ironically condemns some sick people to die by denying them drugs available in other advanced countries which might have cured them; or the prefer-ence for assured illness and death from mining and burning coal over the hypothetical exposure to radiation from a possible accident in a nuclear plant. It is the import restrictions that encourage inefficient industries to hide behind import barriers instead of lowering costs, improving their products and be-coming efficient, or releasing their resources to other industries that can compete. It is occupational licensing which instead of protecting the public from incompetent practitioners so restricts entry as to reduce service and provide a monopoly rent to those who are admitted to the occupation. These are the governmental impacts which when combined with generalized rapidly increas-ing government spending and related growth in money supply led to the rapid inflation of the 70's.

"DEFICIT SPENDING GENERATES INFLATION"

Monetarists contend that there are other inflationary ten-dencies intrinsic to our government's policies. By deficit spend-ing, the American public is led to believe that a new government spending program is costless. The taxpayer (who, of course, is not a professionally trained economist) only notices that he is not required to pay new taxes *directly* in order for the new spending program to go into effect. He therefore does not challenge the lawmaker as he would if he were taxed directly as a result of a new government spending program. (Few taxpayers of the past real-ized that they pay the cost of many new programs in the form of higher consumer good prices. How many have actually under-stood that inflation is fundamentally due to government eco-nomic policies?)

Too many laws have been quickly passed without any weighing of the pros and cons the way individuals do when spending their own money. The associated costs do not have to be explicitly considered, much less provided for in the legislation. Worse yet, by deficit spending (that is spending more than one receives as income), the government typically borrows from commercial banks *and* the Federal Reserve Banks. Chapters 5 and 6 have demonstrated that more money then results. This additional money, in the absence of a proportionally increased output of final goods, is simply inflationary. Moreover, the sale of additional quantities of government bonds raises the rate of interest. As already suggested earlier in the book, private investment in new plant and equipment falls off as interest rates rise.* Indeed, as inflation progresses, illusory profits arise reflecting the under-depreciation of buildings and equipment and the valuation of inventory at low acquisition costs rather than much higher replacement costs (see Chapter 13). Uncertainty increases. As company officials become more and more uncertain about past and future policies, they tend to invest less than they would have done otherwise. The rate of increase in output declines.

Recent Government Attempts to Reduce Unemployment Have Promoted Inflation

So when government spends more in order to reduce unemployment, inflation takes place. (Recall Figure 13.1.) Consider also the following scenario: Suppose that government regulatory agencies—such as OSHA (Occupation, Safety, Health Administration), EPA (Environmental Protection Agency), CPSC (Consumer Product Safety Commission), CAB (Civil Aeronautics Board), and others—intensify their rules, and new programs such as CETA (Comprehensive Employment Training Act) are enacted by Congress. A result is increased paperwork and uncertainty. Interest rates go up because of deficit spending. People put more and more of their savings into precious gems, real estate development schemes, and the like. Thus the supply of loanable funds decreases, and interest rates continue the trend upwards. Business uncertainty continues to increase.

As inflation increases, illusory business profits are taxed, minimum wages are raised as well as business costs, prices rise again, and consumers go on non-buying "strikes." Investment falls.

---

*Interest rates would rise even if the money supply is expanded in the vain hope of keeping them down. This is actually the result because inflation due to a relatively increased supply of money causes lenders to require higher interest returns; this follows because each dollar of interest at higher price levels (higher CPI) is of lower value than it used to be.

"*COULD IT BE* THAT THE INFLATION IS CAUSED BY UNIONS AND BUSINESS MONOPOLIES RATHER THAN GOVERNMENT?"

The Carter administration tried several times to blame businessmen and union leaders for the inflation of the late 1970s. Meanwhile business and labor, feeling the need to justify their own actions, often blame the other. The myth thus persists that they are responsible for out-of-line prices. Elementary demand-supply curve analysis indicates that unions and monopolists can indeed cause selected high prices, but not country-wide high prices. Economic theory and data indicate that businesses and unions cannot cause rising prices *independent of inflationary governmental policy*.

Individuals often approach this intricate subject by asking, "Did prices cause wages to rise or was it wages (and other resource costs) which pushed prices up?" But these are superficial questions. Wages and other resource costs are just other names for *prices*. If resource prices, including labor, are pushing up product prices, the relevant question is, "What is causing resource prices to rise?"

There *is* evidence that unions are able to gain higher wages for their members than would exist in the absence of unionism. But there is *no* evidence that union wages rise more rapidly than other resource (or product) prices, thereby causing inflation. In fact, as we shall see in a moment, the evidence is just the opposite.

Suppose union members gained a wage increase relative to non-union workers. In addition, suppose the demand for union-made products is inelastic, by which we mean consumers want about the same number of units even though the prices of these products are steadily rising. Total consumer expenditures on union-produced goods would, in other words, go up.* But the higher level of expenditures on union-made products must necessitate a fall in consumer spending on other products, in the absence of expansionary governmental policy. The fall in demand for other products leads to lower prices in nonunionized sectors, offsetting the higher prices in the unionized sectors of the economy. There is clearly no generally rising price level throughout the economy.

---

*Inelastic demand, therefore, means that expenditures vary directly with prices; that is, they rise (fall) when price goes up (down).

172

What if the demand for union-made products were such that a price increase would cause a substantial decrease in total consumer expenditures for them? In other words, what if the demand for union-made products happened to be elastic?* In this case, higher labor costs and product prices in the unionized sector would cause a sharp decline in the acquisition of union-made products. This would imply a decline in the employment of labor and other resources in the union sector. So workers unable to find jobs in the union sector must, and will eventually, shift to non-union employment, increasing the supply of labor in the nonunion sector. This supply shift of labor and other resources lowers costs and prices of nonunion goods. Of course, these adjustments do not take place instantaneously. Over some small period of time, the rising prices might outweigh those that are falling. But rising prices in the unionized sector, we have observed, will set off forces causing downward pressure on prices in other sectors. Certainly, there would be no expectation of continually rising prices—that is, inflation—in the absence of expansionary government policy that generates inflation.**

Empirical Evidence

What about the empirical evidence? Relative to nonunion wages, union wage rates historically fell during inflationary periods and rose during periods of stable prices.*** This is because long-term contracts were not rapidly adjusted to the rising prices. Since they lost ground during prior inflationary periods, it hardly seems likely that unions could be an underlying cause of inflation.

Second, wages in manufacturing (which is the most highly unionized sector in the American economy) actually fell during the 1966–1970 inflationary period when they were adjusted for

---

*Elastic demand means that expenditures vary inversely to prices; they fall (go up) when prices go up (down).

**There is a logically consistent scenario that unions (or businesses with monopoly power) indirectly cause inflation. It goes as follows. Higher union wages cause unemployment. The market adjustment process will not immediately lead to a reallocation of resources and full employment. The temporary unemployment will cause government to follow an expansionary policy that will cause prices generally to rise.

***See Albert Rees, "Do Unions Cause Inflation?" *The Journal of Law and Economics*, October 1959.

changes in consumer prices. A similar pattern was present during the 1950–1952 and 1955–1957 inflationary periods. The obvious question is, "How can falling real wages in the most highly unionized sectors be pushing prices up?" The answer is that the inflation does not result from union wages.

Third, price increases during the inflation of the late 1960's and early 1970's have been more pronounced in the service, medical care, food processing, agriculture, and government sectors. In general, these sectors are not highly unionized.

In summary, while unions could cause the prices of union-made goods and services to be high, neither theory nor evidence suggests that they could have caused the continual rise in prices of the late 1960's and 1970's.

What about greedy businessmen? Corporate profits have declined both as a share of GNP and as a percentage of sales during each of the three major inflations since World War II, as shown in Table 14.2. These declining corporate profits do not suggest the business sector as the culprit in the inflationary game. Of course, businesses raise their prices during inflation, but this is in response to the demand and cost conditions generated by inflation.

TABLE 14.2

Inflationary period	Consumer price index (1967 = 100)	Corporate profits as a percentage of GNP	Manufacturing Corporation profits as a percentage of sales (after taxes)
1950–1952			
1950	72.1	13.2	7.1
1952	79.5	11.5	4.3
1955–1957			
1955	80.2	11.8	5.4
1957	84.3	10.3	4.8
1966–1973			
1966	97.2	11.0	5.6
1969	109.8	8.6	4.8
1973	133.1	8.5	4.6

SOURCE: U.S. DEPARTMENT OF COMMERCE.

174

If firms can gain by charging higher prices, they will do so independent of inflationary conditions. But when will firms in the aggregate be able to gain by raising their prices? Only when aggregate demand is such that they can still sell their output at the higher prices.

What about the monopoly power of big business? The same logic that explained why unions could not cause rising prices applies to big business. If higher prices in a so-called "monopoly business sector" result in an increase in total spending in that sector, then demand, and therefore prices in the non-monopolized sector would decline. On the other hand, if purchases in response to the higher prices happen to fall so that there is a decrease in spending on the goods produced by big business, then fewer resources would be demanded by this sector. This would cause the supply of resources to the nonmonopoly sector to expand, placing downward pressure on costs and prices there. As with unions, business monopoly power could explain selected high prices, *but not continually rising prices throughout the economy*.

The blame for inflation, just as the credit for a stable economic environment, belongs to those in charge of monetary and fiscal policy. For obvious reasons, while politicians readily accept credit for stability, they are reluctant to assume responsibility for inflation.

"THE SHIFTING TRADE-OFF CURVE"

Monetarists have gone several steps beyond the claim that expansionary government policies involving fiscal deficits and vastly increased money supplies are inflationary. They propose that not only are deficits inflationary, but they increase unemployment notwithstanding the old idea of a trade-off. (The joint occurrence of unemployment and inflation, to repeat, is called "stagflation.") To appreciate their view, let us start with an inflation. Recall from Chapter 13 that there is an increasing tax-take on illusory accounting profits. This, we know, reduces business replacement of capital and investment in new technologies. Meanwhile, the consumer's loss to inflation continues to generate more and more uncertainty on his part. Any fears by labor and business of wage and price controls tend to induce a quick anticipatory *upward push* in wages and prices.

More and more women enter the work force to supplement

INFLATION, UNEMPLOYMENT, AND STAGFLATION

FIGURE 14.1

TRADE-OFF THEORY OR PHILLIPS CURVE

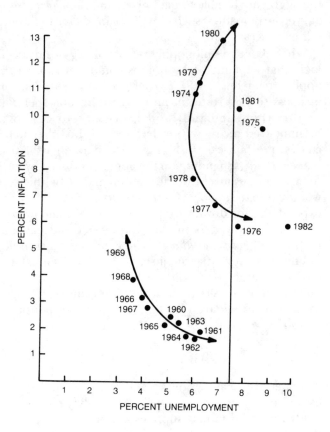

UNEMPLOYMENT		CPI INCREASE
YEAR	(%)	(%)
1982	9.7	6.1
1981	7.6	10.4
1980	7.1	13.0
1979	5.8	11.1
1978	6.0	7.7
1977	7.0	6.5
1976	7.7	5.8
1975	8.5	9.1
1974	5.6	10.7

their husbands' decreasing real income. Monetarists point out that young people, some former housewives, and the less skilled workers who are hurt by Congress' raising of minimum wages beyond levels that firms would pay *remain unemployed*; in fact, more become unemployed. Suddenly it is clear from Figure 14.1 that the trade-off curve has clearly shifted dramatically up and to the right. (Apart from the shifting, the trade-off itself does not conform to a pattern for 1975, 1981, and 1982.) Manifestly, the large amount of government spending which, in the past, associated a 6% unemployment rate with less than 2% inflation, more recently associates a 6% unemployment rate with 8 to 11% rates of inflation. As more and more government spending takes place to reduce a rate of unemployment that is too high, deficits grow larger.

The steadily larger deficits increase inflation and unemployment. This follows, in part, because each increase in governmental activity has been associated with increased unemployment compensation benefits. Worker disillusionment with personal income has increased, so search time for new jobs has increased, also. In addition, the underlying full employment rate appears to have moved from, say, 4% to 4½% to 5% to 6%. (Note that this is why economists have recently begun to disagree on what in fact is full employment in the United States.)

Recollection of past standards unfortunately leads many in Congress to propose a 3% full employment target rate, as they did in the original 1975 Humphrey-Hawkins bill. They raised this rate slightly to the somewhat more realistic 4% target in the second (1977) draft of that bill. Monetarists would say, however, that 6% is alone realistic now, and that a 4% target would prove to be extremely inflationary and utterly disastrous. In fact, they would say government cannot maintain unemployment even at a 6% level if it continues to deficit spend *and* to effect arbitrary controls on the economy.

"SUMMARY OF AND OTHER FACETS OF THE UNEMPLOYMENT-INFLATION DILEMMA"

You may have wondered before what could be worse than either unemployment *or* inflation. The answer is both high unemployment *and* high inflation at the same time. But let's review for the moment.

INFLATION, UNEMPLOYMENT, AND STAGFLATION

Our discussion of the economy's trade-off between un-employment and inflation was a simple view of how the economy *once worked*. This trade-off model of inflation and unemployment really explained how the economy operated between 1960 and 1970. Since 1970 the Phillips curve model has not worked well at all. (The curve simply shifted to the right, as in Figure 14.1.) Since 1970 we have had tendencies for increasing unemployment *and* inflation. The joint occurrence of unemployment and inflation is called stagflation. But why is it that the single Phillips curve model no longer truly depicts our economy?

"STAGFLATION: UNEMPLOYMENT AND INFLATION COMBINED"

Not all economists agree on the answer to the above question. But two very important reasons for stagflation can be stressed.

(1) Recall the slight but rather steady rise in the nation's CPI after the depression years. Consumers thus have long been subject to a steady rise in prices in the United States. More recently, they have expected the price level (CPI) *to rise substantially*. This expectation has itself been a cause of inflation. If people expect prices to go up, they increase spending now, and this helps account for more inflation.

(2) There exists in the United States a growing mistrust and even resentment towards business. Big business is blamed for high prices today. At the same time, our government officials have passed more and more anti-business rules and regulations. In this hostile climate, it is small wonder that many business leaders think twice before they try to increase their output and use of the factors of production. These leaders themselves compound the problem when they seek governmental protection from competition rather than keep government away from their field of activity. In terms of the circular flow of economic activity, businesses are not investing enough. If the money saved in the circular flow of economic activity is not put back into the flow as investment, the size of the flow will shrink—unemployment rises. The productivity of those who *are* working is not increased.

"STAGFLATION AND THE FUTURE"

What should we really do about unemployment and inflation in the United States? This is not an easy question to answer. In fact, a complete answer cannot be given in a book on this level. Nevertheless, some thoughts on the matter can be entered here for consideration, and we shall go well beyond our present suggestions later in the book.

First, the recent continuing and massive government spending must be brought under control. Repetitive government deficit spending is not the way to solve unemployment. It makes inflation worse.

Second, a new look must be taken at government programs designed for the unemployed. While many of the programs which reduce the financial difficulties of the unemployed are desirable, these same programs also increase the time someone can remain frictionally unemployed and not suffer financially. While this may appear to be humanitarian, we must at least recognize that unemployment rates which once were valid (e.g., the 3% limit) no longer apply. Statutes based on illogical dreams can only compound the problem—not help solve the problem.

Third, and most important, government spending and regulations must be limited to practices which do *not* destroy individual initiatives and freedom. Simply eliminating government excesses, number of agencies, and size of the bureaucracy will go a long way towards fulfilling this need. Claiming we want tax reductions to benefit only the poor may well destroy the initiative and productivity of all. The poorest pay no income taxes.

"FINAL STATEMENT"

All steps proposed above move toward a common objective: improving the overall free enterprise *climate* in the United States so that sufficient business investments are encouraged. There are grounds for optimism here. In fact, change in the long-continued tax emphasis favoring consumption rather than private investment was indicated by a February 28, 1980 report of the Congressional Joint Economic Committee. On that date, the committee proposed as its *solution* to inflation the need to stimulate private investment and thereby to gain economic growth. The 1980 statement reflected an increasing concern with the slowing down of productivity per worker, and also recognition that long-run improvements in the American economy were needed. Mr. Carter's desire (expressed earlier in that same week) to eliminate the proposed fiscal year 1981 deficit was echoed by corresponding policy changes in the House and Senate committees. These changes in approach to the galloping inflation of 1979 and early 1980 attested to the beginning realization by the nation's leaders of the underlying causes for the upward price spiral. The election of 1980 strongly indicated public concern with recent economic events. It brought into practice supply-side economics, to the specifics of which we now turn.

CHAPTER 15:
THE SUPPLY-SIDE FACTOR
IN KEYNESIAN
ECONOMICS

In our regard, supply-side economics is simply Keynesian economics from a different viewpoint. This so-called new economics places *special emphasis* on an *income determinant* — supply — that was fundamentally conceived by Keynes as a dependent variable; it is not so regarded by supply-siders. To understand the importance of this, we must recast the Keynesian system of thought more formally in this and the following chapter than in earlier chapters in the book. For the moment, let us note that in the basic Keynesian formulation, any increase in aggregate demand spending (AD) was conceived to increase output (hence income) by the amount of the initial increase in AD times a multiplier. This multiplier equalled the reciprocal of the marginal propensity to save.* We shall explain the basic multiplier concept in detail below.

"THE KEYNESIAN MULTIPLIER"

Suppose the aggregate demand (AD) for American goods by consumers, businesses, governments, and foreigners goes up by a certain amount a day. For simplicity, imagine a business firm (Company F) now purchases $5 more per day of electrical services from Mr. A than it had purchased in the past. So, A receives a $5 increase in income per day. Assume next that *as a result*, A tends to spend $2.50 extra each day. Let B regularly receive the $2.50 that A now spends for services performed by B. Assume next that B also spends fifty percent of the new $2.50 added income that is received from A. Thus, B spends $1.25 extra compared to B's past expenditures. This means that C receives new extra income. And we will imagine C also spends fifty percent of the extra received. It can be shown that A's spending plus B's spending plus C's spending, etc. will rise by a total of $5. Of course, each of the expenditures by A, B, C, . . . meant new income to B, C, D, . . .

---

*More technically, it is the reciprocal of the marginal leakages.

The new $5 total of *extra* spending by A, B, C, . . . equals the $5 worth of *extra* income received by B, C, D, . . .

A's *original new income receipt of $5* resulted in a final *total* of $10 of new income. So when AD went up initially by Company F's $5 expenditure, incomes (GNP) rose by a total of $10. A multiplier of 2 resulted from the propensity of A, B, C, . . . to increase their consumption by fifty percent as their incomes went up. That propensity to increase consumption is called the marginal propensity to consume, MPC. It is shown symbolically in Keynesian economics as $\Delta C/\Delta Y$, where the symbol Δ stands for the word "change" and the letters C and Y stand for the words "consumption" and "income." In our example, the change in consumption out of a change in income, i.e., $\Delta C/\Delta Y$, equalled $\frac{1}{2}$.

"THE MULTIPLIER VIEWED IN MORE FORMAL DETAIL"

The simple multiplier stemming from $\Delta C/\Delta Y$ can be demonstrated to equal the number 1 divided by $(1 - \Delta C/\Delta Y)$. And since out of any $1.00 *change* in income, a person can either change consumption or change savings or both, $\Delta C/\Delta Y + \Delta S/\Delta Y = 1$, where $\Delta S/\Delta Y$ (the marginal propensity to save, MPS) is the change in savings out of the unit change in income. It follows by simple subtraction that $\Delta S/\Delta Y = 1 - \Delta C/\Delta Y$. Thus the multiplier can be viewed either by reference to the change in savings or to the number 1 minus the change in consumption that results from a unit change in income. Since the simple multiplier is equal to $1/(1 - \Delta C/\Delta Y)$, and the denominator $(1 - \Delta C) = \Delta S/\Delta Y$, the multiplier also equals $1/(\Delta S/\Delta Y)$. And $1/(\Delta S/\Delta Y)$ is the same thing as the reciprocal of the fraction saved, i.e., $\Delta Y/\Delta S$. Most simply viewed, the multiplier is therefore equal to $\Delta Y/\Delta S$.

It suffices for our purposes to view the multiplier as basically dependent upon the proportion of the change in income that is consumed. The greater the proportion consumed, the less is the proportion saved, and hence the greater is the multiplier. If $\Delta C/\Delta Y = \frac{1}{2}$, then $\Delta S/\Delta Y = \frac{1}{2}$; the reciprocal of $\Delta S/\Delta Y$ is the multiplier, in this case 2. If $\Delta C/\Delta Y = \frac{2}{3}$, $\Delta S/\Delta Y = \frac{1}{3}$, and the reciprocal of $\frac{1}{3}$, namely 3, is the multiplier. If $\Delta C/\Delta Y = \frac{4}{5}$, $\Delta S/\Delta Y = \frac{1}{5}$, the multiplier is 5 . . . if $\Delta C/\Delta Y = \frac{9}{10}$, $\Delta S/\Delta Y = \frac{1}{10}$, the multiplier is 10.

M.L. GREENHUT   C.T. STEWART

"GOVERNMENT SPENDING AND THE MULTIPLIER"

In the Keynesian system, a $10 billion increase in government spending (i.e., G) along with a multiplier of 5 would raise the nation's income (Y) by $50 billion. If unemployment existed before the new spending, output was conceived to increase by an equivalent $50 billion in the *real* value of goods and services produced.

Suppose the $50 billion increase in the nation's output (income) still left a large number of people unemployed. Then the government could raise its budgeted spending an additional $10 billion in the next period above the level resulting from the prior $10 billion increase in spending. Since the level of income of the people had already risen, we can propose that the public would tend to save a little more out of this gain in income; thus a slightly smaller multiplier would now apply than formerly.* Suppose the new multiplier is four instead of five; that is, $10 billion will initiate a new wave of $40 billion increased income deriving from the new lower multiplier of four. Given the *total* change in aggregate demand of $40 billion, real output of goods and services will go up by the same $40 billion. It goes up by the same amount as the increase in government spending times the multiplier because unemployed resources are assumed available at this time, and because the *productivity* of the labor force (based in part on the public's willingness to work and the prevailing technology) tends to be constant over short periods of time. The result of the increases in aggregate demand of $50 billion plus an additional $40 billion will be a perfectly matching increase of $90 billion in aggregate supply, according to Keynes.

---

*Recognize here that as people become wealthier, they tend to save a little more out of each unit increase in income than they would have when they were poorer. That is, the MPC falls a little as the MPS, accordingly, rises a little. Assume an increase in income of $10 originally caused an increase in consumption of $8, MPC = 80%. Suppose an additional increase in income of $10 next induces a $7.50 increase in consumption (MPC = 75%). It follows that the new MPS is 25%. The multiplier being the reciprocal of 25% is now 4. *In reality*, if the original multiplier were 5, we can expect a miniscule decrease in it (for example, to 4.999) as aggregate income rises over the short periods of time during which the economic expansion may take place.

THE SUPPLY-SIDE FACTOR IN KEYNESIAN ECONOMICS

"THE SUPPLY-SIDE CRITIQUE"

The economy conceived of by Keynesians was, therefore, one which assumed that the government itself is as acceptable a spender *in general* as are businesses and individuals, that is, government spending was conceived to have the same impact as business or consumer spending. But *supply-side* fiscalists say that this is really not so! They contend that government spending leads to an increased bureaucracy, more regulations and controls over people, wasteful projects, greater taxes, *ad nauseum*. The effect is that as income (output) rises over the years because of increased government spending, the private sector tends to become less and less productive. The impact of this is that while nominal income may rise, say by $90 billion, because of a spending increase by government, *real* output (goods and services) may rise by, let us say, only $75 billion in value, even though some labor and other resources remain unemployed. The $15 billion difference between dollar incomes received and real output produced, in other words, reflects a rise in money prices (inflation) alone.

Let us put the argument of the supply-siders as follows: As government increases its share of the economy, it raises taxes. Higher tax rates in turn dampen the stimulus of additional government expenditures. High marginal tax rates discourage work and investment, i.e., they dampen supply responses to increased public spending. Such a dampening effect implies a progressive tendency toward inflation at higher and higher levels of unused resources, stagflation. The tendency as government grows is for it to divert resources from the private sector to less productive uses; this accentuates inflation at rising levels of unemployment.

"SUPPLY-SIDE CRITIQUES IN DETAIL"

(1) Imagine you are earning $30,000 a year. Suppose everytime your income had risen by $5,000 in the past, your marginal tax rate had risen a few percentage points. You recognize that if now you receive another $5,000 increase in income, the federal government will snatch 30% by way of income taxes, your state will take 10% more, and social security will take 6% of the increase; in fact, you might even recognize that 4% of your extra spending would go in the form of sales taxes. The upshot is that in real

personal gains you net only 50% of your increase in gross income. Sooner or later the risk, the uncertainty, the wear and tear on you of earning the extra $5,000 (when viewed at only 50% of that figure) will prove insufficient to warrant taking on the extra investment, or work, or new job. So you stop being more productive.

(2) High marginal tax rates drive some labor and resources from market to non-market activities. Individuals have recognized the advantage in recent years in doing their own repair work rather than hiring others, as they might have in the past. For example, if a person could earn an extra $100 by extra job effort while netting only $50, and it would cost $60 to hire another person to do some house repair work, the "worker home-owner" in question may well decide to do the repair work himself, instead of hiring another. In practice he would forsake the employment of another and use his own time for house work rather than further effort on his job. In effect the nation gains only the $60 house repair work rather than the $160 increase in the nation's output that would have resulted otherwise.

(3) High marginal tax rates divert productive resources to non-productive activities. It is well known that high marginal tax rates cause people to hire tax accountants, tax lawyers, investment consultants, etc. The nation's tax advisory (tax saving) industry thrives, but little real goods benefits result. We become a nation of paper workers, as businessmen, company managers, physicians, artists, blue and white collar workers all spend less time working while devoting more time to figuring out how to reduce their tax liabilities. Taxpayers in many brackets spend undue time in developing income and expense records just in case of audit, besides hiring professionals simply to keep their tax lives as palatable as possible. Investments are directed toward minimizing taxes rather than maximizing economic returns. A smaller output of real goods and services results.

(4) High corporate tax rates subsidize much business waste. For example, suppose a vacation in Acapulco costs $5,000 and carries a $2,500 value to an individual who owns his own company. Suppose the company pays — in rounded percent — a 50% tax rate on income. Out of $5,000 extra company income, it would pay $2,500 in taxes. Let the balance be paid to the individual owner-manager as personal dividend income. Assume the individual is also subject to a 50% (personal) income tax rate. He

would, therefore, net $1,250, much less than the cost of and even the value of the desired vacation in Acapulco. Change the above scenario! Let the company send the same owner-manager to Acapulco on a business trip, spending the $5,000, which is not subject to tax. The owner-manager therefore does not receive the $1,250 net, but instead takes a $5,000 vacation that he would have paid $2,500 for. The upshot is a personal gain of $1,250, in effect at the expense of the members of society who cannot use company expense accounts for personal advantage. Company airplanes, plush business offices, vacations in Mexico provide affluence to many people in replacement of real production.

(5) Higher taxes, in addition to discouraging work and risk-taking investment, discourage saving. The individual income tax permits deduction of interest payments on debt. An individual who borrows $1,000 at an interest rate of 16% must pay $160 in interest per year. But if he is in the 50% federal income tax bracket, he reduces his tax payment by half of $160, or $80. His effective rate of interest is 8%; with an inflation rate of 10%, he would be borrowing at a *negative* 2% rate of interest. A poor fellow who is at the 20% federal income tax bracket only saves twenty percent of $160 of taxes due to debt, or $32; thus he pays an effective rate of interest of 12.8%. (Notice how the poor are losers under this facet of our income tax laws whereas most members of Congress preach their concern for the poor.) Meanwhile, interest and dividend income that is received from invested savings are taxed at the full rate. In fact, income in the form of dividends is taxed twice, first as income to the firm, and second when distributed to stockholders. Thus our tax system encourages borrowing and consumption and discourages savings and investment relatively. Those in higher tax brackets, who could do more of the saving, are the ones who are most encouraged to borrow and consume instead.

(6) Supply-siders go on to assert that there exists a natural tendency for inflation even in the presence of large numbers of unemployed. This assertion violates the traditional Keynesian thought which viewed inflation as something resulting only from excessive spending at full employment levels. Moreover, the inflationary process viewed by supply-siders does not require the standard monetarist perspective of excessive creation of money. It suffices that the increase in output fails to match nominal income gains. In particular, income support policies, including

unemployment compensation, that are fixed over long periods of time at a high proportion of previous earnings, are also tax-free income. They, along with food stamps, medicaid, and other programs (all of them meritorious to some extent), allow many to prolong unemployment, to postpone their return to active job searching. Their demands for goods are not matched by production. In this way, they contribute to the coexistence of inflation with substantial unemployment.

(7) Supply-siders go on to present one final problem in using the government sector as the vehicle for bringing about full employment. According to their argument, proliferations of government expenditures and related programs, to the extent they are not financed by higher taxes, not only generate deficits, money expansion, and inflation, but they also raise interest rates above the levels that would exist if government were a less prominent part of the business world. The competition of government agencies in the market for credit "crowds out" private borrowing and the investment and productivity gains dependent on it.

"GOVERNMENT BUDGETS AND SUPPLY-SIDE ECONOMICS"

People worry about the budget deficit and well they should. Unfortunately, however, the impact of the federal government on interest rates *and* our money markets is much greater than that resulting from its "on budget" items alone.

"OFF-BUDGET EXPENDITURES AND GUARANTEES"

There are major off-budget federal entities whose transactions are excluded from budget totals and from budget reviews *and ceilings*. When these off-budget outlays are financed by Treasury borrowing, they generate additional debt which is subject to the *statutory debt limit*; when they are financed by the entities' own borrowing, however, no statutory limit applies. *In either case*, the debt is part of the the gross federal debt. The U.S. Postal Service, the Rural Telephone Bank, and The Housing for the Elderly or Handicapped Fund are examples of off-budget entities.

Besides off-budget Federal entities, there are government-sponsored enterprises that were partly or fully owned by government, but typically converted later on to private ownership. The Federal National Mortgage Association and the Federal Home Loan Banks and Home Loan Mortgage Corporation are government-sponsored (privately owned) enterprises created to carry out loan programs to support housing. Other prominent programs deal with agriculture and education. Under these programs, the enterprises in question often lend funds to people, loans which are then guaranteed by the federal government. Federal government guarantees of the debt of those who borrow funds from government-sponsored enterprises make it easy to sell the guaranteed note on the market at a premium, thus obtaining new funds for new (additional) loans.

The greater the number of loans made by private "government-sponsored" firms, the greater the demand for loanable funds and hence the higher are the interest rate levels in the economy, all other things equal. The magnitudes of these off-budget demands as well as the on-budget demands for loanable funds by the U.S. Treasury Department (and its FFB arm) are given in Table 15.1. (And see the Appendix to this chapter for further details.)

TABLE 15.1

FEDERAL AND FEDERAL-RELATED BORROWING
(IN BILLIONS OF DOLLARS)

Fiscal Year	Direct Treasury	Federally-Sponsored Enterprises	Guaranteed Loans	Total Federal & Federal-Related Borrowing
1960	.2.2	0.4	3.0	5.6
1970	5.0	11.0	1.9	17.9
1980	70.5	21.4	32.4	124.3
1981	75.4	27.8	51.3	154.5

"THE PUBLIC DEBT AND THE NATION'S SAVINGS"

Irwin Kellner* pointed out that though the U.S. public debt is

*Irwin Kellner, *Economic Report, The Manufacturer's Hanover Bank,* November, 1981, pp. 2, 3.

only about one-third of our GNP vis a vis noticeably higher ratios for other countries, it is *not* the GNP that the debt should be compared to; rather, the public debt should be compared to the stock of savings. Kellner notes that according to the Federal Reserve Board, the economy generated about $196 billion in savings in 1981, including pension fund contributions, personal, and business savings. Though this large sum was 15% greater than it was in 1980, its growth was smaller than that of federal-related borrowings, which rose by 24%. He goes on to observe that this one year typifies the last two decades. In particular, federal plus federal-related borrowings have risen in the U.S.A. from about 19% of savings in 1960 to 25% in 1970, to 73% in 1980, and to almost 80% in 1981. The amount of funds available to the private sector is sorely limited today. This helps account for the high interest rates in 1981, our small amount of business investments, low productivity, and the recession that began then. It also helps account for the decade of general unemployment with inflation, and serves accordingly as one illustration of the concern of supply-side economics.

"THE SUPPLY-SIDE MULTIPLIER"

The supply-side arguments propose, in contrast to our original multiplier formulation, that if Company F purchases $5 of extra electrical services from Mr. A, he does receive an additional $5 of course; however, because of income tax paper work involved, EPA, CPSC, OSHA, etc., inspections and requirements, just like his competitors, Mr. A either turns out inferior services or less services than in the past. This result applies to the $2.50 Mr. A spends of the additional $5 earned, which $2.50 is received by B. And it applies to B, who in turn spends $1.25, *ad infinitum*. In sum, money income will rise by the same $10 total, and in appearance output increases by $10. But in reality, the increased output is lower in value, either in quality or quantity, than that which resulted in the past. The income receipt dollars are the same, while the *real* goods and services amount that is produced (i.e., the quality and real quantity of the GNP) is smaller than in the past. The money income of $10 is associated with what is in fact a smaller GNP as the increase in GNP of $10 simply involves inflated money values *per unit of good* (pound, foot, etc.) *produced*.

THE SUPPLY-SIDE FACTOR IN KEYNESIAN ECONOMICS

"WHY DID KEYNES IGNORE THE AGGREGATE DEMAND/AGGREGATE SUPPLY INDEPENDENCE?"

It would be natural for the reader to wonder why Keynes assumed for periods of less-than-full employment that an increase in aggregate demand (AD) would generate a corresponding (perfectly matching) increase in the aggregate supply (AS) so that the price level would be basically unchanged? Why is it that now an increase in government spending (hence AD) under conditions of less-than-full employment generates inflation? Is the Keynesian theory simply wrong? Our answer is probably already evident to you. Keynes was writing at a time when government represented a microscopic part of the economy; regulations were relatively few, income tax laws were comparatively simple, and marginal tax rates low. Given a catalyst such as a substantial increase in government spending, Keynes anticipated that incentives to save and invest would be substantial, and private investment combined with truly needed government creation of goods and services would increase output (AS) in perfect correspondence to increasing demand (AD). For reasons already noted, the substantial growth in government paperwork, in income taxes, etc. has eroded the dependency of supply on demand.

"SUPPLY-SIDE ECONOMIC POLICY"

Unlike the government spending demand-side Keynesians, supply-siders claim that a need exists to prop up business investment (Keynes' I function). They stress the idea that a rise in AD attributable to an increase in I will carry with it an increase in supply, which increased supply can match the increased income *at the (same) existing price level.* They would expect the Fed to be obliged simply to match the increased real output with a proportional expansion of money.

Among measures to stimulate business investment, supply-siders include: (1) a reduction in marginal tax rates and (2) shifting the bias in the tax system away from consumption and borrowing towards saving and investment. The encouragement of IRAs, reduction in capital gains taxation, more liberal depreciation allowances are steps in that direction. Some supply-siders recommend a shift in emphasis from the taxation of income to the taxation of consumption, via national sales and excise

190

taxes, or a value-added tax. (See the Appendix to the book.) Tax deductions for interest payments on consumer borrowing remain a significant antisavings, proconsumption bias, which helps keep interest rates high. Another measure would be (3) to stop the inflation-creep of personal income tax brackets by indexation, which will be done starting in 1985.

Supply-siders, no less than demand-siders, will differ on the details of the policies they would recommend, but not on the priority of investment nor on the need to improve the responsiveness of supply. They feel that government regulation is too often obstructive rather than constructive, excessive, unnecessarily costly in compliance, and that the share of national resources diverted from the private sector to governments is too large to permit satisfactory growth in productivity or sustained high levels of employment. However, to *fully indicate* the role of supply-side economics, some further basic analysis is needed. This is the objective of the following chapter.

"FINAL STATEMENT"

Supply-side economics is based on the idea that demand does not necessarily elicit supply. Briefly put, it asserts that alternative types of demand will elicit differential outputs of goods and services. Thus a rise in AD may or may not be associated with an equivalent increase in real GNP *even if it takes place at a time of unemployment*. Supply-siders agree that the Keynesian model must be expanded to include variable supply responses to changes in demand. Their full system of though is presented formally in the chapter that follows.

APPENDIX TO CHAPTER 15: ON AND OFF-BUDGET ITEMS

"THE SIZE OF ON AND OFF-BUDGET ITEMS"

Most of the excluded outlays of off-budget Federal entities, such as the Student Loan Marketing Association, are incurred for carrying out loan programs. A special government bank, the Federal Financing Bank (FFB), handles most of the off-budget outlay needs that are financed by the entities' own borrowings. It does this typically by purchasing the debt securities of a public enterprise, such as the Rural Telephone Bank and the Pension Benefit Guaranty Corporation. In addition, it provides funds directly for the specifically authorized purposes of government-sponsored, privately owned enterprises, oftentimes buying up loans that were originated by the private groups sponsored by the government.

Consider only the years 1960 and 1981 that were recorded in Table 15.1. These years are indicative of the changes that have taken place over all interim years. Note that the borrowing in 1960 on the public deficit resulted in $2.2 billion of new U.S. Treasury debt. Most significantly, these Treasury outlays *did include* the off-budget federal entity outlays of the Postal Service and some for NASA and TVA. The $0.4 billion figure for federally-sponsored enterprises involved such activities as the Federal National Mortgage Association, while the guaranteed loans total of $3.0 billion led to *total federal and federal-related borrowings of $5.6 billion.* The total growth to the 1981 level reflects the fact that the 1981 government deficit was 78 percent of direct Treasury borrowings, at the level of $58 billion, while direct Treasury borrowings for federal entities amounted to an additional $17.4 billion. However, the federal deficit and the total treasury borrowings comprised only 37% and 49%, respectively, of Washington's 1981 total impact on the market for funds that free-enterprise must also tap. *Including guarantees of $51.3 billion, the 1981 total of federal and federal-related borrowings was $154.4 billion.* Its guarantee *in effect* pushes the borrower to the head-of-the-line for the public's savings

CHAPTER 16:
A FORMAL VIEW OF
SUPPLY-SIDE ECONOMICS

For an appreciation of problems from the supply-siders' view-point and a fuller understanding of supply-side economics, we shall present the Keynesian framework of thought in a more formal way than was done earlier in this book. In the process, we shall see that supply-side economics is much more than a trickle down policy, as was suggested by many in 1981; it is also much more of a formal scientific system than even Mr. Stockman, for example, understood it to be.

"SUPPLY-SIDE ECONOMICS AND THE KEYNESIAN FRAMEWORK"

Classical Keynesian economics can be presented by elementary diagrams. Let's do that here, deriving as a result many insights into both the Government spending route and the Reaganomics supply-side route to growth and high employment.

"KEYNESIAN GROWTH DIAGRAMS"

Consider panel (a) in Figure 16–1 below. View it as a map. A one-unit walk to the east from the origin 0, plus next a one-unit

FIGURE 16.1

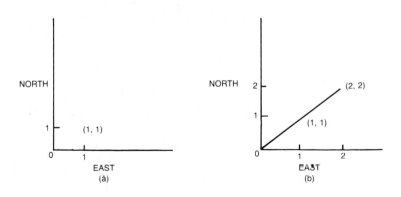

FIGURE 16.2

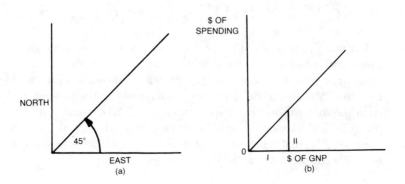

walk to the north would place you at point (1,1). Let us then take an extra unit walk to the east and another to the north; connect point 0 with point (1,1) and with point (2,2), thus obtaining panel (b). Redraw all of this as Figure 16–2, panel (a), where we extend our line and do not record points (1,1) and (2,2) specifically. Now the slope of the line in panel (a) is at a 45° angle, one unit to the east for each unit to the north. The consequence is that the triangle drawn in panel (b) of Figure 16–2 has two equal sides (I and II). Any point along the 45° line has a horizontal measurement (EAST = I) equal to its vertical measurement (NORTH = II). It then follows that if side I stands for the nation's GNP in $, side II shows the same $ of GNP. That GNP, we shall see, need not necessarily be equal to the aggregate demand (AD). We shall refer to the vertical axis in panel (b) as $ of spending (AD) to distinguish it from the $ of GNP viewed along the horizontal axis.

Aggregate Demand, Consumption, and GNP

We found earlier in the book that aggregate demand is the sum of C+I+G+E. We also proposed earlier in the book that in the short run people tend to increase their consumption by smaller amounts than their increases in income. That is to say, we tend to save increasing proportions of our increases in income. Any consumption line C will thus have a smaller (flatter) slope than the 45° line. In fact, if we assume that people will consume a positive quantity even should the nation's GNP be zero, in effect living off their past accumulated wealth (inventories), a consumption line at the zero level of GNP would start at a point such as (A) in panel (a) of Figure 16–3. And since the slope of the consumption line is flatter than the 45° line, we have the consumption line (labelled C) of panel (a). The intersection of this line with the 45° line at point X has a unique meaning. The consumption of the people equals the GNP they produced. (Remember side I equals side II along the 45° line.) No longer would the public be consuming more than was produced, as they would at point (A). Recognize further that at greater levels of income than point X, such as point (P), the consumption amount MN is less than the GNP amount MP (= OM). It follows that positive savings NP exist at point (P).

FIGURE 16.3

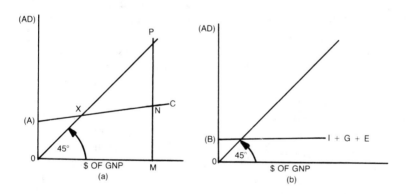

(a)   (b)

I, C, and E, and GNP

Keynesians lump I+G+E together when working with a simple model. For further simplicity we will imagine this composite of spending to be constant regardless of the level of GNP. So we draw the I+G+E line of panel (b) Figure 16–3 parallel to the horizontal axis, placing it at level (B) along the vertical scale. In effect, regardless of how far to the right one looks along the

197

horizontal axis (that is, regardless of how great is the $GNP produced), the I+G+E total (read upward vertically to the I+G+E line) is unchanged at the level (B).

Aggregate Demand, C+I+G+E, the Multiplier, and GNP

Figure 16–4 below combines the I+G+E line with the consumption line C. Its panel (a) shows the sum of the two as the C+I+G+E line. Recognize that at point Y_U, the sum of C+I+G+E (which is the aggregate demand AD) equals the nation's GNP. (Again side I always equal side II along the 45° line.) So we are in the Keynesian equilibrium. But suppose that Y_U stands for 10% of the labor force unemployed. Keynesians would propose that an increase in G to G', which would raise the I+G+E line to the dashed I+G'+E line, would by elementary addition also raise the C+I+G+E line to C+I+G'+E. For simplicity, let us suggest from Chapter 15 that if government spends $5.00 more than it used to spend, A's income rises by $5.00. Let A then spend $2.50 which B receives; so B spends $1.25 more, etc. The triangle GHJ in panel (a) of Figure 16–4 depicts both the total change in income (via the length GH) and the change in consumption (via the length HJ). Unemployment falls from Y_U to the lower unemployment level, Y_{LU}. The increased consumption to $Y_{LU}J$ from Y_UG plus the increase in government from G to G' combine to lead to the greater GNP of Y_{LU}. Recognize further that because consumption is provided by the C line, and at GNP level Y_{LU} is equal to $Y_{LU}J$, the quantity JB is *not* consumed; *and* this quantity (consisting technically of savings, taxes, and imports) equals I+G'+E. (Let us repeat, side I equals side II along the 45° line, or by symbols $OY_{LU} = Y_{LU}B$; so the difference between $Y_{LU}P$ and $Y_{LU}J$ must be I+G'+E. In sum, intersection of AD with the 45° line provides the Keynesian equilibrium, where I = S, or more generally, I+G+E = S+T+M.

The new GNP (at the Keynesian equilibrium point) is—to repeat—Y_{LU}, a lower unemployment level than Y_U. But we assume that it is unfortunately still a level less than the full employment level. So let us suppose next that G is increased to G''. Panel (b) of Figure 16–4 proposes a raised AD to the new C+I+G''+E line and hence equilibrium at Y_F, the full employment level. This is what Keynesian economics contended. Simply raise G enough and the economy will reach full employment.

FIGURE 16.4

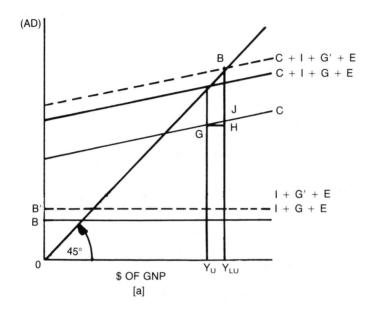

[a]

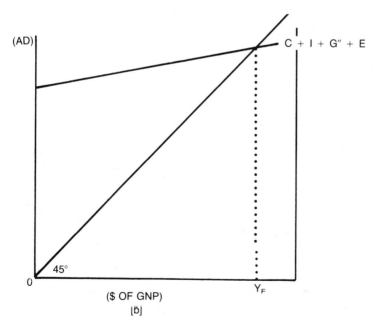

[b]

A FORMAL VIEW OF SUPPLY-SIDE ECONOMICS

Aggregate Demand Elicits Its Own Supply

The Keynesian model presumed that aggregate demand elicits the necessary supply. Thus an increase in aggregate demand, for example an increase in G, will produce an increase in output (GNP).

Keynesian Inflation

Keynesians recognized that if from Y_F in panel (b) of Figure 16–4 we added still another increase in G to say G''', or if E rose or if I rose or if people changed their consumption habits by trying to consume more, any or all of these when the economy was already at capacity (full employment), the result of the rise in AD would be an increase in prices. In other words, the real GNP would be constant beyond Y_F but the nominal (money) income GNP would rise. What they did not recognize is what the supply-siders claim has happened in recent years: inflation at less than full employment, as illustrated below.

"THE SUPPLY-SIDE REVOLUTION"

Consider Figure 16–5. Let C+I+G+E intersect the 45° line at Y_U. Suppose G is increased under political pressure because of the large numbers of unemployed (in effect the number of

FIGURE 16.5

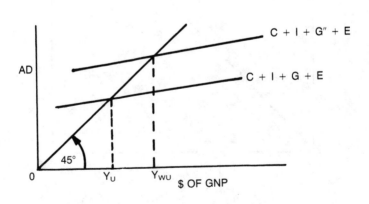

unemployed may be increasing because of a developing recession). Raise the level of aggregate demand AD to $C+I+G''+E$; nominal income may actually rise to Y_{WU}, but at Y_{WU} we mean that real income has actually fallen, with Worse Unemployment occurring. How can this take place? Supply-siders suggest that as government spends, A spends, B spends, C spends, ..., etc. And while many new services may be in the process of being created as a result of these expenditures and the output related to them is rising, other forces exist which are decreasing output; in particular, the heavy tax bite on industry and on consumers, the concern with government spending related to the increase in G to G'', and regulations (EPA, OSHA, CPSC, CAB, FTC, IRS), some of which require an output-contracting retooling of industry, lower output. Though the magnitude of I stays the same or declines less than G increased, total (industrial) output decreases. If furthermore G is increased more than T increases, deficits arise. If the Fed prints the money to buy the deficit, the seeds of runaway inflation really take root. People will then tend to shift from their normal consuming patterns toward buying (more) gems, gold, jewelry, attending more garage sales, and recycling used cars; at the same instance, their savings will move towards land speculations and tax-exempt municipal securities. Meanwhile, the paper profits of companies provide higher tax receipts for government but less liquid financial positions for firms. Uncertainty about regulations and future controls discourages research and development (R&D) expenditures. Short term, quick payoff investments are sought by firms rather than the more productive heavy capital investment. If actual output rises at all, so that Y_{WU} is really not worse unemployment, but slightly improved unemployment (i.e., a somewhat lower level of unemployment), the downswing in productivity nevertheless is a factor. Further increases in G to G''', G'''', . . ., may well be associated with further declines in productivity, more deficits, more M, greater inflation, and steadily rising uncertainty.

People slow down on the job. They seek fringe benefit company vacations, go on strike, accept unemployment compensation payments more readily than heavy taxable jobs. They take more time while unemployed to find satisfactory employment, and their wives and children enter the work force without prior skills. The economy in general runs down. Increasing $GNP proves to be essentially nominal dollar increases in output, as inflation rather than real increased production characterizes the economy.

Increases in AD May Not Stimulate Increases in Real Output

Supply-siders conclude that increases in aggregate demand may not elicit equivalent increases in the goods and services which would improve our real standard of living. The resulting demoralization causes a slow-down in the economy even though the multiplier and nominal GNP are working normally. Supply-siders contend that real economic growth depends on the source and type of increase in demand. They assert that in order to obtain an increase in AD which always elicits an increase in output, we must typically increase I, not always G, under conditions of unemployment. If I and thus supply increases, the economy's AD and real output can generally be expected to remain high compared to the outcome of excessive attempts to use G as the prime vehicle for economic growth.

Supply-Side Economics and Inflation

To illustrate further the supply-siders' theory, return in your mind to late 1981 or early 1982. Supply-siders will say that any attempt in 1982 to apply the traditional quick fix out of the recession then in progress would imply not only living with deficits, but having the Fed buy the new debt. In the process, the federal funds rate would fall, and also interest rates in general. But this, of course, immediately reflects the expanded money supply (M). In fact, not only is there an immediate increase in M (reflective of our government's spending of the money created by the Fed), but at the same time excess reserves are created. These excess reserves enable banks to multiply the amount of new demand deposits. So, from the deficits, unduly large increases in the supply of money take place, further whetting the fires of inflation.

We have seen that inflation carries its own set of supply-side evil forces. Individuals use funds to join in speculative schemes rather than saving and investing their funds in the markets. When government becomes more and more prominent in the business world, tax rates rise, and diverse expenditures of the kind noted above are favored. Worse yet, everyone wants in on the government spending, including consumer advocates, professors opting for research funds, would-be civil servants seeking jobs, environmentalists, and the attorneys who try to win for them. As business starts floundering from the lack of innovation and investment, lower output of business firms appear in the form of OSHA, EPA, and CPSC investigations. Uncertainties as to the meaning of laws for the protection of workers, public health, and consumer safety go along with uncertainties in the tax-law interpretations. They generate a maze of regulations by lawyers which other lawyers cannot decipher.

"KEYNESIAN AND SUPPLY-SIDE ECONOMICS: AN INTEGRATION"

We can now compare directly the early Keynesian applications with the supply-side interpretation. Begin in Figure 16–6 at income $Y_u = 10\%$, that is, 10% of the labor force is unemployed at that income level. Imagine that G is increased to G' so that AD becomes $C+I+G'+E$ in panel (a). Alternatively, let us gain an increase of I to I' in panel (b). Imagine each of the changes, via the multiplier, raises GNP from A to B, and hence incomes to the $Y_u = 8\%$ level of unemployment.

Suppose next in panel (a) that G is raised again to G''. In fact, let the budget be balanced and let the Fed abstain from undue increases in the money supply. Even in the most favorable case for a large government sector, according to conservative analysts, the impact will prove unfavorable sooner or later. A large government sector, even if not characterized by deficits, and an unduly expanded money supply, and therefore high inflation, will still be faced with high interest rates via off-budget growth along with G'' compared to G. Retooling of industry to meet regulations, related uncertainties, punitive tax levels needed to support the big government, all will involve a slowdown in productivity and in growth of output by the industrial sector; it will do this even if I remains constant.* An economic system centered on a large

---

*Actually, the decreased productivity noted above would coincide with inflating costs and prices. Technically, constant I and increased G'' would be in nominal terms only. In real terms, the sum of I+G+E would be, let us broadly suggest, unchanged. Supply-side economics is simply Keynesian economics viewed from the standpoint that inflation may associate with unemployment when G in effect crowds out productive I. The full rigor of Keynesian economics thus applies to supply-side economics. In turn, supply-side economics cannot be simply derogated as a trickle-down theory; rather, effective challenge must involve demonstration that increased real G does *not* involve decreased real I.

A FORMAL VIEW OF SUPPLY-SIDE ECONOMICS

FIGURE 16.6

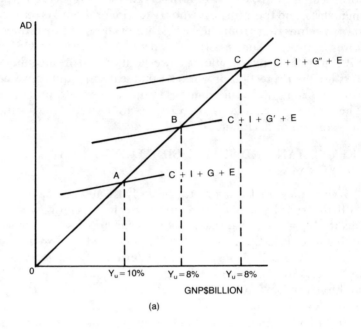

(a)

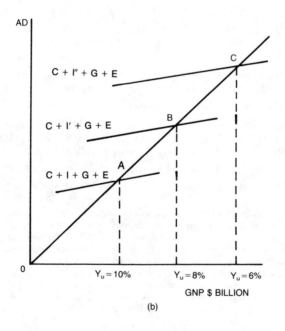

(b)

government sector can also be expected to cater to voter groups in countries such as the United States. Expanded entitlement programs can be expected. All of the above would cause the nation's growth of real output to slow down regularly. So prices would continue to inflate *even without budget deficits and even without undue money creation by the Fed*. Nominal GNP alone would rise from B to C while Y_U could remain at 8%. Panel (b) alternatively demonstrates the supply-siders' view of the effect of raising I to I″, with Y_U falling to $Y = 6\%$.

"HOW WOULD SUPPLY-SIDERS INCREASE EFFECTIVE I?"

How would supply-siders increase effective I? Tax cuts of the Kemp-Roth order will encourage new investments in time. Budget cuts in entitlements and number of civil service employees, simplification of tax reporting and thus reduction in costs associated with preparing tax forms and paying taxes, *and* elimination of or simplification of many regulations and controls over people, will cause business firms to raise their spending on capital inputs. For example, instead of many of the OSHA and CPSC pressures on business, simply strengthening the *rights of workers* to health and safety at work *and of consumers* to safe products would be productive ways of solving these social/economic problems. These solutions can be accomplished *for example* by having the government provide free legal services to workers and consumers harmed by company negligence. The effective result would be self-policing of business without bureaucratic controls and decision-making imposed on firms. Punitive level tax costs for unnecessarily hazardous work conditions or for harmful products can also be imposed; the effect of this would be that businesses and industries would serve as their own policemen.* The return of decision-making to individuals in the private sector, the elimination of capital gains tax and of unduly high levels of personal

---

*In place of EPA regulations by civil servants, applying the bubble concept between companies could simplify pollution controls. Thus a pollutant emission target can be set for an area, leaving companies free to decide who will reduce emissions and how, with those finding it most difficult and expensive to eliminate their pollution paying others to clean up the air sufficiently. Here, too, the effect would be improvement of our environment with minimum use of the government bureaucracy.

and corporate taxes, would bring interest rates down via increased savings. It would, in turn, raise investments manifold. This is the path to sustained non-price inflated economic growth that supply-siders believe can be reached.

Supply-side economics goes well beyond tax reductions. Tax cuts alone do not suffice. Most important is the need to decrease the size of government. Congress has been the fundamental economic problem of our time, according to the supply-sider. Supply-siders hope that the legislators of the future will conceive of ways to help all Americans gain greater freedom; thus they seek simplified record keeping, fewer federal agency regulatory impacts, and minimum size government while still fulfilling the public's social and economic objectives. They — as other concerned Americans — want sufficient income for health and personal care of all. But they stress more than do the original Keynesians the need for freedom in enterprise, freedom in job selection, freedom to join unions or not, and a wide range of alternative opportunities. By encouraging investments and productive work efforts, supply-siders contend that the legislators of the future can accomplish what those of the recent past only gave lip service to.

"FINAL STATEMENT"

Keynesians believed that increases in demand induce matching increases in real supply up to the point where the economy reaches capacity outputs (full employment). Any increases in aggregate demand (AD) beyond this level can only induce inflation in basic Keynesian theory. Supply-siders, on the other hand, believe that we have experienced a slowdown in growth and thus are subject to stagflation because increases in aggregate demand have not elicited sufficient increases in output, even when substantial unemployment existed. Their explanation is that when government became too large, increased public spending chiefly financed paperwork services while regulations also reduced productivity. They claim that the higher taxes needed to finance the increased government spending had disincentive effects on work, savings, and investment. Moreover, large public deficits forced the government to compete with the private sector for increasingly scarce funds. This raised the cost of capital for investment and generated inflationary expectations which further decreased savings. They argue, in addition, that all of this discouraged the *most productive investments* by making longer-term investment prospects even more uncertain than they otherwise would have been. Whereas traditional Keynesians stressed the merits of using government spending to expand aggregate demand, supply-siders *at the most* would favor policy measures that encourage the most productive of private investments.

INTRODUCTION TO PART SIX ON CURRENT ECONOMIC POLICIES

This concluding part of the book applies the economics of our prior pages in the context of our most recent economic events and policies. In a sense, it views *with optimism* the original design of the Reagan administration; it views *with alarm* the most recent (early 1983) concessions of the Reagan administration to the Congress of the United States and the possible return to the spend and tax policies of the sixties and seventies.

Let us pose a question here about deficits and the high interest rates that stem in part from the crowding out of private sector demands for funds by the federal government's demand for funds. Our question to you, the reader, is this: Suppose the prevailing prime interest rate is high, say at ten percent because of a large deficit, and you were paying the same taxes as in the past. Would you be willing to spend more (or invest more in plant and capital) if more of your dollars were being taken by a new tax while the interest rate was dropping to nine percent? Under which circumstance would you feel wealthier or more willing to spend, invest, borrow, or, let us say, take a chance? In considering *your answer*, please keep in mind the many previous statements in this book which claimed that an economic policy desirable in one period of time (for example, no increased taxes during a recession) may be undesirable at another time (for example, no increased taxes during inflation). Moreover, keep in mind the idea that a reduction in the government deficit resulting from higher taxes *may* lower interest rates in the short run because the demand for loanable funds decreases while the supply of loanable funds is *presumably* unchanged. However, a rapid economic recovery with unchanged taxes and a deficit could generate higher incomes, and higher incomes signify less need for certain government expenditures, higher tax receipts, and decreasing deficits. Which avenue is the best: (1) raise taxes now so that we have a balanced budget notwithstanding greater government expenditures, or (2) let the deficit remain and have a more robust recovery? Though a *substantial* deficit *may well be disturbing*, would not the best solution in the 1982–1983 period have been to eliminate governmental wasteful spending while letting full recovery get underway as

completely as possible without imposing greater taxes? *These issues*
and their analysis comprise the general subject matter of Part Six
of the book.

Excerpts on Government Spending from an Editorial Page in the
Wall Street Journal, *8/8/81*

The core untruth in the budgetary fiction the president has
been persuaded to peddle to the American people is the assertion
that the president will get $3 in "spending cuts" from Congress
for every dollar in tax increases he permits. Among people who
have some acquaintance with the budget-making labyrinth, this is
a joke. The trade-off is closer to $3 in tax increases for every
dollar in spending cuts.

The three-for-one fiction was concocted by the Office of Management and Budget and Congress to resolve a deadlock that was
delaying congressional action on the First Concurrent Budget
Resolution for fiscal 1983. As presented to Mr. Reagan, the
president would get $284 billion in "spending cuts" over the next
three years if he would but agree to allow Congress to raise taxes
$98 billion.

That $284 billion sounds like a lot of money until you examine
what it really represents. The compromise actually was designed
to spare Congress the difficulty of cutting the growth in appropriations.

You calculate "spending cuts" in Washington by first setting a
"base line," which theoretically represents what the government
would be spending three years from now if you simply let programs follow their natural tendencies to balloon. If you project
the base line high enough, you can project some enormous
savings, and Congress didn't stint. It projected fiscal 1985 spending at over $1.1 trillion and deducted its $284 billion in "spending
cuts" from that. *Voila!* Fiscal 1985 spending still comes out at $881
billion, up *only* 21% from the current fiscal year.

But let's examine the $284 billion, most of which involves no
congressional action at all. A large chunk, some $36 billion,
consists of so-called "management savings," meaning things the
president could theoretically do on his own, like sell more oil
leases if anyone would buy them. This whole area deserves the
utmost skepticism, as a Federal Reserve Bank of New York study
recently indicated. Worse yet, some of the "savings" are achieved

merely by revising economic forecasts. Over $100 billion is achieved, for example, merely through more optimism about interest costs.

Finally, we get down to what Congress actually intends to cut from the base line. Here it is most instructive to look at what is happening in Congress right now, as it tries to make appropriations bills conform to what it promised in the concurrent resolution.

.

.

.

. . . A projected cut in dairy price supports, for example, will be attained by giving the industry what amounts to a cartel, letting it make up for lost budget money by charging consumers higher prices. And "savings" in Medicare are arrived at by requiring employers to continue health insurance coverage for retirees—in other words a hidden tax. We're told that Dan Rostenkowski's House Ways and Means Committee wants to count this large sum as both a "savings" and a tax to get credit for deficit trimming on both sides of the ledger. "If I tried to do that in a bank, I'd be arrested," says one congressional aide.

.

.

.

. . . larger point is that Congress clearly has no intention of curtailing federal spending. The president is allowing himself to be made a participant in, or victim of, a hoax.

PART SIX:
THE 1980's, GOVERNMENT, AND ECONOMICS

CHAPTER 17:
ON PRICE CONTROLS, AND THE 1980s

The British Tory Party under Margaret Thatcher favored a substantial reduction of government spending, in effect reestablishing fiscal conservatism, and in general reversing the trends toward socialism that prior labor governments had been fostering. In addition to returning certain industries to the private sector, the main thrust in the first year of her prime ministership (1979) was to avoid excessive printing of money. Simply put, Monetaristic policies (and theory) were to replace Keynesian policies (and theory) in the political-economic arena of Great Britain.

"THE THATCHER GOVERNMENT"

Mrs. Thatcher's accomplishments in the first year of office were praiseworthy. Britain's stiff income tax rates (particularly in the higher brackets) were lowered, albeit at the expense of sharp increases in sales taxes. Government spending and government aid to troubled industries were cut. Resale to private owners of some of Britain's nationalized companies was begun. Government wage guidelines and dividend controls were abolished as well as the "Price Commission" that had authority to block industrial price increases. Even the exchange controls, which for over thirty years had limited the amount of money Britons could take in or out of the country for business or personal use, were eliminated.

The inflexible determination of Mrs. Thatcher and her supporters became subject to "nit-picking" before year's end. Economic trends are not quickly reversible, and *inflation continued to rise*, up to 20 percent. At the same time *unemployment increased to* 5.3 percent of the work force. Promised future income-tax cuts were being downplayed by Parliament's refusal to go the full route with Mrs. Thatcher. Meanwhile, *interest rates rose* to over 15 percent on home mortgages. (Notice how comparable the British data were with those of the United States.) The greatest concern among her followers was the recognition that Monetarist policies and goals are slow moving—that two or three years at least would be required before they would have the desired effect. Apparently Parliament, labor union officials, and the general public *were not willing to wait that long.*

By the end of 1979 critics were claiming that too many mistakes were being made: the credit screws were too tight and the budget should not be cut in the face of recession. Others were concerned about the time required for monetary changes to work out. They argued that big cuts in government spending to reduce the budget deficit would work faster than would decreases in the growth of the money supply. But the spending cuts that were effected in 1979 were actually modest; they merely eliminated the increases previously planned by the Labor party.

Continued high budget deficits were forecasted for 1980 and 1981, as budget cuts appeared difficult to effect—even with the conservative party's dedication to reduce government spending. Further income tax cuts also appeared remote. One of the most critical complaints heard in late 1979 was that Mrs. Thatcher tried to do too many things too quickly. Mrs. Thatcher's insistence that government should not regulate wages was being met by a 21 percent pay increase at Ford Motor Company's British unit. And union leaders were contending that the Tories were "kicking the working class in the pants" by increasing unemployment, inflating prices, and smashing the nation's health service. One would have thought—on the basis of Labor party claims—that Great Britain had been a rapidly developing economic and political *power* under the stewardship of their party.

"WHAT NOW IN GREAT BRITAIN"

Great Britain, as the United States, continued to experience inflation in 1980; in fact, its inflation was worse than in the United States and had been going on for a longer period of time. So the economic problem there, in many ways, was (and remains) much deeper than here.

By early 1980, the Tory party's deference to political pressures had begun to be evident by a backsliding from its original program. Obsession with a balanced budget had already led Parliament to *increase taxes* rather than to provide investment incentives to businesses. Of all things, a windfall profit tax on North Sea Oil, which had been *raised* from 45% to 60% in 1978 by the labor government, was raised again in early 1980 to 70% by Mrs. Thatcher's government. This was indeed a surprising change in practice (from monetaristic practices), particularly in a country where business leaders have been especially reluctant to invest in capital improvements. Meanwhile, *social welfare programs appeared out of control* and extra-large returns to civil servants continued. Total public spending in proportion to GNP was budgeted *upwards* from a 42% rate for the fiscal year ending April 5, 1980 to 42.5% for the year ending April 5, 1981. To pay for this *increased* spending by government, taxes were scheduled to rise by 22.6%. As a result, the private sector continued to be starved for resources, and likely increases in interest rates were projected. Most surprisingly, the growth in the money supply continued to be excessive, until quite recently. One thing was clear—the strong union-based control of politicians was so deeply entrenched that return from a highly regulated state back toward a laissez-faire state was proving to be more difficult than Mrs. Thatcher had hoped. What was taking place in the United States during this same period of time?*

"THE CARTER ADMINISTRATION PROGRAM"

By April, 1980 the Carter administration's program for controlling inflation had been clearly defined. The growth of money supply was to be held back partly by high Fed discount rates.

---

*We might observe here in final note of Great Britain that its economy appears to be improving in early 1983, although its overall picture is still mixed. The main gain is the sharp drop in the inflation rate, from over 20 percent in 1980 to less than 5 percent currently. Pay increases have been moderate and interest rates have fallen. Another bright spot is a sharp rise in productivity, especially in manufacturing. Investment appears to be picking up at last. And the economy grew slightly last year after two years of decline; it is expected to do better this year. Unemployment, however, is still some 13 percent of the labor force. The combination of high welfare payments and heavy taxation of low wages continues to make work not worthwhile to many. Some strikes have been defeated, others averted, as the economic realities and Thatcher's determination sink home. But the government so far has failed to reduce the total burden of taxation, primarily because of inability to curtail expenditures.

Severe constraints on the spending of consumers were finally being imposed. In addition, increased taxes (chiefly due to higher incomes and the windfall profit tax on oil) were projected to help balance the budget and to slow down the inflation. Unfortunately, controlling inflation by bringing about recession is a debatable and dangerous practice, especially since breaking down the inflationary psychology in an oligopolistic economy could require substantial unemployment. The Carter-Volcker policy appeared to many to portend great risk, not only to the stability of the American economy but to its political-social base as well. To project a gradual decrease in inflation at the cost of substantial unemployment could well intensify social tensions. Those who would be hurt the most would *not* be experienced workers laid off from given jobs; rather, unemployment compensation payments and labor union payments would keep most of these individuals relatively content. Instead, it would be the younger worker, even the young college graduate with important new skills, who would bear the brunt of the program. Most fundamentally, the policy would not deal with the structural sources of inflation: low private capital investment, low savings, low productivity, excessive government red tape, and excessive public spending. Would wage and price controls be a better way to stop inflation? Senator Ted Kennedy was claiming they would.

"MANDATORY WAGE AND PRICE CONTROLS FOR THE 1980's?"

Economists, many politicians, and a rather large number of the American public—who were concerned with the idea of squeezing inflation by increasing unemployment—actually began to advocate involuntary wage and price controls in late 1979 and early 1980. We must, accordingly, evaluate the pros and cons of these controls.

"ARGUMENTS FOR THESE CONTROLS"

Those in favor of involuntary wage and price controls were contending that: 1) Average hourly compensation in the country had increased by about 9% in 1978 while average hourly output had increased only about 1%. The 8% or so residue thus represented an underlying hard core of inflation. By limiting wage-price increases, inflation would be reduced, if not eliminated. 2)

It was claimed that the Carter administration's policy of producing a moderate recession would not work; it would simply disadvantage certain workers and small companies, in many cases unduly so. 3) A sharp recession would, in fact, be necessary, requiring a substantial reduction in spending and a sharp cutback in the money supply. It was estimated that only a 1% decrease in inflation would take place for every $200 billion of decreased GNP. Under wage and price controls, the 200/1 ratio would fall toward 100/1. 4) Proponents of wage and price controls finally argued that within a year or so after the controls were imposed, inflation would be cut to 5% or less, at which time the controls could be removed.

Supporting Arguments that So-Called "Uncontrollables" are Controllable

Certain questions immediately arise: What about prices that are not controllable? Would not rising food costs due to a drought, or rising prices due to OPEC controls, or the rising interest rates partly within and partly outside of the control of the Fed, tend to bring down the controls? The answer to these questions was "No," according to the proponents of wage and price controls. They argued that an alert economic policy which would include deescalation of agricultural price supports (imagine the House Agriculture Committee's reaction to this) and effective management of agricultural reserves, besides limiting the amount of land set aside in soil banks, would help reduce sky-rocketing food prices. Moreover, *rationing* of gas would limit the impact of OPEC. Finally, the wage and price guidelines themselves would not only lower the inflation rate, but in the process would stop the rise in interest rates. They concluded, accordingly, that the *uncontrollables* were in fact *controllable*.

"ARGUMENTS AGAINST THESE CONTROLS"

Those who were against wage-price controls stressed the arguments that: 1) Controls, in effect, suspend the individual's freedom of choice. This occurs because *governmental* decision making substitutes for *individual* decisions. 2) Cheating and corruption often takes place when people are subject to wage and price controls. 3) Controls would require at least 4,000 regulators in place of the 200 that were supervising the voluntary wage and price guidelines of the Carter administration. 4) Controlling oil prices would reverse the nation's current energy policy and place the country at the mercy of OPEC. And by not controlling oil, or selected farm products, or housing, or the interest rate, the "Pandora's Box" for other decontrols would open up. 5) The real need in the country as of 1980, they asserted, was to increase business investments. That increase would enhance worker productivity, while more bureaucratic regulations would have the opposite effect.

Supporting Arguments that Controls Would be Regimenting

It was further contended that controls would have to be imposed on more than 10 million business establishments and wages set for many millions of workers. Regulations of this magnitude would build up pressures for the decontrol of many products and many industries. As a matter of fact, the Nixon wage and price freeze of 1971–1973 curbed inflation for only about six months, as prices started to rise *rapidly* by late 1972; in fact, by early 1973 they were rising more than 6%, an increase greater than the inflation rate of 1970. It was also noted in further reference to the history of the Nixon wage and price freeze that shortages quickly developed in copper, zinc, aluminum, and lead. World prices of these minerals had risen rapidly in that period, providing an export boom and causing subsequent shortages of them in the United States. Among other products that were *victimized* by the 1971–73 wage-price freeze were paper products, in particular newsprint. An extreme shortage occurred in "mine roof bolts," which hampered coal output—the bolts that *were produced* were exported to Canada and then imported back into the United States in order to avoid the American controls on them. The Nixon wage and price controls also resulted in producers slaughtering livestock and poultry rather than undergoing substantial marketing losses. Many agricultural economists assert that the reduction of the size of herds due to the Nixon controls continued to affect the American economy as late as 1980.

It was also contended by those who object to wage-price controls that well before March, 1974 (when the controls were taken off by the Nixon administration), fertilizers, zinc, aluminum, auto tires, furniture, paper products, coal, shoes, and many other products had already been decontrolled. They further contended that if we are to limit the prices on housing in the 1980's, how would millions of homeowners who plan to sell their houses be controlled? Instead of only 4,000 regulators, perhaps as many as 200,000 bureaucrats would be required to police a strong wage and price control program in the 1980's, as George Meany claimed would be necessary.

"CONTROLS AND MACRO POLICY"

Practically every economist in the United States agrees that sooner or later controls fail and a free enterprise economy is left where its basic monetary-fiscal policies would have placed it. Many who favor price controls insist they would not repeat the error of the Nixon administration, but rather would impose a tight macro policy. Nevertheless, a fundamental critique remains. A fair and equitable system of controls would require a substantial bureaucracy; the paperwork in the country would become even more time consuming and costly than in the late 1970's. This paperwork reflects income without any production of goods. The effect would be more budgetary red ink.* Most significantly, during the early periods of time after enactment of controls—when *wages and prices would indeed be held down*—a strong tendency would prevail to pursue an expansionary macro policy. This likelihood possibly serves as *the most important reason* to prefer almost any proposed panacea for inflation to wage and price controls. But what panacea would the present authors favor?

"DIAGNOSING THE PROBLEM: SUPPLY-SIDE ECONOMICS AGAIN"

Before settling on the best remedies for the stagflation of the 70's and early 80's, a final diagnosis of causes is needed. What makes the present economic situation quite different from previous inflations is the "snail's pace" growth in productivity in the late '70s, and its recent declines. Decreased productivity is basically inflationary even with a balanced budget and a small public

---

*One of the authors of this book was a price controller during the Korean war. In his opinion, the costs and delays in processing complaints alone are significantly damaging to efficient economic activity.

sector. Therefore, the traditional policies of fiscal and monetary restraint for coping with inflation, although necessary, would not be sufficient.

The average rate of increase in productivity (output per unit of input) was 2.8% a year between 1948 and 1966. This annual average dropped to 1.6% between 1966 and 1973, and dropped further to 0.8% between 1973 and 1978.* The year 1966 was an approximate turning point, the beginning of protracted inflation initiated by increased commitments in Vietnam without timely changes in tax or other policies.

What would have happened to total output and to price levels had productivity grown since 1966 at the same rate as it grew between 1948 and 1966? This is a complicated question to which we can here attempt only a simplified answer. Output in 1978 would have been 25% higher than it turned out to be, assuming an unchanged input of productive factors. Since in fact part of the increase in productivity would have led to an increased supply of productive factors (including capital), output in 1978 (assuming unemployment rates unchanged) should have been more than 25% greater than it was.

What would have happened to prices? As a very rough estimate, the tradeoff between productivity and price increases for the post World War II period appears to be − 1:3; that is, a one percent drop in the annual rate of productivity increase is associated with roughly a three percent increase in the consumer price index. (See Table 17.1.) On the basis of this historical relation (which could change), one can estimate that if the 1948–1966 rate of productivity gain had been maintained, inflation between 1973 and 1978 would have been close to 2% rather than at 8%. In 1979, productivity declined by 1.2%. By using the − 1:3 relation, and knowing that the *decline* in productivity for 1979 totaled 2% from the 1973–1978 value, one could have predicted inflation in 1979 at 14% (it was actually 13.3%).** We obtain this last figure since

---

*John Kendrick, "Productivity Trends and the Recent Slowdown," in William Fellner, ed., *Contemporary Economic Problems 1979* (Washington, D.C.: American Enterprise Institute, 1979), p. 33.

**The estimated negative 1.2% in productivity is based on labor productivity only whereas the productivity data shown in Table 17.1 reflect all productive resources and hence are in a slightly different context than the − 1.2% figure mentioned above.

TABLE 17.1

PRODUCTIVITY AND PRICES

	Productivity Increase	Price Increase
1948–1966	2.8%	2%
1966–1973	1.6%	5%
1973–1978	0.8%	8%

the negative 1979 productivity was 2% less than in the 1973–78 period; and therefore the inflation rate would rise by 6%.

Of course, the above numerical relation assumes a more direct correspondence between productivity and inflation than is really the case. Besides low productivity, big public deficits associated with substantial growth of money will generate inflation. Furthermore, inflation brings about inflationary expectations which, in turn, stimulate the fires of inflation further. The combination raises the numerical relation more than would otherwise be the case. We contend, accordingly, only that *given the slowdown in productivity and the government policies of recent decades, prices have been rising at a 3/1 rate with respect to each slowdown in productivity.*

"CAUSES OF LAG IN PRODUCTIVITY GROWTH"

What are the causes of the lag in productivity growth? Such knowledge is essential in designing appropriate responses. Whatever policies restore our past growth rate in productivity would also *reduce* the rate of inflation. The causes are complex, numerous, and not yet completely understood. Some, such as OPEC price increases are beyond our control, although we could have avoided policies increasing our dependence on imported oil. The increased proportion of the labor force consisting of inexperienced workers is largely the outcome of the earlier baby boom and will soon cease to be a depressing factor. Some other causes, however, are the result of past policies and are within our control. The immediate causes are *inadequate investment* and a *change in the composition of investment,* reducing its contribution to growth. But why? William Fellner suggests that

221

"Some of the recent difficulties are apt to be related directly to the political process. The list of such 'suspects' includes uncertainties and distortions created by inflationary policies; tax disincentives reducing the amount of investment in productive activities that are risky for the individual investor; and the specific uncertainties, reduction of competition, and burden of paperwork caused by administrative controls and regulations. Another suspect is a legal-institutional setting conducive to a lessened emphasis on competence and work effort. . ."*

Lagging investment is in part the result of inadequate resources for investment, in part the result of depressed expectations of profit. The large and increasing share of government in the economy and the huge deficits financed by borrowing reduce the share of resources, including credit, that is available to business; it drives up the price of credit. The resulting inflation reduces the real value of business depreciation allowances, based as they are on historical costs. Business profits decline, and so do business savings. The expectation of more inflation eventually persuades individuals to consume more and save less. Incentives to invest are also decreased by the growth of government, the effects of inflation on tax liabilities and expected profits, and the magnification of uncertainty caused by unstable prices.

More important than the inadequate *amount* of investment is a change in industrial *composition* which has the effect of decreasing possible gains in productivity. Diversion of investments to comply with regulations, to protect business from prosecution, to reduce pollution, to protect employee health and safety, have already been stressed in the book.** This type of cost expenditure does

---

*William Fellner, "The Declining Growth of American Productivity: An Introductory Note," in Fellner, Editor, *Contemporary Economic Problems 1979* (Washington: American Enterprise Institute, 1979), p. 4.

**There are many who believe worker health and safety, as well as consumer product safety, require government interference. In contrast, M.L. Weidenbaum, *Business Government, and the Public* (Englewood Cliffs, New Jersey: Prentice Hall, 1981) stresses the misguided policies of the Consumer Product Safety Commission and those of the Occupational Safety and Health Administration. With respect to the former, he argues in favor of better information to consumers and allowing market competition to play a more important role; he wants the firm to seek advantage over the rival by stressing the safety of its product(s). As for the latter, he critiques standards being set by government officials rather than analyzing causes of injury and choosing appropriate ways to eliminate them, such as tough enforcement of liability.

not increase capacity, but reduces it; it also does not lower the cost of production, but raises it. Its contribution to productivity is negative.

Beyond the impact of regulation, there is the outcome of inflation on the *composition* of capital investment. Because inflation magnifies *risks*, businesses concentrate investment on minor improvements with little risk and almost immediate payoff; they avoid the costly innovative investments that take a long time to pay off and which in turn would offer the possibility of major gains in productivity and capacity. In particular, firms reduce their commitment to the investments with the greatest uncertainty and longest gestation period, in effect cutting down on research and development work. Ultimately productivity growth depends on previous research and development activity. Neglect of research and development is one of the most damaging consequences of recent public policies and attitudes.

"A PROPOSED PROGRAM TO COMBAT INFLATION"

We shall discuss our program for the current economic malaise in this country in three steps. Initially, we shall recall from earlier pages the art of economics, the reason why economists often appear to disagree with each other. After this is done, we shall briefly evaluate President Reagan's program. Then we shall draw our final conclusions.

"THE ART OF ECONOMICS"

Two economists who accept the same theoretical framework may disagree on their "preferred policy." For example, *even if* two economists accept the Keynesian framework of thought as their model, *even if* they agree the economy is in a state of recession, and *even if* they agree government should cut taxes to provide the spark to revive the economy, they may very well disagree on the *specific tax cut* that is needed. One may assert great fear of Russia and contend that an increase in business investments must take place; this economist would therefore tend to favor accelerated depreciation allowances and the like. The other may argue that being poor remains the number one problem, and favor a tax cut to increase the well-being of the poor; in effect, this economist would want to increase consumption in the country.

Disagreements may be found among economists who subscribe to different theories; for example some economists may contend that the Monetarist framework will explain more completely certain economic conditions than Keynesian economics; or there are supply-side theorists who rather than stress the demand side effects of C + I + G + E, borrow from the other side of Keynesian economics in evaluating the conditions affecting productivity, investments, and savings. (The next chapter of this book explains why we neither regard ourselves as Keynesians, Monetarists, or for that matter Supply-Siders.) Disagreements among economists as to the most applicable theory for a given situation is, therefore, intrinsic to the problem of what should be done about stagflation in the United States. Such differences should be kept in mind as we turn to our own policy proposals.

"THE REAGAN ADMINISTRATION ECONOMIC PROGRAM OF EARLY 1981"

The prior explanations in this book of Keynesian and Monetarist economics recognize that the supply-side emphasis on falling productivity and inadequate output can be understood in terms of either of these systems of thought. Let us observe from Keynesian economics that the tax laws of recent years have essentially favored the very poor, and possibly the very wealthy who usually have tax dodges available to them which were either deliberately provided for them in the tax bills or accidentally discovered by the tax lawyers and accountants in their employ. The majority of income recipients, ranging from, say, the $12,000 to the $120,000 income class, find themselves restricted in their wealth accumulation and their incentives to work. For those in the upper part of this group, savings are placed in land speculation schemes, in gold, jewelry, and other get-rich-quick ventures; or else the very conservative among them place their savings in insured tax exempt municipals, horse breeding, vacation condos, and the like. Their savings tend *not* to be returned to the economic system in the form of productive industrial activity. Speaking relatively *and marginally*, construction of new factories with new technologies tends to decrease, and supply-side shortages emerge. At the same time, individuals in this large class tend to opt for more leisure time rather than greater work effort amid excessive taxation. Inflation-caused "tax bracket creep" further

224

induces individuals to seek leisure and to opt for get-rich-quick schemes.

In the development of economic thought, supply-side adherents differ from many Keynesian economists. Nevertheless, we propose that all three viewpoints are actually part and parcel of a broad macroeconomic theory which would recognize that certain *applications* of Keynesian economics in governmental attempts at fine-tuning have failed. This failing is stressed by the monetarists; indeed the inability to fine-tune reappears in part as inadequate output.

For at least the early years of the 1980's, we propose that (1) excessive government spending in the '70s, (2) excessive political scapegoating of industry, (3) the failure to recognize the importance to an effective economy of the $12,000 to $120,000 class of income recipients, and (4) misapplications of Keynesian thought by Congress and a money creating Fed have produced an economy in trouble. This economy will in time require a balanced or surplus budget *along with* a slowdown in money creation; at the same time, a vital need exists to provide tax cuts that would stimulate savings earmarked for use in capital industrial development (and hence greater productivity). What should be done has been clear. Before evaluating further, let us examine some of the critiques that were levelled against so-called "Reaganomics" in early 1981.

Critiques of Reaganomics

Apart from traditional critiques of budget cuts and tax changes needed for the $12,000 to $120,000 and even higher income class, the question has been raised why a supply-side oriented administration continues certain tax shelters and why it does not propose eliminating many interest payment deductions from income taxes. Clearly, these tax devices do not stimulate business capital-forming expenditures; on the contrary, these shelters and deductions have and will have perverse supply-side effects. Another objection is the claim that the administration's economic program does not provide sufficient advantages for investment by small business establishments, nor investment in what economists refer to as "human" capital — e.g., education aids and loans. The criticism has been raised that little encouragement is being given those receiving welfare payments to do *some* work rather than none at all. Most well known of all these critiques is the claim that the administration's receipt and spending projections were based on false econometric premises: namely, that the real GNP will surge at a 4.5% rate between 1982 and 1985, that investment will jump about 5% higher in ratio to GNP than it has been, and that inflation and interest rates will drop sharply.

Counter Arguments

Notwithstanding critiques of the kinds mentioned above, the present writers repeat their fundamental support of the overall program. In their view, except for certain specific improvements which Americans may not really want for many years (such as eliminating many of the tax shelters we have in our present income tax provisions, and possibly eliminating deductions from taxes for interest payments on credit card debt, and the like), we were not nor are we impressed by the opposition. In particular, we believed that if "Reaganomics" had been completely (and realistically) approved by the Congress along the lines of the administration's original tax and spending-cut proposals, there would have been a significant change in public attitudes and expectations. A tendency to increase savings would arise and, at the same time, greater business investments would raise the GNP and the nation's tax receipts, leading eventually to a balanced budget. Desirable projections on investments, the GNP, inflation, and the interest rates could have been realized if the Congress of the United States had fully supported the administration. At the worst, we believe that considerable economic improvement will result in time even if the present course is left alone.

What About Inflation Resulting from Tax Cuts?

What about the claim that the Kemp-Roth type of tax cuts would have stimulated inflation? Our answer to that should be evident from the above. Tax cuts designed chiefly to induce consumption would indeed whet the forces of inflation. In our view, Congress does the most good for the poor by stimulating the work efforts of *everyone* and helping to channel savings into productive industrial pursuits. If any tilt appeared in order in the early 1980's, it was the need to eliminate, if not just to limit, the tax

226

dodges available to the very wealthy. All of this is not to favor *in any form* highly progressive taxing of the very wealthy class. (We favor highly progressive taxes on consumption . . . see the Appendix on the income tax.) Rather, all Americans must dream and aspire to substantial personal economic improvement and have their innovativeness and individualism encouraged. But egregious escapes from taxes are undesirable, and incentives to save could still be fostered; in the process, all classes would benefit from the resulting healthy economy—the poor, the lower middle-income class, the higher-middle income class, and the very wealthy of our country. Tax cuts favoring consumption would be inflationary, while across-the-board tax cuts tend to be productive of greater output; if—in the process—inflationary expectations were reduced, the inflation itself would soon be ended. When tax rates are so high as to discourage savings, investment, and productivity gains, it is possible for a tax cut to reduce inflation and even to increase tax revenues in the long run. It does this through its stimulus to productivity growth. This is the argument underlying the so-called Laffer curve, as depicted in Figure 17.1.

FIGURE 17.1

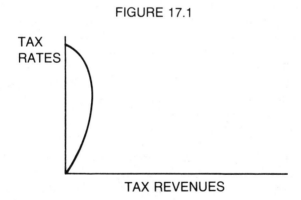

TAX
RATES

TAX REVENUES

In 1981 we believed that if Congress would do essentially what the Reagan administration was proposing—(1) get rid of excessive regulations and paperwork; (2) reduce the tax burden of all Americans; and (3) cut bureaucratic spending *substantially*—the American economy would begin to move forward in the near future.

ON PRICE CONTROLS, AND THE 1980s

"THE REAGAN ADMINISTRATION PROGRAM AS IT APPEARED TO US IN EARLY 1982"

As the reader knows, the tax cuts passed by Congress in the summer of 1981 did conform somewhat to President Reagan's package. To be sure, instead of the Kemp-Roth tax cut or a 10% tax cut each year for three years beginning in January 1981, the cut will total 25% over thirty-three months, and it first began in October 1981. There were other differences. But nit-picking of differences is undesirable and unnecessary. The basic Reagan tax package, including indexing in 1985, was passed. Is it working? Will it work? Our answers are yes. Please note, the fundamental structural change brought about by the administration in 1981 takes time to impact. Businessmen must believe in it. They must see it *not* as a temporary aberration, as was the case in Mrs. Thatcher's first year in office, but something they can rely upon. The consumer has to change his continuing inflationary expectations, and this requires time. From where we started in early 1981 to early 1982 was tantamount to seeing a boy play sandlot football and next seeing him as a college All-American ready to play in the pros in a year or two. Certainly the job is not done. Paperwork is still excessive; deep budget cuts are needed. Tax shelters and the like should be minimized, some avoidances eliminated entirely. The whole income tax law should be restructured and conspicuous consumption taxes imposed (see the Income Tax Appendix to this book). The road to rapid economic growth lies in the future. In our opinion, we are in the process of first getting to that road. What about the huge deficit? Let's delay that matter to the final chapter of the book.

"FINAL STATEMENT"

Inflationary price increases rest on a two-pronged foundation: excessive quantities of money and insufficient quantities of saleable goods and services. Reducing the money supply *alone* will reduce inflation, but at a high cost of unemployment. To increase saleable goods and services output, more private business investment in capital goods and a smaller public sector is required. The elimination of excessive paperwork and selected regulation is sorely needed. Special industrial tax breaks can be offered to firms maintaining or actually lowering their prices in the presence of rising costs. Across-the-board lowered tax rates took place

228

in 1981. Lower marginal rates on interest and dividend income were also established. Reductions in the capital gains tax and even the inheritance tax were set forth, though with respect to the capital gains tax we are still not in the same league as Japan. Also intrinsic to the package is the need to continue to provide accelerated depreciation and other investment incentives. Further tax and budget reductions should be planned. The tax cuts would offset the recessionary effects of decreased public expenditures, stimulate private investment and further tend to decrease inflationary expectations. The immediate impact of this overall program would be to slow down the rate of inflation well below that which voluntary wage-price guidelines could ever achieve. It would also place the United States completely back on the path of economic growth that characterized its past, while augmenting the great advantages the free enterprise system offers the people.

CHAPTER 18:
KEYNESIAN, MONETARIST, AND SUPPLY-SIDE ECONOMICS: WHICH TO USE?

We stated earlier that "our" own policy proposals depend on the position of our country in the world, both economically and politically. Under certain conditions, we would favor Monetarism; under others, supply-side economics; and under still others, more classical Keynesian applications. This chapter will synthesize our views, with particular stress on conditions in early 1983.

"THEORETICAL POSITION"

We believe monetaristic economics provides great insights, but chiefly as a long-run explanation of prices and the level of unemployment. We contend that for short-term uses the theoretical system of Monetarism is too simple, too narrow, and may we say too abstract. Its reliance on the concept of a supply curve of money is troublesome, since what is money and what is the supply of money are subject to dispute. Correspondingly, making Monetarism work requires greater knowledge than is currently possessed by economists.

"PROBLEMS IN MONETARISM"

The simplifications accepted in the Monetarist's demand-supply analysis of money downplay the fact of administered (monopoly) pricing by businesses and unions (e.g., regulated airlines and ALPA, the airline pilots' union); the analysis does not weight as heavily as it should the importance of credit cards and other substitutes for *money* besides the recent growth and extended life of receivables; it underplays the effect on prices of paper bids which never reach contract stage, the increase in bad debts and government bail-outs or prospective bail-outs, to say little about the improved quality of goods which is *not* included successfully in the cost of living indices. Money substitutes are not covered adequately by the concept of money supply. Most of the economic forces just mentioned are conceived of in the theory as influencing the demand curve for money. Sooner or later an excessive supply of money (M1 or M2)* *will support* a high price level; sooner or later an insufficient growth in that supply of money will yield a lower price level. But we emphasize *sooner* or *later* even though we recognize that a squeeze at any point in time on the availability of bank loans (probably more so than encouraging expansion of bank loans) will reduce (speed up) exchanges in the market, besides creating temporarily higher (lower) rates of interest that affect the macroeconomy. Our caveat on the money supply as *the key* determiner of employment and price levels reflects our belief that if the overall economic climate is in conflict with a money crunch (or its opposite), the velocity (turnover) of money and the use of money substitutes (expanded or contracted credit card use) will tend to offset changes in the supply of money, both in the immediate present and the short run as well.**

Indeed, the problems of Monetarist theory extend directly to the question whether the Fed can properly control interest rates and *hence whether* simple annual increases in the money supply as proposed by the Monetarists *could be* stabilizing and sufficient. Consider in this regard the following scenario proposed in greater detail in late 1981 by Mr. Rutledge of the Claremont Institute:

Imagine *you*, and all of us in general, are conceiving of increased inflation in a year or two. All would therefore want to buy land, buildings, carpets, new and used cars, diamonds, and the like; we would tend to sell financial assets such as stocks and in particular bonds. Rutledge professes that people may well switch out of trillions of dollars of financial assets into trillions of dollars of nonfinancial assets. The upshot is a depressed set of prices for stocks and bonds so that rates of interest rise. (Note that if interest

---

*M1 money includes cash and regular checking accounts at commercial banks as well as NOW accounts and other checking accounts at all depository institutions. M2 money essentially adds to M1 money short-term savings accounts at commercial banks and thrift institutions.

**Mr. Lewis Lehrman observed in his article "The Means to Establishing Financial Order," *Wall Street Journal*, Wed., February 18, 1981, p. 20, that the quantity of money during part of 1978 grew by about 30% in Switzerland while its price level rose about 1%. Conversely, the money supply in the United States grew about 5% in 1979 and 1980 while its consumer price index rose about 13%.

rates are at 10%, a $1,000 bond would be issued to pay $100 a year. If rates of interest rise to 20%, that same bond would fall in market value to $500 in order to net 20% for a purchaser; new bonds to be issued must therefore also provide the same 20%.) We abstracted completely in this scenario from the Fed's monetary policy. To be sure, the Fed could enact a tight money policy which would *tend* to decrease the inflationary expectations of the public; or by loose money policy, it could whet inflationary expectations. The main point is that people can act somewhat independently of and counter to the Fed, which in turn *may or may not* strongly influence the public's actions. Interest rates may accordingly remain high or go higher even after tax cuts are passed (as in the August through October period of 1981). The Fed has more influence on the supply of money and its turnover in the long run than it has in the short run.

"PROBLEMS IN KEYNESIAN ECONOMICS"

Keynesian economics originally stressed the idea that by boosting aggregate demand, more and more people could be employed up to the level of full employment. Supply was implicitly considered to follow demand until capacity limits were reached, after which point inflation would result. Monetarists, too, claimed that once capacity was reached, inflation must surely follow. In their scenario, a greater supply of money would generate increased spending and hence employment gains if that increased supply originated in periods of less than full employment. Unlike the Keynesians, however, they further recognized that deficits supported by the printing of money could well generate a rightward shifting of the Phillips curve. Given this precondition, inflation would occur at less than capacity output levels. The Keynesian prescription therefore fails according to Monetarists in that inflation may take place even with less than full employment income. Moreover, according to supply-siders, increasing government demand may not stimulate private sector output.

"PROBLEMS IN SUPPLY-SIDE ECONOMICS"

This book has emphasized the existence of a real world in which monetary valuations play their role. That *real world* includes an economic climate affected by international economic conditions. It includes the basic productivity of a people, the set of freedoms under which they operate, the regulations to which they are subject, and the controls over the market exercised by government agencies, trade associations, business and union monopolies. All of these serve as the fundamental factors affecting economic growth, the ups and downs of business and prices. They constitute the supply-side elements that are vitally important in determining price levels, even though—as noted in Chapter 17—simply maintaining productivity at 1960 levels would not necessarily have meant price level stability in the 1970's and 1980's.

We are thus proposing that inflation *could* take place even in the presence of a modest growth in the money supply that only matches (not exceeds) the growth in productivity. By making government a larger part of the nation's total GNP, an economy tends to generate increased paperwork and other government output valued essentially at cost. This governmental output involves a decreased amount of saleable goods in the market, and hence constitutes what would be a short-run price-increasing force even under a constant supply of money. To the extent that regulations and deficit-driven higher interest rates bring about relative decreases in investments in capital goods, an economy subject to a given supply of money and supply inducing incentives will still find costs and prices rising.

"COMBINING THE THEORIES"

Notwithstanding the disclaimers to Monetarism, *money does count*. No matter how extensive the upward biases of administered pricing, no matter how large the government sector *and* how limited the growth of productivity, etc., there cannot be a generalized, long-lasting double-digit price inflation without a greatly expanded money supply (*or the* institutional development and acceptance of money substitutes). Yet to think of money alone or the supply of saleable goods alone would reflect a myopia with unfortunate overtones. It *is* rather the case that money *does combine with* the state of the arts and the resource base (i.e., the real structural underpinnings of the economy) to promote an expansion or contraction of economic activity, a rising or falling price level, as the case may be. It follows that the Fed and the Treasury must complement each other in order for the economy to find itself once again on the path of economic growth without inflated prices and high unemployment.

"THE ART OF ECONOMICS: WHICH THEORY?"

A final question about theory and its applications remains: Which is the most effective tool: monetary policy or fiscal policy (in which we now include supply-side emphasis)? Alternatively phrased, should the consumption function be altered by government design, should the investment sector be stimulated, should the government sector be expanded, should regulatory agencies be abolished, *ad infinitum*? Our book proposed that what might have worked well at any past moment of time will not necessarily be the best policy at another moment of time. This is, not a "cop-out-plea" at all! It is rather to say that the effect of changes in monetary policy blend with and affect the non-monetary forces in the economy. People learn from experience, so that next time their rational expectations are different from the last time, and so is their behavior. But history does not repeat itself perfectly. The effect of a large public deficit today, or of an excessive increase in M, is different from what it would have been in 1962. Possibly the greatest shortcoming of Monetarism is its reliance on a perfectly competitive microeconomic framework when, in fact, the micro-world of today's free enterprise nations is of spatial oligopoly form.

The one clear policy applicable at all times is the need to minimize the bureaucratic regulations governing a free people. Simultaneously, we must discover ways of having the market resolve the problems raised by externalities, such as pollution and worker health and safety; correspondingly, we must eliminate business monopoly and trade union combinations with their devastating monopoly impacts, as in the airline industry. These are *prime* policies needed at any and every point in time.

"ON DEFICITS, INTEREST RATES, AND REAGANOMICS"

The supply-side application of the Keynesian framework involves the syllogism that a very high tax rate lowers productivity and reduces output (the GNP), thus yielding smaller tax revenues (the so-called Laffer curve). According to supply-siders, it is necessary to find the tax rate level that would encourage greater work effort, increased productivity, and sufficient savings rather than encouraging leisure and investment in tax saving and other less productive ventures. The tax bill originally proposed by President Reagan was designed to produce supply side gains while holding a Monetarist rein on the money supply.

Will Reaganomics prove successful? Let us first note that readers of a book by economists will typically want a definitive statement about the core of the subject matter discussed; and certainly they have the right not to be subject to widely hedged predictions. For these readers, we will rephrase the above question by asking still more bluntly: "Will Reaganomics definitely lead the U.S. economy to a full employment, moderately inflating economy by 1984, 1985, . . .?

No economist can answer the above question without initially mentioning the possibility of an unpredicted war taking place, the death of a leader, the passage of unanticipated statutes, etc. Unpredictable events of the kinds just mentioned will affect economic forecasts. We have no doubts about the basic properties of the Reagan administration's program. What is problematic and doubtful is only the timing of noticeable improvements if the Congress places Reaganomics into effect and stays with it; dates alone are undeterminable since points in time depend on the behavior patterns and policies of the main actors of the play. Consider the following scenario, which we wrote about as a *possibility* in June of 1981. In fact, we shall use our exact wording then, after which we shall bring the discussion to the point where the actual events that have taken place up to early 1983 are interpreted.

Reagan administration budget predictions were predicated, among other things, on the interest rates that the U.S. Treasury would be likely to pay as it finances the 1981–82 projected deficit of around $45 billion. However, if interest rates prove to be higher than those projected by the administration, the deficit could easily rise to the $55 billion order. This in turn would set off greater Treasury borrowings which will have the effect of maintaining pressure on interest rates, causing them to be higher than they otherwise would be. If consumers anticipate tax-cut effects more favorably than do industrialists and stock market investors, bank borrowings by consumers will remain *relatively* larger vis-a-vis business loans than supply-side economists would want. Vitally needed long-term capital expansion loans may, in particular, be delayed. If consumers also happened to encourage their local and state governments to plan water, road, and other improvements, it could well be that besides a large U.S. Treasury supply of bonds, municipal and state bond offerings could glut the market. Interest rates would remain high, possibly going higher than they have been, while the stock market averages fall noticeably. What should be done if this chain of events comes to pass, namely strong nonindustrial demand for loanable funds in the presence of limited supply of loanable funds?

Our answer to the basic question posed above will surprise many readers. In fact, it may appear to contradict our support of the Fed squeeze on the money supply announced by Mr. Volcker in October, 1979, and subsequently carried forth in *erratic* bursts up to mid-1981 (text change to provide date). Assuming withheld appropriations are miniscule and possible budget cuts in the immediate future do not come about, we would favor minor reversal of that policy if the scenario described in the preceding paragraph takes place. We say this even though the squeeze on the money supply to this point in time *was needed.* Manifestly, the scenario noted above would place the economy in a different position from that which marked the end of the Carter years and the beginning of the Reagan years. Over a post "budget *and* tax-cut" period that could be characterized by continuing high interest rates, a slight increase in money growth targets could prove to be desirable if not outright necessary. Supply-side economics, which seeks strong industrial demand for loanable funds and anticipates more rapid real economic growth, must be financed by higher money growth targets than the Carter years required. By moral suasion we hope the Fed will encourage bank loans to businesses up to the time when supply-side savings are brought about. Indeed, not only must the inflation psychology be ended, but apologetic excuses by businessmen and investors who delay capital improvements because interest rates are too high must be terminated.

The supply-siders who supported President Reagan are *in effect* throwing the ball to the business leaders and investors of the country. If they run rapidly with it, Reaganomics will work by 1983. If they "play footsies" with it, it will work, say by 1985 — *provided* the public continues to support the administration so that the nation does not return to the policies of the 1960–1980 period. We, therefore, must hedge on dates, and you can see why that is necessary. How can one predict the economic behavior of uncertain people? But note one thought with respect to which we shall not hedge at all. Either American industrialists and other investors must get "bullish about America" soon, or they could find themselves direct witnesses to the same sorry chain of events that their counterparts in Great Britain and Sweden have experienced. May we sum up our prescriptions as follows:

Hopefully, the Reagan administration forecasts will stay in step with the economic future. The late June budget cuts by Congress were, however, many billions of dollars below the originally proposed level. This raises the demand level for loanable funds. If, further, the scenario on continuing high interest rates that was outlined above does come about, some slight but quick adjustments by the Fed will be needed.[1] If Fed responsiveness does not take place, but the American public and Congress "gut it out long enough," we still would predict that the American economy will be characterized by low unemployment, high growth, and moderate inflation before the next presidential election year.[2] It would only be after a new stable path is gained that serious thought can be given the ultimate aim of Monetarism — namely, to get government, including the Fed, out of the economic policy game. In the interim, the Fed may have to fine-tune its policies to the changing psychology it finds on Wall Street and in the meeting rooms of directors of American companies."*

WHAT HAS IN FACT TAKEN PLACE SINCE THE EARLY SUMMER DATE IN 1981 WHEN THE ABOVE REMARKS WENT INTO PRINT? First of all, interest rates did remain high notwithstanding the tax cuts that were effected. They remained

---

[1]Rates may remain high after inflation has receded unless the Fed responds to the strong demand for loanable funds by *slightly* increasing the bank supply of loanable funds. Note further that in the absence of the Fed supplying more funds, the high rate of interest would be due more to a rising premium required for undertaking activities marked by high risks and uncertainties in place of the high premium previously required by a galloping inflation.

[2]Incidentally, a trouble spot with Reagan administration forecasts is the *sustained, rapid growth rate* that was made part of its basic planning. Again, the business leaders of the country must evidence old-fashioned innovative daring in order for the Reagan administration predictions to occur quickly, as forecast.

*Quoted paragraphs and notes from M.L. Greenhut and C. Stewart, *Economics for the Voter* (Austin: The Lone Star Publishing Co., 1981), pp. 303–304

high partly because of fears of greater budget deficits than those forecasted by the administration and possibly because people still were opting for non-financial asset holdings *relative to* financial assets, as in the scenario derived from Mr. Rutledge's thesis. Worse yet, when they did begin to fall, a deeper than predicted recession took place. This recession had the effect of decreasing government revenues substantially, in the process raising the deficit (actual and projected) noticeably. Clear-cut resolutions to stay with the supply-side game plan were provided by only the President himself *and* Mr. Regan. Other supporters were losing faith or understanding before the game plan had really been placed into effect. What will these deficits do? They will frighten many while giving argument to Mr. Reagan's opponents of impending doom, chaos, etc. . . . as if we had not already survived decades of deficits. More tangibly, the deficits in the presence of a continued tight money policy will mean a crowding out of private borrowers, hence higher interest rates than the levels of risk, uncertainty, and inflation would otherwise require.

"MATHEMATICAL ECONOMICS VS. POLITICS AND PSYCHOLOGICAL REACTIONS"

Economists in general began to opt for a strictly mathematical-statistical science soon after Sputnik rose into the heavens. By developing econometric model building to the point where errors in data and other significant variance-generating components could be handled statistically, they considered their *science* to approach the laboratory certainty of the physical sciences. Unfortunately, the quest for mathematical rigor led them away from the fundamental realities of economics, its roots in psychological-behavioral reactions to economic stimuli. Theoreticians of the new order, the young (or is it new?) Turks searched for *real* causes of recession and inflation, in the process ignoring the psychological basis for each. This is *not* to say that real forces do not exist; it is rather to say that attempts to change aggregate economic trends by altering *real* (exogeneous) economic conditions depend themselves on the short-run important psychological reactions of the main actors in the play. Let us—by reference to 1981–82 and the underlying thesis of this book—explain what government *can and cannot do* by way of economic policies.

President Reagan sought tax cuts in 1981 in belief that productivity would improve and with it supply-side gains would enhance future growth of the GNP. Unfortunately, projected deficits for fiscal 1982 through 1984 were greater than originally conceived. This became much more evident in the latter part of 1981 when the income tax cuts were combined with the revenue cuts projected because of the ongoing recession. High interest rates were accordingly forecast to continue throughout 1981 and most of 1982, and with it Wall Street became more and more apoplectic, or was it apologetic.* Whereas Keynesian theory generally downplays the interest rate factor in *comparison* to an expansionary fiscal stimulus (tax cuts), economists on the Street expressed grave doubts as to economic growth because of these rates. A pessimistic attitude permeated the nation's financial capital, which itself spread to the Board rooms of American companies. McGraw-Hill and other forecasters of capital investment placed them undesirably low. The upshot was that as January faded into February in 1982, both Republicans and Democrats were calling for tax increases, and gloomily predicting still rising unemployment. What should have been done?

Actually a change in psychological reactions was needed, along with better fine-tuning by the Fed. Consider the industrialists who really do not want regulation (i.e., protection from competition by government); consider also those who do not want confiscatory income tax rates; additionally, consider those who want a smaller federal government and/or real programs to help the poor rather than to encourage idleness: Let all these people get *bullish* on the recent tax cuts and America; then, as they announce company capital investment *expansion programs* and begin to place their plans into effect, let the Fed raise its money growth targets so that interest rates do *not* rise at the time when demand for capital funds increases. The Fed could even monetize the deficit and offset the increase in excess reserves by raising reserve requirements. The effect would be a falling real rate of interest *without the classical monetary seeds for inflation* normally stemming from Fed purchases of the debt.

There is also talk that many on Wall Street had been angered by President Reagan's refusal to approve of a massive capital-gains tax restructuring that would have stimulated investments in stocks and bonds. According to this view, the loss in brokerage and other Wall Street incomes led many economists on the Street (e.g. in Salomon Brothers) to reject supply-side economics in their public pronouncements.

Add to the above mentioned forces a downsliding inflation (and of inflationary expectations). The total effect would be to induce many to switch their personal investments from land and real estate development schemes, from gold, gems, carpets, and horse breeding to industrial stocks and bonds. In other words, recognize that people who forecast a rapidly increasing inflation, or expect a repeat of one in the future, tend to cash in securities in order to invest directly in real assets (thus raising interest rate levels), and the opposite holds when direct gains from real assets appear to be smaller because inflationary trends have been curbed. Interest rates normally fall when inflation is being curbed in conjunction with economic growth. The composite result would be a rise in tax receipts and a decrease in the deficit. If Federal Financing Bank growth and federal agency guarantees are curbed, and real budget cuts made, the fall in interest rates plus tax cuts would propel the country forward.

Pursuant to the above, we propose that underscoring economic values are the financial evaluations of the public. What was needed in late 1981, in 1982, and probably for years to come is a "bullish attitude on supply-side economic policies" on the part of industrialists and Wall Street Economists. Of course, many in the initial group want government protection from competition while many in the latter group want the power they would gain from economic planning. Hence many in these groups will seek a return to the days of more and more paperwork and government controls.

"FINAL STATEMENT"

Reduction in off-budget interferences, including the rapidly expanding guarantees of government agencies, would serve to reduce the pressure on interest rates. Moreover, if the public optimistically chooses financial assets over nonfinancial assets, the high rates would be moderated somewhat. In general, we say and repeat again that, if Wall Street and the public in general have been "bullish" on the *overall* supply-side game plan in place of the government managed welfare state of the 1960s and 1970s, the reversal of downward trends projected by the administration could have been faster. But, if the confusion and changing policies plus vested interest influence that has long characterized Great Britain reappear in the United States in 1983, the years to follow will probably witness a backsliding toward new government controls and powers over the American economy and people. Clearly, uncertainties in this regard alone keep long-term rates high. Equally clear, the 1980–1985 period marks a point of no return in our country's history as the nation approaches its most formidable *economic,* if not also *political* crossroad since the depression years, *or* perhaps since the republic was born.

CHAPTER 19:
THE INTEREST RATE, THE DEFICIT, THE TAX PROBLEM, AND REAGANOMICS OF 1983

What accounts for the high interest rates over the period from October 6, 1979 to July 31, 1982, still high in real terms in March 1983? Why would President Reagan propose tax increases when he was brought to Washington by the nation's voters expecting him to achieve spending and tax reductions? Did Reaganomics fail? How would you, the reader of this book, use the economic analysis of prior chapters to answer these questions by yourself? This *brief* chapter will put you to work by suggesting the way you *might* use the tools of economic analysis to resolve issues of this kind and others that will arise in the future. Let's begin with the interest rate. What determines its level? What makes it high or low?

"THE INTEREST RATE"

Consider demand and supply of loanable funds. As we found in Chapters 11 and 12, the greater the demand, the higher is the price (here, the interest rate), all other things unchanged. The greater the supply, the lower is the price (interest rate). What then accounts for the high interest rates of recent years? Let us explain these rates as follows:

Beginning on October 6, 1979, Mr. Volcker (in some ways, President Carter) and certainly the Federal Reserve began to limit increases in the supply of money (hence loanable funds) to smaller increments than was the case over the prior decade. At the same instance, inflation meant losses to lenders, especially those who would lend on a long-term basis. It meant losses because (as we previously observed in our chapter on inflationary impacts) a loan at a given rate of interest, say six percent, meant less *spending power* if repaid a year later during a price inflation of, say, seven percent. Add that to the risk of nonpayment by the borrower and clearly a six percent loan was foolhardy. The rate to be received must therefore cover not only the risk involved, but the inflation. Simply put, the supply of loanable funds under conditions of inflation tends to be restricted. [We shall not draw supply and demand curves for you, as you should be able (and want) to visualize the process in your mind; only rarely will you have a pencil and paper available when you want to use the tools of economics.] Imagine in your mind's eye that the supply of loanable funds (especially longer-term loans) is not increasing as much as the supply of money that was created by the Fed. In fact, for simplicity, keep the supply curve in your mind's eye at the same place for the late 1979 through 1982 period as it was before then. What about the demand for loanable funds? If it increased while the supply of loanable funds remained unchanged, interest rates should rise.

Normal economic growth (resulting from an increasing population, from new entrants—such as women and young people—into the workforce, and even from small productivity gains) involves a rising nominal GNP; it also signifies an increasing demand for loanable funds. This increase stems simply from the fact that even just a nominal dollar economic expansion causes many to seek and need additional funds in order to carry out their activities. In your mind, shift the demand for loanable funds to the right to represent a need for more loanable funds at every relevant interest rate. The intersection of the new shifted demand curve with the unchanged supply curve signifies a higher price for loanable funds (a higher interest rate). [If you want, turn back to Figure 12.3 to see the higher value effect of an increase in demand. In the present context, the interest rate would be plotted on the vertical axis.]

Inflation began to moderate from mid–1981 through mid–1982. Why then did the supply curve remain virtually the same as it was under more inflationary conditions? Why didn't the supply of loanable funds shift to the right since lenders would no longer need a premium for inflation? In still other words, if inflation dissipates or, let us say, is nonexistent, a potential lender should be willing to lend more funds at any given rate than previously. This increase in willingness to lend at any given rate means that the entire supply curve of loanable funds shifts to the right. [If you need to probe deeper into this matter, return to Figure 12.3.] So the demand/supply intersection would then occur at lower rates. This was President Reagan's expectation. What went wrong?

Unfortunately there were strong pressures from lobbies, from the constituencies of federal spending programs and the bureaucracies that are employed administering them, and concern about the electoral consequences of high unemployment rates. These pressures used fears of growing budget deficits and their long term inflationary consequences to urge delay or reversal of some of the tax cuts approved in 1981 instead of insisting on further reductions in federal spending. In fact, modest tax increases were enacted, mainly an additional five cents a gallon federal tax on gasoline. And there was insufficient awareness of the time required for the big payoff from supply-side policies. Large productivity gains come from new plant and equipment in place, and new products; these are the results of increased savings and investment, encouraged by restored confidence, reduced fears of inflation, and improved incentives. This sequence of events cannot take much less than five years.

Note that interest rates were finally falling in early August 1982. They were falling because the Fed was loosening up on money and because the disinflation effect was beginning to dominate along with recession decreased demands for loanable funds. Of course, tax increases would further reduce government demands for loanable funds, all other things unchanged. So interest rates should fall still further. Then many legislators, the Wall Street economists, et al., could say: "See—we moved toward a balanced budget and solved the high interest rate problem." However, what would have happened had President Reagan been able to resist Congressional pressures completely, remaining against all tax increases while insisting on real reductions in public spending? Supply-side economics would propose that the economy would have been stimulated by the deficit and by the assurance that the Presidency was not the captive of Congress and of Washington interest groups. Moreover, the falling interest rate pattern that was already taking place before the tax increase would have been stimulative. In effect, a faster recovery would have occurred than that which could take place given the tax increases. Of course, economic growth signifies increasing demands for loanable funds. The greater the GNP growth rate, the greater is the demand for funds. But this would have been offset by diminishing premium requirements for anticipated inflation and uncertainty. To supply-siders, (1) the expectation that future inflation was no longer imminent, along with (2) steadfastness in purpose to trim bureaucratic waste and unnecessary federal spending, *and* hence (3) the greater certainty of recovery would have released funds from speculative ventures for industrial loan (interest) purposes. More funds going into long-term bond issues because inflation premiums were lower would have provided the needed (capital goods expansion) source of funds for American industry. A real recovery could have been generated, far superior to the restricted growth the tax increase will allow.* Has supply-side economics failed? No! Only its post 1981 Reaganomics version failed somewhat. Consider the following:

Besides the tax increase (which is anti supply-side economics), the victory of the Washington establishment over another president is manifest in the fact that government spending projections for 1982 are estimated at 24.1% of GNP compared to the 21.9% existent during fiscal year 1975's recession. Indeed, compare it with the 22.5% that took place during the last year of the Carter administration. As was noted in an editorial of the *Wall Street Journal* (August 10, 1982, p. 26): "For that matter, at 20.5% of GNP, taxes are higher today than the 18.9% in 1975 or 20.1% in 1980 — so much for the 'failure' of supply-side economics." Unfortunately, Reaganomics today is no longer the supply-side economics that was set forth in Chapters 15 and 16. Rather, it is a curious mixture that can best be described as Washington in confusion.

To understand the above contention, recall from our supply-side chapters that steadily decreasing American productivity, including a one-year negative change in productivity during the late seventies, signified an impending structural economic collapse in the nation. Major reasons for the declining productivity were said to be the heavy personal income tax rates which encouraged absenteeism (leisure), and unfortunately decreased investments in capital good expansion. In the very short run,

---

*Recognize from Keynesian economics that a tax increase acts as a drag on an economy. This manifests itself in a slower growth than might occur otherwise (e.g., lower productivity). A lower rate of growth signifies an increased possibility of loss in capital good investments (hence greater uncertainty). This in turn signifies higher interest rates than would otherwise exist, *ceteris paribus*. The fact is the 1982 tax increase separated Reaganomics from supply-side economics. Relatively speaking, it promotes higher interest rates over time than would have arisen otherwise.

supply-siders agreed that the raising of taxes by Congress in August of 1982 (with President Reagan's approval), in apparent intention to eliminate deficits and to gain a balanced budget in a few years, would encourage Wall Street; the result would indeed be some decrease in interest rates. In the longer run, however, supply-siders argue that the decreased productivity associated with the higher tax bill must increase the uncertainty (risk) premium required by lenders. Hence the higher tax bill would, in time, produce higher interest rates than those stemming from the deficit alone.

From a strict Keynesian perspective, an increase in taxes decreases savings. This signifies a smaller decrease in the excess demand for loanable funds than that which would otherwise be projected from the greater tax receipts (and any related decrease in the deficit). In general supply-siders object to the increased taxes of 1982, even going so far as to claim that over time it would have unfavorable impacts on the interest rates compared to the faster economic growth that strict adherence to supply-side policies would have promoted. What can be done in the future to protect against the tendency of legislators to spend and tax excessively as they cater to lobby interests seeking special favors?

"CONCLUSIONS"

The press has repeatedly reported President Reagan's defense of his budget deficits. "A necessary evil," he called them in response to a congressional drive to "narrow the deficit." But this drive was also a pretext to raise taxes. Why the backsliding we have noted, why the concessions? For one, politics is the art of the possible, and in order to obtain sufficient support to implement policies we consider vital it is often necessary to support (or not oppose) other policies with which we disagree but which we consider to be of secondary importance. There is bargaining in the political as well as in the economic marketplace; without it there are few trades, few decisions.

Why the lack of overwhelming support for what we "know" is the correct policy, which drives us to accomodate strange bedfellows? There may be shared goals, but differences of opinion on how best to attain them, which derive from different views as to the causes of current problems *and* the effectiveness of alternative policies. Which taxes to raise, how much? What money supply target to aim for, and when to change targets? These differences can be narrowed by better information and education. There may be more fundamental, intractable differences, in values and goals, which are not reducible through better information. Pacifists and supporters of a strong defense are unlikely ever to arrive at a common policy; neither are devotees of urban living and addicts of suburban life. Then there are conflicts of interest, not based on ignorance or on conflicts in values. Tobacco farmers cannot be dissuaded from production by any evidence the Surgeon General may provide on the harmful effects of smoking. Domestic manufacturers cannot be persuaded that they should be driven out of business by cheaper and/or superior imports in the interests of the consumer. They may perhaps be bought off — helped to adjust and consequently reduce their opposition.

To be sure, ideas have consequences, and therefore the opinions of important groups should not be ignored; they affect behavior. If important segments of society anticipate inflation, even if their fears are unfounded, their expectations will lead them to consume and borrow more, to save and invest less, and this behavior will promote inflation.

Given the realities of political life in a democracy, theories cannot be adequately tested, and this is what is happening to Reaganomics and supply-side economics. For the programs they recommend cannot be fully implemented.

This brings us to the subject of decision-making through democratic processes in a pluralist society. How do we deal with issues on which there is no consensus? We agree on a procedure for arriving at decisions: elections, legislatures, judges, juries. And we develop methods for eliciting and promoting the views of those who share interests and values. These methods are known as lobbies, whether or not the organizations are registered as such or simply behave as lobbies in influencing legislation, executive decisions, administrative procedures. The list is immense, spanning the vast range of interests, values, goals encompassed in our society: business and labor organizations, government agencies, philanthropic societies, the Sierra Club, the National Rifle Association, the American Medical Association, the Ford Foundation, *ad infinitum*. In a population of 230 million people, they are essential as intermediaries between single individuals and central governments or society at large. There are "good" lobbies and "bad" lobbies, interests well represented and ineffectively advocated, but without these groups little can be accomplished.

Unfortunately the distribution of influence in a representative democracy is distorted, primarily from differences in the ease of organization. Producers tend to be more influential than consumers because their interests are concentrated and the number of actors may be small enough for ready collaboration. They can afford to be well informed and represented. Consumer interests are diffuse, and the number of actors very large. Beneficiaries of specific government programs find it easier to be up in arms than taxpayers at large. Those threatened by large losses (import-competing industries) are more alert and effective on the average than those who have the potential for large gains (industries with export capabilities).

Elected officials stand to gain through public spending in their states and districts. Bureaucrats advance in pay and prestige with the size of their staffs and of the budgets they administer; they have a vested interest in perpetuating existing programs and procreating new programs. It was in this context that two economists argued recently against the use of government as a means of assuring economic growth. "For the politician, income, prestige, power, . . . are derived from only one source: tenure in public office . . . the taxpayer who sleeps soundly because of the security provided by constitutional and statutory protections on public debt is profoundly naive about the wiles of politicians and public employees." They advised that this statement ". . . should not be interpreted to mean that politicians and public employees are, as individuals, more devious and dishonest than individuals who work in the private sector. Neither public nor private sector employees are inherently 'saints' or 'sinners'; neither group has a monopoly on horns or halos. All individuals, regardless of the sector in which they work, serve their own private interests first and foremost."*

The distortions in the distribution of influence, and the biases in the behavior of elected officials and bureaucrats, suggest that deficits and inflation may be occupational diseases of democracy. Fortunately the educated, informed, articulate taxpayer and consumer also has a disproportionate influence in the land. It is our hope that this book may contribute toward strengthening this

---

*James T. Bennett and Thomas J DiLorenzo, *Underground Government* (Washington, D.C., The Cato Institute, 1983), pp. 11, 16.

countervailing influence. They will more readily vote incumbents out of office who cater to lobby interests at the expense of the nation at large. Better balance between the interests of constituencies and the nation is needed if our country is to avoid the political-economic errors of the past.

"FINAL STATEMENT"

This book was written with deep concern on our part over the future of the American free enterprise system. We believe supply-side economics is a fundamentally correct system of thought, with roots in formal Keynesian economic science. Because it is not just simply a trickle-down to the poor from the wealthy theory, or just a set of empty statements, *as many politicians have claimed,* our concern has included the political outcry against it that has been so extensive. This politics has gone to the point of implying that supply-side economics failed even before the October 1981, and especially the July 1982, dates which first marked its actual start in practice. In fact, it basically will not have gone into effect until July 1, 1983 and then really will not have been proven or disproven by the American use of its principles until the end of the decade, *if it can ever be proven empirically right or wrong.*

The facts of economic life are that: (1) Twenty years of government profligacy cannot be turned around in three months, three years, or even a decade. (2) Regulatory interferences and off-budget expenditures, which President Reagan's supply-side people may never control sufficiently, tend to destroy any so-called laboratory tests of any form of Reaganomics. (3) Also uncontrollable are our legislators, if not also our judges who repeatedly alter their interpretations of the laws that govern the free enterprise system. (4) We agree with the Austrian school of economic thought in proposing that statistical testing of economic theory, especially testing of a macroeconomic theory which depends upon a myriad of changing political/social forces, is not possible. Instead, we must verify or refute supply-side economics by tests of its logical structure of thought and self-contained truths. The theory can only be disclaimed by formal demonstration of its logical contradictions. Until that is done, the writers of this book propose that the supply-side twist to Keynesian economics that we set forth in Chapters 15 and 16 should serve as a guide to the economic policies of the federal government. Certainly too much of federal government handouts go to the wealthy, the civil servant, the college professor, and in general those who know how to make their money and position lead to the reelection of those who take care of the people who promoted them to power. A real democracy and free enterprise system involves limited controls over others, requires alternative opportunities for all, and most particularly maximizes the opportunities for free choice by the people.

THE INTEREST RATE, THE DEFICIT, THE TAX PROBLEM, AND REAGANOMICS OF 1983

APPENDIX A: SIMPLIFYING THE CURRENT INCOME TAX SYSTEM

The American income tax system is an absurdity, better yet, a monstrosity. Past Congressional failures to stave off lobbyist pressures have led to such a complex system of laws and legal escape hatches that a large industry has been created to interpret, implement, and circumvent it. The incredible amounts of paperwork forced on taxpayers, the need to hire expensive accountants and tax attorneys, and activities of a government agency, IRS, which interprets Congressional statutes, are major reasons for the reduced productivity of the workers of the country. Double taxation of dividends in the existing laws, tax shelters, capital gain provisions, and the taxation of interest have combined to discourage investment in American industry. These disincentives have compounded the loss of productivity due to the paperwork imposed on the nation's taxpayers.

Potential taxpayer revolt is at hand. It can be avoided. This appendix presents a simplified income tax proposal that was offered by Robert E. Hall and Alvin Rabushka in the *Wall Street Journal* on December 10, 1981. Their proposal is incomplete in our view: we favor selected modifications to their plan. This appendix presents the Hall/Rabushka proposal exactly as it was set forth by them. We then indicate modifications to the Hall/Rabushka plan which would resolve objections to their plan.

The Hall/Rabushka Proposal to Simplify Our Tax System

"Despite recent progress in lowering rates, the tax system remains a disgrace. It is in dire need of simplification and reform. The tax system is inordinately big, filling volumes of codes, complicated by hundreds of credits, exemptions and special provisions. Many taxpayers need expensive professional help to fill out their returns. Each act of Congress complicates the system further. Widespread evasion is apparent on interest, dividend and other forms of household or professional income. Tax shelters are commonplace. Estimates of the size of the underground range from tens of billions of dollars to several hundred billion. In short, we have a system that fosters contempt for the law, and simultaneously discourages productive economic activity.

We have recently worked out the details of a simple income tax, imposed at a low uniform rate on a comprehensive measure of income. The tax would be founded on the following principles:

1. All income should be taxed only once, as close as possible to its source.
2. All types of income should be taxed at the same rate.
3. The poorest households should pay no income tax.
4. Tax returns for both households and businesses should be simple enough to fit on a postcard or on a single page.

A major problem with the current system is its helter-skelter taxation of business income. Corporate income is taxed first under the corporate tax and again under the personal tax on dividends. Income from proprietorships and partnerships often evades tax, or is taxed lightly. We propose a single business tax on all types of income other than wages.

A uniform rate of 19% would replace the current range of rates. The current rates now stretch from actual subsidy of highly leveraged tax shelters with large interest deductions to rates as high as 80% that are imposed on income earned by stockholders.

The proposed new 19% business tax applies equally to all forms of business — corporate, partnership, professional, farm and rentals and royalties. The base for the tax is gross revenue less purchases of goods and services and compensation paid to employees. In addition, a capital recovery allowance is deducted for investment in plant and equipment. No deductions are permitted for depreciation, interest or payments to owners in any form.

Even for a multibillion-dollar corporation, the business tax return would fit easily on a single page. It would look like this:

1. Gross Revenue from sales

Costs

2. Purchases of goods and materials
3. Compensation paid to employees
4. Other direct costs
5. Total costs (lines 2, 3, and 4)
6. New Revenue (line 1 less line 5)
7. Purchases of capital equipment and structures
8. Taxable income (lines 6 less line 7)
9. Tax (19% of line 8)

10. Tax carry-forward from losses in previous years
11. Tax (line 9 less line 10)
12. Tax payment (amount on line 11 if positive)
13. Carry-forward to next year (amount on line 11 if negative).

In place of the hodge-podge of investment incentives in the tax system now, we propose the use of straightforward first-year write-off of all business investment. First-year capital recovery is a great simplification over the complicated depreciation deductions and investment credits in present law.

The net revenue of U.S. business in 1980 was $803 billion. Under the new business tax we are proposing, capital recovery allowances would have been $317 billion, leaving net taxable business income at $486 billion. A tax rate of 19% would have yielded $92 billion; that would be about half again the revenue from the actual corporate income tax in 1980 of $64 billion. Despite a much lower tax rate, the extra revenue comes from the much wider tax base, including unincorporated business, and from taxing business income at the source.

Under the simple tax system, all business income would be taxed only once, at its source. Household receipts of interest, dividends and capital gains would be after-tax income. Though wealthy households might receive large amounts of these types of income, it is important to understand that the taxes on such income have already been paid. Taxing business income at its source has the important practical benefit of taxing the large amounts of interest and dividend income that escape taxation under the current system.

With comprehensive taxation of business income, taxation of capital gains should be eliminated at the level of the individual. The value of a security or other interest in a business is the capitalized value of its after-tax income, and so already embodies the appropriate tax when business income is taxed at its source.

Our simplified tax system also includes a comprehensive tax on the earnings of individuals.

Most income in the U.S. is a compensation for work. In the proposed tax, compensation is broadly defined as anything of value received by workers from employers, including cash wages and salaries, the market value of fringe benefits and contributions to public and private pension plans.

To limit the tax burden of poor families, we propose a set of personal allowances. Taxes would be 19% of compensation in excess of the following allowances:

Married Couple	$5000
Single	3000
Single/Head of Household	4500
Each Dependent	600

Except for the personal allowances, no deductions of any kind would be permitted, including interest deductions.

The individual tax return for the compensation tax would look very much like the illustration accompanying this article. It would fit on a postcard.

In 1980, total compensation in the U.S. — including fringes and pension contributions — was $1,596 billion. We estimate that personal allowances in 1980 would have been $420 billion, leaving taxable compensation of $1,176 billion. At a rate of 19%, tax revenues would have been $223 billion. By comparison, the personal income tax in 1980 yielded about $225 billion.

At the outset, the simple income tax, with common flat rates of 19% on business income and compensation, would raise revenue equal to about 12% of GNP, the same as the current combination of corporate and personal income taxes. Though our system would stabilize revenue as a fraction of GNP, it would probably produce more revenue that the government needs to maintain existing programs.

Low marginal tax rates would draw economic activities from the underground economy into the formal market, where they are recorded as part of GNP. Businesses and individuals would spend less time worrying about the tax consequences of their actions and concentrate instead on earning higher incomes. On these grounds, we believe that the revenue needs of the federal government could be met with tax rates as low as 16% or 17%, rather than the 19% needed to reproduce current revenue at current levels of GNP.

The benefits of tax reform are not merely economic. The complexities of the federal tax system now foster contempt for government and make petty criminals out of a large fraction of the population. A simplified tax with low marginal rates would help restore confidence in government and would support the basic honesty of the American people."

(Messrs. Hall and Rabushka are senior fellows at the Hoover Institution, Stanford University. Mr. Hall is also professor of economics at Stanford.)

The obstacles to all plans of this kind are the vested interest groups who profit from the existing morass of regulatory intrusion on free choice: the tax lawyers and accountants who profit from the present system, the "restaurant beneficiaries" of the tax, the mortgagees and construction people who believe interest cost deductions induce people to buy houses, the MD lobbyists who believe medical deductions encourage visits to doctors *and* extended stays in hospitals, and so on. The biggest obstacle will be found among the legislators in Congress who find advantage in yielding to these lobby groups rather than promoting the nation's well-being.

A Federal Sales Tax Inclusion

The authors of this book would propose adoption of the Hall/Rabushka proposal along with a highly progressive federal government imposed tax on expensive consumer goods and services, for example, luxury cars, yachts, big television sets, furs, special microwave units, expensive jewelry, freezers, large home uses of electricity, etc. This tax would provide some of the egalitarianism sought by the federal income tax with two special, unique attributes: one, the very wealthy who wanted to consume *could not escape* this tax, as they virtually do the income tax; two, there would be no paperwork by householders in connection with paying the tax. Also, the government's revenue base would rise somewhat and the projected deficits for fiscal 1983 and following years would be reduced.

Other Modifications to Hall/Rabushka

A decided shortcoming of the basic Hall/Rabushka tax proposal is its failure to encourage risk capital. This shortcoming will be especially significant in future years because increasing complexity of business *and* international competition will place a greater premium on more daring ventures. A nation primed for industrial advances, if not leadership, must encourage enterprise, particularly highly innovative and hence risky initiatives.

A related shortcoming is its failure to recognize that many actions in the past were taken in the belief that the tax deductions of the U.S tax laws would hold throughout time. For example, elimination of tax savings through mortgage interest deduction would amount to a breach of faith for those who purchased a house through borrowed funds rather than renting.

The above noted shortcomings tend to offset the basic advantages cited previously in this appendix for the Hall/Rabushka plan. To remedy these shortcomings, we would modify the Hall/Rabushka proposal as follows: A special capital loss deduction could be allowed in defining taxable (earned) income. In the event an investment loss occurs, it can be deducted from taxable income, thereby saving the investor federal taxes to the extent of 19% of that loss. Purchases of primary and secondary residences which involve mortgage payments should have similar tax deduction, with the interest paid on the residence serving to reduce the person's taxable income. These provisions would involve much smaller tax saving under our modified Hall/Rabushka plan than currently applies for most taxpayers; this is so because of the low tax rate under Hall/Rabushka compared to the marginal tax rates currently existing. Most importantly, the proposed modification would encourage risk-taking and the acquisition of homes in contrast to the Hall/Rabushka plan, which does not recognize capital losses and interest expenses.

State and local property taxes could also be deducted from the concept of taxable (earned) income in computing the Hall/Rabushka tax, albeit the present authors would propose otherwise. Moreover, to simplify record-keeping of people on company expense accounts, we propose that individual reports should *not* be required; instead, IRS checks on companies alone would be in order, and then only to make sure that company expense allowances conform to the nation's laws.

Capital gains above a significantly large amount should be taxed. This item means that the typical capital gain by middle class income recipients — and even upper middle class income people — would not be taxed. To repeat, we would propose taxing only significantly large gains, the kind that substantial investments combined with significant speculative profit would generate. In no case should a capital gain tax be imposed on residences. It is absurd to require people concerned with jobs, family problems, health, crime, wars, etc. to maintain records on every house purchased and sold over the years. In corresponding manner, we would tax dividend and interest income *above very substantial levels,* which again means only the truly wealthy would be subject to taxes on original earned income plus tax on the savings their income produced. The vast majority of American citizens would be free to invest in speculative ventures, to save via stock market and bank deposit acquisitions without multiple reporting to government (hence record-keeping) of their activities. [No federal consumption tax would be needed if the proposals of this paragraph were added to the Hall/Rabushka plan.] Gifts between family and friends should be allowed without reporting and record-keeping up to at least the very substantial sums per year that would only involve the *extremely wealthy.*

As far as charitable contributions are concerned, we could be dogmatic. If they are indeed *charitable,* they will continue to be made without special tax favor. Indeed, the federal government should not (nor do we believe it must) legislate the morality which stands behind charitable donations. At the most, charitable contributions should be allowed only to the point where they do *not* serve as the vehicle for the extremely wealthy to virtually avoid paying an income tax.

There exist today many tax *favored* investments, the owners of which would suffer (confiscatory) loss under the Hall/Rabushka proposal if they were not protected otherwise. For example, investment in municipal and state government bonds usually carries almost thirty percent lower interest returns than those on corporate bonds of equivalent risk. Precipitous drops in their market values would take place, *ceteris paribus*, under the basic tax plan. We would propose that these and similar investments require special consideration, for example a *reduction* in the income tax otherwise owed by the taxpayer, say by the amount of thirty percent of the total interest paid on the municipal or state bond.

Arguably, there may be other special adjustments that are needed. For some individuals, extra large medical expenses should carry special tax reductions. Most taxpayers are, of course, insured by governments and/or by private carriers and therefore do not need special tax treatment. Nevertheless, Congressional study of this matter appears to be desirable to protect the few who may incur undue medical costs with no recourse to government or insurance.

APPENDIX B:
THE PROBLEM WITH
VESTED INTERESTS

We observed in Chapter 17 that the biggest problem, and possibly an insurmountable one, for the Thatcher government in Great Britain is rooted in the large civil service force and the entrenched labor unions, each of which has been (and will) strongly resist changes away from the government provided welfare state of recent years. The following editorial from the *Wall Street Journal* of December 8, 1981 points to similar problems in the United States for any administration proposing change in entitlements or other practices that (appear to) favor some special group.

'Strikes, Riots, Vandalism'

One of the loudest screams yet from a wounded bureaucracy was produced last week by underlings in the Department of Housing and Urban Development, which David Stockman & Co. has targeted for some judicious budget cuts. It revealed more than the screamers know.

A draft appeal from the department, quite naturally leaked to the press, predicted nothing less than civil insurrection if Mr. Stockman gets his way. According to news stories, the HUD leftenants warned that cutting back federal rent subsidies would lead to "rent strikes, riots, vandalism and irreparable damage to projects."

We wonder if these people, in their fear and anger about the threat to their own positions, had any idea of what their remarks imply. They were suggesting that their clients out there in the housing projects are not the helpless indigents the public housing lobby has been describing in the past. Rather, they are people who are likely to resort to extreme violence if someone tampers with their dole.

Now, we are quite well aware that no single description fits any large group, and the group referred to here is large indeed. What interests us most is the way the HUD officers think about the responsibilities of government. It seems that they have somehow developed a philosophy that says hard-working, tax-paying citizens who choose to support themselves can be legitimately asked by the government to bribe a violent underclass just to keep it quiet. Worse still, their concept even implies a bit of sympathy for that violent underclass if it chooses to respond to cutbacks with "rent strikes, riots, vandalism and irreparable damage to projects."

Such attitudes—and they have become all too common among welfare state bureaucrats—are sheer madness, because they put government in the position of actually encouraging a breakdown of social order. When government suggests to people that the dole is their right and implies that they might be justified in violent reaction if it is reduced or removed, what kind of behavior should it expect to engender?

Indeed, it has not escaped our notice that a great deal of that kind of behavior the HUD people describe has already been taking place, even during the expansion of the rent subsidies the bureaucrats think are so palliative. A massive rent strike occurred in New York's Co-op City not long ago and we are convinced it grew out of nothing more than widespread expectations by the tenants, many of whom are not poor by any measurement, that the state owed them cheap housing. As to vandalism and riots, have any of the HUD officers had the nerve lately to walk through some of the projects they are using tax money to support? We have little doubt that a great many are like Chicago's Cabrini Green, which Mayor Jane Byrne described not so long ago as little more than a sinkhole for crime and violence. The Pruitt-Igoe project in St. Louis was ultimately razed because its population became unmanageable.

The HUD bureaucrats will fight violently and use their usual channels in Congress to try to thwart Mr. Stockman's efforts to bring the massive federal housing program under control. But they are very naive if they think the leak of their protest memo did anything to help their cause.

EPILOGUE

Specific legislation of the United States including the Full Employment Act of 1946 and the Humphrey-Hawkins Full Employment Act of 1979, have established a broad set of goals for the American economy. Among these are full employment, stable prices and economic growth. But, we have seen that it is only from a growing economic pie that a system can raise the well-being of the entire population: economic growth is not only the best way of reducing poverty; it is the only way.

National economic policy has been misdirected for the last several decades. Undue emphasis has been placed on the wants of the beneficiaries of our generous welfare state. This emphasis has undermined the sources of economic growth and lowered our overall rate of growth. Government spending on entitlement programs—with generous cost-of-living adjustment programs—has diverted an increasing share of our national income from the productive sectors of the economy to the retired, the unemployed and the unemployable. The federal government has done this via tax and transfer policies which have weakened the relationship between effort and reward for workers, savers and investors. At the same time inflation, resulting from government spending exceeding government income, has increased the annual federal deficit, and thus encouraged consumption which discourages both savings and investment. In this process, nearly everyone has suffered, but the poor in whose behalf much of this was done have suffered the most.

Professors Greenhut and Stewart state that Keynesianism, monetarism, and supply-side economics are not conflicting theories of how the economy works, but limited perspectives stressing different factors. The authors state that the differences between them are not between right and wrong, but rather as to which is the most appropriate under particular circumstances: at a time when people are overburdened by taxes, the appropriate diagnosis is not underconsumption. Likewise, demand feeding is not the recommended treatment under pressures of large deficits and low household savings.

However, we have learned that the simplified Keynesian demand-feeding theory of economic growth can result in runaway inflation. Therefore, the limiting of the supply of money is essential in affecting interest rates and price trends. The main task of our time is to change the expectations of inflation that have become entrenched by a decade and a half of inflationary policies and experience. Confidence in future price stability is fundamental to restoring incentives to save and invest. But, controlling the money supply does not attack the basic problems of the tax-transfer system and the federal regulatory excesses which have caused two of the nation's fundamental economic problems.

Everyone agrees that cutting the deficit is a high priority, but as the authors argue, stopping the growth of government welfare spending is of primary importance. This—not higher taxes—is the way to cut the deficit and, more importantly, to restore the conditions for sustained growth which can alone eliminate poverty. Income and employment are at stake, so too is the historic full range of opportunities and scope for individual freedom of choice that all Americans seek.

Edwin J. Feulner, Jr.
President
Heritage Foundation

INDEX

INDEX

INDEX